ENTANGLED

A HISTORY OF AMERICAN METHODISM, POLITICS, AND SEXUALITY

ASHLEY BOGGAN DREFF

NEW ROOM
BOOKS

Entangled: A History of American Methodism, Politics, and Sexuality

The General Board of Higher Education and Ministry leads and serves The United Methodist Church in the recruitment, preparation, nurture, education, and support of Christian leaders—lay and clergy—for the work of making disciples of Jesus Christ for the transformation of the world. Its vision is that a new generation of Christian leaders will commit boldly to Jesus Christ and be characterized by intellectual excellence, moral integrity, spiritual courage, and holiness of heart and life. The General Board of Higher Education and Ministry of The United Methodist Church serves as an advocate for the intellectual life of the church. The Board's mission embodies the Wesleyan tradition of commitment to the education of laypersons and ordained persons by providing access to higher education for all persons.

The name New Room Books comes from the New Room, a historic building in Bristol, England, and place of John Wesley's study. Built in 1739, it is the oldest Methodist chapel in the world.

Entangled: A History of American Methodism, Politics, and Sexuality

Portions of chapters 1 and 3 were previously published as follows. They are used here by permission: Ashley Boggan, "A God-Sent Movement: Methodism, Contraception, and the Protection of the Methodist Family, 1870–1968," *Methodist History* 53, no. 2 (January 2015): 68–84. Ashley B. Dreff, "American Methodism and 'The New Morality'" *Methodist History* 56, no. 3 (April 2018): 149–59.

Scripture quotations marked KJV are taken from the King James or Authorized Version of the Bible.

Scripture quotations marked RSV are taken from the Revised Standard Version of the Bible, copyright 1952 [2nd edition, 1971] by the Division of Christian Education of the National Council of the Churches of Christ in the United States of America. Used by permission. All rights reserved.

ISBN 978-1-945935-32-9

18 19 20 21 22 23 24 25 26 27—10 9 8 7 6 5 4 3 2 1

Manufactured in the United States of America

HIGHER EDUCATION & MINISTRY
General Board of Higher Education and Ministry
THE UNITED METHODIST CHURCH

This book is dedicated first and foremost to Erik Dreff, my husband, interlocutor, and best friend.

Thank you to Harvey, my son, whose smile is a daily inspiration.

Thank you also to my family, Kurt and Rebecca, Emily and André. You all raised me in the United Methodist tradition and taught me the values of inclusiveness.

CONTENTS

ACKNOWLEDGMENTS
IX

INTRODUCTION
American Methodism and American Politics
1

1

A NEW AMERICAN METHODIST SEXUALITY
Methodists and Birth Control
19

2

AMERICAN METHODISM AND SEXUAL REVOLUTION
Togetherness, Divorce, and *Playboy*
61

3

THE POLITICAL TURN
American Methodists, the New Morality, and Sex Education
107

4

AMERICAN METHODISM AND THE POLITICS OF ABORTION
149

5

AMERICAN METHODISM AND HOMOSEXUALITY
A Breaking Point
205

CONCLUSION
263

SELECTED BIBLIOGRAPHY
271

INDEX
279

ACKNOWLEDGMENTS

This book is the product of seven years of research, and therefore, I have many people to thank. My professors at the University of Chicago Divinity School first introduced me to the complex history of The United Methodist Church and encouraged me to continue my research into this denomination's history with a PhD from Drew Theological School. The people I encountered at Drew changed not only how I understood theology but how I understood gender and sexuality. Conversations with my peers opened my eyes to the beautiful complexity and fluidity that make up our individual identities. Thank you to my doctoral advisor, Dr. Morris L. Davis, who guided me through inquiries into how Methodists have understood race, region, and gender. Thank you also to Dr. J. Terry Todd, a member of my doctoral committee. Your classes catered to my interest in Methodist sexuality and piqued my interest in the rise of the New Christian Right, two subjects that I will continue to interrogate.

Thank you to the staff at the General Commission on Archives and History of The United Methodist Church. Not only did you all provide me with a job while I was a doctoral student, but you introduced me to the wealth of information available at GCAH. Thank you to Frances Lyons for fulfilling what seemed like endless requests for scans. Thank you also to Dr. Dale Patterson and Mark Shenise for the incredible insights into the historic gems that GCAH has to offer. You two were not only wonderful bosses; I consider you great friends. I must also thank the Reverend Dr. Fred Day, who encouraged, published, and praised my research along the way. Finally, thank you, GCAH, for providing me with the Women in United Methodist History Research Grant. Those funds supported necessary lodging and travel to further this research.

Thank you to the staff at the Connectional Table of The United Methodist Church, the ladies on Higgins Road. Dr. Amy Valdez Barker, you were a wonderful mentor and a needed reminder that the focus of The United Methodist Church should be its mission. Cynthia Dopke and Dr. Meredith Hoxie Schol, you two helped me understand the worldwide nature of our denomination and how entangled current conversations are within our institutional boundaries. I truly miss working with you three, especially discussing the future of the church in our after-work sessions at Gino's.

Thank you to the publishing staff at the General Board of Higher Education and Ministry. Kathy Armistead, your edits and comments vastly improved this manuscript. Thank you for taking a chance on a new scholar.

Thank you to my family. Mom and Dad, you all raised me in the United Methodist tradition. You taught me to question everything, and you taught me the value of inclusivity. I hope that this book makes you proud that your daughter is an expert on Methodist sex. Emily, my sister, you were the first person to teach me how to debate and how to form arguments. Thank you for letting me occasionally win.

Finally, thank you to my husband, Erik, and my son, Harvey. Erik, you put up with me throughout the dissertation process and throughout the continuous edits and re-edits of this manuscript. Thank you for letting me process out loud and thank you for being my chalkboard. Thank you for pushing back on certain points and helping me fine-tune my arguments. Thank you for the foot rubs, the back rubs, and the philosophy lessons. I could not ask for a better partner or a better father for our son. Our journey as parents is just beginning, and I cannot wait to see where it takes us. Harvey, the dissertation that forms the base of this book was written while I was pregnant with you. Thank you for the small kicks that kept me writing until 4:00 a.m. I can honestly say that without your nudges, I would not have finished my dissertation in such a timely manner. You are an inspiration to me, and I hope that your father and I raise you to be a justice warrior, fighting to break down all systemic barriers that keep people from being able to live and serve as they deem fit.

INTRODUCTION

AMERICAN METHODISM AND AMERICAN POLITICS

I n 1965, the Reverend John V. Moore of Glide Memorial Methodist Church preached a three-week sermon series that sought, in his words, to "test . . . the 'new morality'" and provide his congregants with a framework to evolve from "morality," or "codes or conduct expressed in laws and customs" that are imposed on persons from "parents, church, the Bible, or the state," to situational "ethics," a system that "aris[es] from within individuals rather than imposed upon them by some external authority."[1] The goal of the sermon series was to teach his congregants to "integrate [their] sexuality into [their] person-hood."[2] If sexuality was considered an integral part of one's God-created self, a person should be allowed to make his or her own sexual decisions based on the ethics of the situation at hand. Reverend Moore considered this the best way for a person to construct sexuality and sexual experiences in a way that honored one's relationship with self, with others, and with God.

Two years later, Charles Keysor, a Methodist minister in Elgin, Illinois, sparked a different type of revolution in the Methodist denomination. He, via the bur-geoning Good News Movement, sought to limit the expression of the "new morality," and instead called for a return to what may be understood as a rule-based morality, one reliant upon the infallible authority of Scripture, which lists right from wrong, moral from immoral. The dichotomy between Rever-ends Moore and Keysor cannot be overstated in its implications for the future polity, doctrine, and social awareness of the newly formed United Methodist Church.[3] From its inception in 1968, the denomination was highly politicized

---

1   John V. Moore, "Chastity and the Pill (Consideration of Ethics and Sex)," January 24, 1965, 1, 3.
2   John V. Moore, "Man, Sex and the Gospel," January 10, 1965, 2.
3   See Russell E. Richey, Kenneth E. Rowe, and Jean Miller Schmidt, *Methodist Experience in America,* vol. 1 (Nashville: Abingdon Press, 2010) for more. From here on the *Methodist Experience in America*, vol. 1, will be cited as *MEA*, vol.1.

regarding human sexuality because United Methodists were not united regarding the treatment of persons who identified as lesbian or gay.

The goal of this book is to trace the Methodist sexual narrative alongside and together with the larger sexual narrative in American history. This book will show how American Methodists discussed, debated, and discerned human sexuality, broadly defined to include birth control, divorce, sex education, abortion, and the rights of persons who identify as gay and lesbian, in the twentieth century. American Methodists typically are active participants within American politics, and as such, their understanding of Methodist sexual morality cannot be fully understood without being placed in the history of American politics, specifically, the rise of the New Christian Right and the perceived threats to its white, heterosexual base. Furthermore, the history of American politics and the rise of the New Christian Right cannot be understood fully without an examination of American Protestantism. Religion and politics are intertwined throughout American history, and their relationship becomes especially entangled with sexuality after the revolutions of the 1960s. One reason The United Methodist Church is currently at an impasse is that some of its members have brought, and continue to bring, American political rhetoric into a conversation about Christian morality. The conflation of American Protestantism and American politics is not a unique phenomenon within The United Methodist Church. Historians of what has come to be called the Christian Right or New Christian Right have spent countless pages outlining how, when, and why American politics and American Protestantism formed a symbiotic relationship.[4]

As American politics became increasingly obsessed with and divided on the moral parameters of human sexuality during the late 1960s, so, too, did American Methodism. I argue that United Methodists became divided once they were asked to confront nonheterosexual and nonmarital sexual expression; and they remain divided because they cannot untangle political rhetoric from Christian

---

4   George M. Marsden, *Fundamentalism and American Culture,* 2nd ed. (New York: Oxford University Press, 2005); Axel R. Schafer, *Countercultural Conservatives: American Evangelicalism from the Postwar Revival to the New Christian Right* (Madison, WI: University of Wisconsin Press, 2011); Daniel K. Williams, *God's Own Party: The Making of the Christian Right* (New York: Oxford University Press, 2010); Molly Worthen, *Apostles of Reason: The Crisis of Authority in American Evangelicalism* (New York: Oxford University Press, 2014); J. Brooks Flippen, *Jimmy Carter, The Politics of Family, and the Rise of the Religious Right* (Athens, GA: University of Georgia Press, 2011); Neil J. Young, *We Gather Together: The Religious Right and the Problem of Interfaith Politics* (New York: Oxford University Press, 2016); Darren Dochuk, *From Bible Belt to Sun Belt: Plain Folk, Religion, Grassroots Politics, and the Rise of Evangelical Conservatism* (New York: W. W. Norton, 2011).

concepts of sexuality. Prior to the 1960s, Methodists largely agreed upon necessary changes to their understanding of sexual morality, as is evident in the acceptance of birth control as a form of responsible Christian marriage (chapter 1) and divorce as an unfortunate, but sometimes necessary, part of responsible Christian living (chapter 2). These changes to the Methodist understanding of sexuality and marriage were largely accepted because they were limited to the confines of heterosexual, Christian marriage. However, once the conversation shifted to include the sexual actions and identities of persons not legally married (that is, teenagers, single women, and persons who identify as lesbian or gay), the conversation became a heavily divided and politically charged debate, one held in the pulpit, the pew, and the ballot box.

American society was also trying to grapple with forms of sexual expression that were just becoming public. While some sought to embrace sexual expression, others took advantage of what they believed to be a moral void. The New Christian Right emerged in this decade as a religio-political powerhouse dedicated to bringing back their notion of sexual morality to American society, politics, and Protestantism. Alongside this, American Methodism took a political turn in the early 1960s when the Methodist Boards of Education and of Social Concern adapted "the new morality," a situational ethic that allowed well-informed persons to make their own determination of what sexual acts were good or bad, and used this ethic to design a sex education course called *Sex and the Whole Person*. However, instead of providing Methodists with a new model for moral decision making in light of the sexual revolutions, the new morality encouraged "evangelical" or "orthodox" Methodists (defined below) to bring rhetoric from American politics into the denomination's conversation about sexual morality.

There are many problems with using the term *evangelical*. First and foremost, there is no agreed-upon definition as to who or what constitutes an evangelical. Journalist Jonathan Merritt, in an article for the *Atlantic*, quipped, "To the pollster, [*evangelical*] is a sociological term. To the pastor, it is a denominational or doctrinal term. And to the politician, it is a synonym for a white Christian Republican."[5] He argues that, depending on the definition used, evangelicals compose either 7 percent or 47 percent of American society today. As

---

5   Jonathan Merritt, "Defining Evangelical," *Atlantic*, December 7, 2015, https://www.theatlantic.com /politics/archive/2015/12/evangelical-christian/418236/.

a religious term, it has historically and theologically been defined as one who spreads the gospel. In the academic arena, American religious historians tend to use David Bebbington's 1989 definition, which identifies evangelicals as those who emphasize conversionism, activism, Biblicism, and crucicentrism.[6] Despite the repeated use of Bebbington's definition in the academic realm, it is no longer satisfactory for what an evangelical is. With the rise and political reign of the New Christian Right over the course of the 1970s and 1980s, the term *evangelical* became more of a political designation in America, "a catch-all term for politically conservative Christians."[7] *Evangelical* was associated with those persons who were pro-life, anti–Equal Rights Amendment, and anti–same-sex marriage; and evangelicals tended to support political candidates whose platforms upheld these stances. In fact, the term *evangelical* has become so conflated with American politics that it can no longer be understood as solely a religious term.[8]

To make matters more complicated, there are religious persons who still identify as evangelical in its traditional sense. This is where the definition becomes even more convoluted. Persons who would identify as politically progressive use the term in its traditional religious form: one who desires to spread the gospel. Likewise, persons who would identify as politically conservative use the term in its traditional religious form: one who desires to spread the gospel. Both of these groups not only seek to spread the gospel; they have the same goal of improving society through social action campaigns and political involvement.

American United Methodists are all evangelical in that they desire to spread the gospel. United Methodists live into the denominational mission to make disciples of Jesus Christ for the transformation of the world. However, throughout this book, I refer to groups of "evangelical Methodists" and "progressive Methodists" as religio-political entities. For this book, it is best to define both evangelical Methodists and progressive Methodists according to how they approach sexuality. Evangelical and progressive Methodists often have the same goals: spread the gospel and transform society for the better through social

---

6   David Bebbington, *Evangelicalism in Modern Britain: A History from the 1730s to the 1980s* (London: Unwin Hyman, 1989).

7   Merritt, "Defining Evangelical."

8   Darren Dochuk, "Evangelicalism," in Philip Goff, ed., *Blackwell Companion to Religion in America* (Hoboken, NJ: Wiley-Blackwell, 2010), 541.

intervention. Where they differ is how they understand human sexuality. *Evangelical Methodists* argue that sexual morality should be based solely upon an infallible scriptural authority. They tend to be anti-abortion, anti–same-sex marriage, and against the ordination of LGBTQ persons. They refer to themselves as "evangelical" or "orthodox" Methodists, and they tend to be members of certain caucus groups, such as the Good News Movement, the Wesleyan Covenant Association, Transforming Congregations, and others. *Progressive Methodists* advocate for a balance between scientifically informed and scripturally informed sexual morality. These Methodists tend to understand sexuality as fluid and encourage frank discussions of all aspects of human sexuality, including nonheterosexual identities and premarital sex. They tend to be pro-choice, pro–same-sex marriage, and advocates for the ordination of LGBTQ persons. They tend to be members of caucus groups such as Reconciling Ministries Network, Queer Clergy Caucus, Love Your Neighbor, and a few others.

Admittedly, these are not neat categories, and some Methodists fall into one camp or the other based on the specific sexual topic. For example, some might believe that sex education should be scientifically informed and include frank conversation, but they also believe that abortion destroys human life. Likewise, both groups spread the good news of the gospel, and thus both can be categorized as *evangelical* in the strictly religious use of the term. For these reasons, many might critique my use of the terms or my trying to categorize Methodists into two camps. Some might see this as encouraging or supporting the divisiveness of the denomination. I recognize that these are problematic categories and welcome critiques of my use of the terms. However, these labels and the subsequent categorization of Methodists is necessary for the project at hand. Furthermore, any shying away from the fact that The United Methodist Church is divided is a break with reality. In the 1970s, as more and more caucus groups emerged within United Methodism, Methodists became increasingly divided as to how one should understand sexuality: does Scripture stand alone as an infallible authority, or is it one authority among many? This difference of interpretation, marketed by different caucus groups, created a United Methodist fissure in 1972, when the denomination tried to define human sexuality amid rapid social and sexual change. In order to understand the tangled web of American Methodism and American politics, certain designations and categorizations must be made, and the terms *evangelical* and *progressive* are not only apt but necessary for this project.

This book presents the histories of Methodist denominations (including the Methodist Episcopal Church, the Methodist Church, the Evangelical United Brethren, and The United Methodist Church) alongside the political reactions to changes in sexuality of American evangelicals and progressives. Using queer theory as a theoretical lens, this book will untangle the web of sexuality, religion, and politics. Queer theory examines different points of history and seeks to understand sexuality at that specific time. For example, in Ancient Greece, sex was primarily about power; it had less to do with romantic love. Sex "functioned as a way of marking individuals in a political order."[9] The active person claimed power over the passive person, and the biological sex of the two did not change the meaning of the act.[10] Queer theory's goal is to "place the question of sexuality as the centre [sic] of concern, and as a key category through which other social, political, and cultural phenomena are to be understood."[11] At its most basic, queer theory uses sexuality as the launching point through which to examine all other aspects of society. For the past forty-six years, United Methodists have placed sexuality as the primary lens through which they have discerned how to be in ministry with one another and the world. The way United Methodists understand sexuality has affected the denomination's history, doctrine, polity, mission, and evangelism. How Methodists define sexuality has altered how they understand marriage, ordination, and personhood. By untangling how Methodists have historically constructed sexuality, we can better understand why United Methodists are divided theologically, socially, and politically.

Using the methodological tools of queer theory, this book seeks to understand American Methodist concepts of sexuality according to their specific social and political contexts. Queer theorist Kathy Rudy argues, "Homosexuality (or for that matter heterosexuality) does not exist in a transhistorical, transcultural, or natural frame."[12] Sexuality cannot be understood as an historic, geographic, or cultural constant. It is fluid and must be analyzed according to a specific time, place, and space. This book will provide the social, political, and

---

9   Kathy Rudy, *Sex and the Church: Gender, Homosexuality, and the Transformation of Christian Ethics* (New York: Beacon Press, 1998), 90.
10   Rudy, 90.
11   Andrew Edgar and Peter Sedgwick, eds., *Key Concepts in Cultural Theory* (London: Routledge Press, 1999), 321.
12   Edgar and Sedwick, 89.

religious context for the stances on human sexuality taken by the General Conference of The United Methodist Church over the course of the twentieth century. Given space limitations, this study will deconstruct sexuality over the span of one century, looking only at the United States and persons who are classified as white.[13]

Throughout the twentieth century, white American Methodists reconsidered their stances on birth control, divorce, sex education, abortion, and the rights and status of gay and lesbian persons. American society has consistently changed its understanding of sexuality too. In early America, sex was primarily for procreation; during the nineteenth century, sex evolved into a love-based act that enhanced marital intimacy. From there, the American understanding of sexuality began to include persons not legally married—the single person, the teenager, the person who identified as LGBTQ. Only through a queer theory lens can the ever-changing stance of United Methodists regarding human sexuality be fully understood, for it allows us to map the fluidity of sexuality alongside the rapid social and sexual change of the twentieth century and the political response to this change.

While queer theory is the main methodological tool, this book is in conversation with historians of the New Christian Right, American Methodism, and American sexuality. Robert O. Self, in his book *All in the Family*, argues that two phrases or ideas shifted American political rhetoric in the 1960s: first that "citizens have *a sex*" and second that "they *have sex*."[14] Self argues that in the first half of the twentieth century, "the universal subject of modern democracies was assumed to be a white heterosexual male." The revolutions of the 1960s forced American politicians and ministers to interact with and minister to those who were not white, heterosexual men. Similarly, the idea that citizens have sex was not recognized publicly until the 1960s revolutions, as prior to that, sex was deemed an act meant to be discussed and performed only in private. Prior to the 1960s, the "national mythology" of the "white middle-class nuclear family

---

13 Methodist sexuality drastically changes when Methodists from the worldwide denomination are considered, because the denomination claims members in African and Asian countries, each of which has its own cultural context and history. Methodist sexuality also drastically changes when African American or black Methodists are included, for they, too, have a different history of sexuality, even when limited to the United States. The work of deconstructing the sexuality of African American Methodists and Methodists outside of the United States needs to be done, but it is too large of a task for this book to accomplish.

14 Robert O. Self, *All in the Family: The Realignment of American Democracy since 1964* (New York: Hill & Wang, 2011), 4, emphasis his.

headed by a patriotic and heterosexual male" dominated. Self argues that the revolutionary climate of the 1960s shook the basis of this mythology as white women, persons of color, and persons of nonheterosexual identity demanded acknowledgment and equal rights under the law.[15]

Another historian of the Christian Right, Daniel K. Williams, argues that in the 1960s, a "grassroots campaign to save the 'traditional' family" began and fought against the Equal Rights Amendment, against abortion, against secular humanism in education, and against gay rights.[16] This book seeks to delve into the arguments made and histories explained by these two authors and provide a micro-level examination of how the rise of the New Christian Right—and its emphasis on Christian morality as a necessary part of American politics—affected American Methodism.

Other scholars have contributed to this conversation. Methodist scholar Jane Ellen Nickell argues that Methodist debates surrounding race, gender, and homosexuality have parallel histories because African Americans, women, and persons who identify as LGBTQ have, across Methodist history, been a threat to white, male power. When threatened, Nickell argues, white men, specifically those of the Methodist clergy, reaffirm a "social structure" that favors white, male, heterosexual power as "God's intended plan." Thus, "deviation" from this authority, she argues, is "seen as a threat to the divine order."[17] This book accepts Nickell's premise and builds upon it. The expansion of sexual morality opens the door to dismantling white, male, heterosexual power, specifically their power to define what acts are "good" or "bad."

Historian Heather R. White created an alternative history of gay rights in America with her book, *Reforming Sodom*.[18] She argues that liberal Protestant clergy were key agents in advancing the homophile movement. In order to sustain this argument, she uncovers how the Bible's condemnation of same-sex acts is a modern-day invention, translated into the Revised Standard Version of the Bible in 1946 by liberal Protestants who wanted to make sexual expression healthy for heterosexual couples. Inadvertently, this translation created

---

15   Self, *All in the Family*, 4–5.
16   Williams, *God's Own Party*, chaps. 6 and 7.
17   Jane Ellen Nickell, *We Shall Not Be Moved: Methodists Debate Race, Gender, and Homosexuality* (Eugene, OR: Pickwick Publications, 2013), 3.
18   Heather R. White, *Reforming Sodom: Protestants and the Rise of Gay Rights* (Chapel Hill, NC: University of North Carolina Press, 2015).

a category of unhealthy sexuality: homosexuality. Built into their new notion of healthy sexuality, however, was the basis for involvement in the homophile movement, which allowed some Protestant clergy to provide space for the gay liberation movement to garner support. The following will show how American Methodist clergy were active agents in expanding the limits of sexual morality. Chapter 5 will delve into how American Methodist clergy worked with the gay rights activists in the early 1960s.

The works mentioned above largely discuss the history of white persons who, through their privileged positions, have controlled the historic narrative. This book, too, is largely a history of white, middle- and upper-class Methodists, for they are the ones who have controlled the Methodist narrative, holding the majority of agency leadership, the larger urban pulpits, and the majority of delegate seats at General Conference.

HISTORY AND DOCTRINE

The spread of American political rhetoric into Christian morality has not only affected the denomination's current discussions of the moral parameters of human sexuality; it has also affected how Methodists tell their history and explain their theology. Methodists tend to prioritize history over doctrine. If anyone doubts this, refer them to the 2016 *The Book of Discipline of The United Methodist Church*, where "A Brief History of The United Methodist Church" precedes "The Constitution" and the "Doctrinal Standards and Our Theological Task."

Methodism did not begin with a doctrinal disagreement. It began as a missional movement within the Church of England. It is the story of this movement and its history that make Methodism, in all of its forms, unique. However, even though Methodism is defined by its history, the story that is told can often vary according to an individual's political leaning. This phenomenon is not unique to American Methodism. History at large is dependent upon the speaker. What is unique about Methodism is how closely linked its history and its identity are.

One history of American Methodism emphasizes social reform. Those who promote this version often emphasize the Methodist stance against slavery, its involvement in the Social Gospel, and its support of civil rights. Another history emphasizes Methodist evangelism. Their story focuses on Methodism spreading across the frontier, camp meetings, and its missional efforts on other continents. These distinct histories and their subsequent theological constructs, which prioritize social reform or evangelism, exist simultaneously within what is now called United Methodism, leading their proponents to have very different constructs and sometimes conflicting meanings of what it means to identify as United Methodist today.[19]

The basis of these discrepancies lies in history. From its founding through the mid-nineteenth century, Methodism (as defined to include the Methodist Episcopal Church, the Methodist Episcopal Church South, the Methodist Church, and the United Brethren in Christ) was *evangelical*. Scholars of American religions typically define *evangelical* using David Bebbington's quadrilateral; historian Martin Wellings argues that Methodism adheres to Bebbington's definition of evangelicalism.[20] However, in Wesleyan terms, a nineteenth-century evangelical can be defined as a person who (1) adheres to the spirit of the gospel, (2) experiences religion (justification), (3) performs good works (holiness or sanctification), and (4) is active in the Methodist connection. To elaborate, (1) John Wesley was known as "a man of one book," the Bible, and most of his sermons and his brother's, Charles's, hymns were hermeneutical. (2) John Wesley's conversion experience was described as a "strange warming of the heart," and creating a similar experience was a primary focus of nineteenth-century Methodist preaching and gathering. (3) Aiding those less fortunate (both physically and spiritually) was essential to Wesley's own ministry and the ministry he sought to replicate in the Methodist movement. And (4) the Methodist connection, with its hierarchical system of class, bands, societies, itinerant preachers, district superintendents, and bishops, was established to maintain social and personal accountability and to maximize conversions. In this sense, Methodists, from inception through the mid-nineteenth century, were staunch evangelicals.

Toward the end of the nineteenth century, Methodist history and theology split into various camps; and around 1890, German biblical criticism became a new way for theologians to interpret Scripture using critical thinking based in

---

19 For more about the different stories Methodists tell about themselves, see Ted A. Campbell's book *Encoding Methodism: Telling and Retelling Narratives of Wesleyan Origins* (Nashville: New Room Books, 2017).

20 Bebbington's quadrilateral is: (1) conversionism, or the belief in an instantaneous change of heart, faith, or life; (2) activism, or the spread of the gospel to others in order to ignite their conversion; (3) biblicism, or a belief in the Bible as sole authority; (4) crucicentrism, or the emphasis of Christ's sacrifice on the cross as salvific moment. Bebbington, *Evangelicalism in Modern Britain*, 2–17. Martin Wellings, "Methodism and the Evangelical Tradition," in *The Ashgate Research Companion to World Methodism*, ed. Martin Wellings, Peter S. Forsaith, and William Gibson (Burlington, VT: Routledge, 2013), 225.

historical, philosophical, and scientific inquiry. Scholars questioned, or posited as scientifically unfounded, certain biblical stories, such as the garden of Eden, the Great Flood, and the virgin birth, although these were still regarded as holding valuable moral and theological lessons. Biblical interpretation, subjected to rational, scientific examination, and Protestant liberalism, was grounded in rigorous method and consequently developed as the primary mode of theological interpretation for mainline Protestant denominations, including the Methodist Episcopal Church (MEC).[21] Around the turn of the twentieth century, as older MEC seminary professors retired, "the theological leadership of American Methodism change[d] hands almost completely" and instituted a "shift," which "signaled the end of one theological era and the beginning of another."[22] This shift was most evident in graduates from Boston University School of Theology, Drew Theological Seminary, Garrett Biblical Institute, and the Iliff School of Theology.

These histories become more convoluted after the 1960s, when partisan politics intruded on the denominational scene and further split the newly formed denomination. Historically, Methodists were not apolitical. They campaigned against slavery, for women's suffrage, and were largely responsible for Prohibition. However, these social action campaigns were largely the work of one or two caucus groups (the Women's Christian Temperance Union, for example). After the 1960s, United Methodism witnessed the rise of multiple political caucus groups. These groups exist on the fringes of United Methodism and advocate for certain social stances based on their own version of United Methodist history and theology and their individual political leanings. Throughout the end of the twentieth century, they burst into the life of The United Methodist Church in unprecedented numbers and divided United Methodists according to political platforms. Most of these political caucus groups emerged to push the denomination toward a specific understanding of human sexuality. This book examines how, after 1960, these groups worked to create new, or maintain existing, sexual moralities. Across the first half of the twentieth century, Methodists worked together to rearticulate what constituted Christian sexuality, in order to accommodate cultural and social change, specifically the use

---

21   Marsden, *Fundamentalism and American Culture,* 17–19.
22   Robert E. Chiles, *Theological Transition in American Methodism: 1790–1935* (New York: Abingdon Press, 1965), 65.

of artificial birth control and divorce. However, with the sexual revolution of the 1960s and the subsequent rise of the New Christian Right, sex became increasingly politicized. As free sexual expression began to include persons who were neither white nor heterosexual, white heterosexual men and women began to reassert their power. They tried to control the narrative through censoring sex education, prohibiting the legalization of abortion, and denying the rights of LGBTQ persons. Until this point, American Methodists had adjusted their construction of sexuality to be apt for the time, as chapters 1 and 2 will show. In the 1960s, American Methodists attempted this one last time with the "new morality," a moral framework with which not all could agree.

THE "NEW MORALITY"

A product of the mid-twentieth century, the "new morality" has a complicated history, because a variety of ethical frameworks have claimed the label or its definition. According to John G. Milhaven and David J. Casey, a new "trend of ethical thought" often called "'situationism,' 'situation ethics,' 'contextualism,' [or] 'the new morality,'" stressed "the concrete situation and the one absolute Christian value of love, while de-emphasizing the importance of absolute laws in discerning what a Christian ought to do."[23] The topic of Christian ethicists such as John A. T. Robinson and Joseph Fletcher, the new morality was "a radical 'ethic of the situation,' with nothing prescribed—except love."[24] This "new look" of Christian ethics was first written about by Joseph Fletcher in 1959; and by 1963, Bishop Robinson proclaimed "the new morality" as a Christian moral framework.[25] Its theological roots lie in the work of liberal theologians of the early-twentieth century who, like Borden Parker Bowne, began "to see the essence of Christianity, the significance of the original gospel, as something human, as simply a summit of human thought and experience, from which other human thought and experience differs only in degree."[26]

For these theologians and ethicists, God's command to love was primary and called persons to serve the world around them. In order to properly serve

---

23   John G. Milhaven and David J. Casey, "Introduction to the Theological Background of the New Morality," *Theological Studies* 28, no. 2 (June 1967): 213.

24   Milhaven and Casey, 213.

25   See Joseph Fletcher, "The New Look in Christian Ethics," *Harvard Divinity Bulletin* 24, no. 1 (1932?): 7–18; John A. T. Robinson, *Honest to God* (London: SCM Press, 1963); Joseph Fletcher, *Situation Ethics: The New Morality* (Philadelphia: Westminster Press, 1966).

26   Milhaven and Casey, "Introduction to the Theological Background," 219.

the world, the person had to understand the context around him or her, which "requires human experience and reflection on what makes up the situation as well as requiring the light of faith."[27] Ethicists, such as Joseph Fletcher, took this basic idea and emphasized the love of God and of neighbor. When applied as an ethical framework, "the situationist . . . holds that whatever is the most loving thing in the situation is the right and good thing." Social reform or acts oriented towards "justice" are "nothing other than love working out its problems," for "love and justice are the same, for justice is love distributed."[28]

When applied to sexual ethics, however, the new morality faced staunch criticism as "nothing but a philosophy of sexual libertinism."[29] Ethicist Elwyn A. Smith argued against this perception of the new morality. He believed that "the new morality is the most demanding ethical concept in the market places of ideas" for "only the most mature persons are capable of practicing it." Only a truly mature person can place love of God and love of others above oneself. Only a truly mature person can fully understand a situation and prioritize love. Only a truly mature person can transform love into social reform. He stated it best when he said, "Rules are for the weak; emancipation is for the mature."[30]

Fletcher's view can easily be applied to Wesleyan theology and social ethics. John Wesley believed the mark of a Methodist to be a desire to do good works and to live into the commandment to love God with all of one's heart, soul, and mind and to love neighbor as oneself. Thus, the new morality, defined as an ethical framework that prioritizes actions of love for God and others as the determining ethical factor, is an appropriate framework for Methodists to discern ethical situations. Methodist theologian Leon O. Hyson argued that

> love is the central Christian virtue which Wesleyan ethics elaborates. It is a composite principle which incorporates the personal and social dimensions. . . . The whole heart, mind, and soul committed to God in a loving relationship, and the same intensity of love or quality of love which is bound up in self-love is to be expressed toward the neighbor.[31]

---

27 Milhaven and Casey, 222.

28 Milhaven and Casey, 238.

29 Elwyn A. Smith, "Notes on the Practice of the New Morality," *Pittsburgh Perspective* 7, no. 4 (December 1966): 23.

30 Smith, 26.

31 Leon O. Hynson, "Christian Love: The Key to Wesley's Ethics," *Methodist History* 14, no. 1 (October 1975): 45.

During the twentieth century, Methodists wrestled with how to construct a sexual ethic that was biblical, Wesleyan, and applicable to the changing society. The new morality offered them such an ethic, as it was grounded in acts of love. By the mid-twentieth century, urban churches increasingly demanded clergy that were attuned to social change; and thus a specific type of graduate emerged from leading Methodist seminaries, trained in historical criticism and later elected bishops and heads of Methodist general agencies. Thus, by the mid-twentieth century, the urban pulpits and administrative ranks of Methodism promoted a more progressive form of Methodism. These clergy emphasized social reform through support of the civil rights movement and aligned the denomination with larger trends of social and sexual change, specifically, the support of sex education in the public schools, the legalization of abortion, and the homophile movement.

GIVE ME THAT OLD-TIME RELIGION

Other Methodists continued what they considered a more traditional route of theological interpretation, one that was suspicious of biblical criticism. By the 1920s, this Methodist voice was represented by Harold Paul Sloan and his Methodist League for Faith and Life. Their main concern was to reform the Course of Study in order to prevent seminary students from reading "modernist" texts such as those that advocated biblical criticism. In the 1950s, Bob Schuler continued these efforts to fight "modernism" in the denomination and began the call for a return to "historic Methodism."[32] These leaders echoed the concerns of some earlier Methodists, that Methodism was too concerned with culture and not concerned enough with personal religious experience and social accountability. They remained committed to the idea that proper Christian morality would naturally lead to proper sexuality—defined as heterosexual, monogamous, and within marriage—and they maintained this view through the sexual revolutions of the 1960s. They, too, embraced certain changes in family life, but believed that some Methodists were failing to protect family life from a multitude of social, political, and moral threats. Sloan and Schuler were never successful in organizing and maintaining a unified voice within the denomination.

---

32   Howard Glen Spann, "Evangelicalism in Modern American Methodism: Theological Conservatives in the 'Great Deep' of the Church, 1900–1980" (PhD diss., John Hopkins University, 1994), 39–41. See chapters 1–3 for more information on these two.

INTRODUCTION

However, in the 1960s, Charles Keysor began the Good News Movement and successfully organized what came to be called "orthodox" or "evangelical" Methodists behind a common voice and agenda, the return of historic Methodism and its emphasis on personal religious experience.

THEOLOGICAL PLURALISM AND THE POLITICAL CAUCUS

Thus far, American Methodism has its roots in a variety of histories and theologies, all of which are connected to larger trends in American Protestant evangelicalism and Protestant liberalism. In the early-twentieth century, when other mainline denominations divided along "fundamentalist" and "modernist" lines, the Methodists did not, at least not with the same effect. Instead, the Methodist Episcopal Church, the Methodist Episcopal Church South, and the Methodist Protestant denominations united in 1939, despite a multitude of theological, social, and political differences.[33] Then in 1968, when the Evangelical United Brethren and Methodist Church united to create The United Methodist Church, General Conference delegates affirmed the core doctrines of both predecessor denominations. They believed the denominations had a unified theology, grounded in historic Wesleyanism.

However, within the Methodist Church, significant theological disagreements, which existed since the mid-to-late nineteenth century, were not addressed in the 1968 merger. This lack of theological unity resulted in the rise of political caucus groups in the late 1960s and further polarized United Methodism and obfuscated its identity as a united denomination. In 1968, the General Conference of the newly formed The United Methodist Church upheld "theological pluralism . . . as a principle" for "reappraising and applying the Gospel."[34] Theological pluralism is best understood as "a living and dynamic theological tradition in which five distinct languages are spoken, including evangelicalism, radicalism, ecumenism, liberalism, and Wesleyanism."[35] Theological pluralism was the solution to allowing multiple histories and theologies to coexist in one

33 For more on this merger and its problems for the successor denominations, see Morris L. Davis, *The Methodist Unification: Christianity and the Politics of Race in the Jim Crow Era* (New York: NYU Press, 2008).

34 "Our Theological Task," *The Book of Discipline of The United Methodist Church* (Nashville, TN: The United Methodist Publishing House, 1972), 69. Hereafter cited as *BOD* with the year following.

35 Jason E. Vickers, "American Methodism: A Theological Tradition," in *The Cambridge Companion to American Methodism*, ed. Jason E. Vickers (Cambridge: Cambridge University Press, 2013), 33.

denomination; yet it unknowingly allowed these histories and theologies to develop into concrete ideologies, which still exist on the edges of United Methodism and whose advocates promote their own history of United Methodism and their own definitions of what is "essential" to United Methodist theology. These differences become predominantly clear in discussions of sexuality.

The formation of political caucus groups in the 1970s reflects the influence of American politics on American Methodism. Their formation should not be understood as negative, for they continually challenge the status quo. Ken Rowe, renowned historian of Methodism, argues that "caucuses, quotas, and church politics are neither new nor un-Methodist—nor are they bad, per se."[36] He bases this argument on the fact that Methodism itself was originally a "caucus," a renewal movement, within the Church of England. Since then, its history, doctrine, and polity have evolved continuously through the work of caucuses. This is not only distinct in one branch of the Methodist tradition; other branches, such as the Evangelical United Brethren, also experienced division, unification, and changes in their doctrine and polity due to the power and influence of caucuses.[37] Caucuses, for Rowe, are grassroots movements that seek to change policy in some way. They inform the power centers of the denomination of how the people in the pews feel about certain policies.[38] He argues:

> Caucuses provide necessary balance to connectional authority . . . They enriched our understanding of the gospel, refocused our mission, and redistributed our power . . . Every generation of Methodist, Evangelical, and United Brethren has had its independent characters and cantankerous caucuses, who would not be put down by episcopal authority or by majority vote. Many of the issues they championed required an extended campaign before the church bowed to reform.[39]

Rowe argues, "The turbulent sixties marked the coming of age of Methodism's caucus tradition," and in response to the "highly centralized remodeling of 1972," the work of caucuses has never been more important.[40] As of 1999, Rowe counted at least twenty caucuses actively working to reform some part

---

36 Kenneth Rowe, "How Do Caucuses Contribute to Connection?" in *Questions for the Twenty-First Century Church*, ed. Dennis M. Campbell et al. (Nashville, TN: Abingdon Press, 1999), 256.
37 Rowe, 243.
38 Rowe, 244.
39 Rowe, 256–57.
40 Rowe, 255.

of United Methodism. The caucuses that this book will discuss became increasingly political and polarized around sexuality by the end of the 1970s. Each caucus formed to fight for or against a specific cause, and many of their current agendas revolve around sexuality. By the end of the twentieth century, they worked with like-minded caucuses, especially during General Conference, to push through broad agendas that would direct the denomination toward maintaining its current construction of sexual morality or rearticulating United Methodist sexual morality. These causes are easily divided into two broader camps, depending upon their stance on human sexuality. Those who work to rearticulate sexual morality are the Methodist Federation for Social Action, Affirmation, and Reconciling Ministries Network. Those who work to maintain the current sexual morality are the Methodist League for Faith and Life, the Good News Movement, Lifewatch, the Confessing Movement, Transforming Congregations, and the Wesleyan Covenant Association. These groups and their members do not agree on all aspects of their individual agendas; however, around General Conference, they form a broad coalition to promote an overall agenda in hope that legislative changes promote or prevent changes to United Methodist constructions of sexuality.

Throughout this book, we will see how Methodists are trying to discern how sex is related to God and how sex is related to and different from sexuality. When chapters 1 and 2 begin, most Methodists believed that "proper" sex was between one man and one woman, for the purposes of procreation, and in the confines of a monogamous Christian marriage. This limited definition of proper sex was challenged to create new frameworks for a Methodist sexual ethic. From the 1930s through 1950s, Methodists developed a new sexual ethic that allowed for the acceptance of artificial birth control and divorce as a realistic part of modern Christian marriage. With continued changes in American constructs of sexuality, this sexual ethic evolved into "the new morality" by the mid-1960s. The new morality was divisive. It was exalted in some Methodist circles, for its allowed Methodists to experiment with frank forms of sex education, to promote the legalization of abortion, and to be involved with the homophile rights movement. However, not all Methodists welcomed the new morality. For the same reasons that some Methodists exalted the framework, other Methodists despised it. The stark divide that currently exists within United Methodism arose during the 1960s, with debates on the new morality and its application in sex education. The divide intensified when United Methodists used the new morality to accept abortion and homosexuality, two aspects of sexuality that have been increasingly debated since the 1970s in both American Methodism and American politics. Since the beginning of the twentieth century, Methodism has been divided—historically, theologically, and socially—on what it means to identify as (United) Methodist. This book examines one aspect of the debate: sexuality.

The chapters will be divided along chronological and thematic lines. Throughout the first half of the twentieth century, Methodists worked together to rearticulate sexuality in order to accept the use of artificial birth control within the confines of Christian marriage and the reality of divorce as a necessary option for Christian marriage. Once sexuality began to include those persons who were not legally married—the teenager, the single person, or persons of non-heterosexual identity—Methodists began to disagree and work against each other. They formed political caucus groups, whose arguments were reflective of American politics, to aid their efforts to sway the denomination in one direction or the other. Each chapter begins with a brief synopsis of American changes in sexuality and family life. It then explains how American Protestantism responded to these changes. Finally, it turns to Methodist sources—primarily published sources in the form of Methodist periodicals and pamphlets, published caucus materials, legislation to General Conference, and statements found in the *Discipline*—to determine how Methodists responded.

1

A NEW AMERICAN METHODIST SEXUALITY

METHODISTS AND BIRTH CONTROL

S ex is no longer a problem to youth. It is a fact." In December 1941, Marjorie Charles wrote these words for a forum on college relationships coordinated by *motive* magazine [*sic*], the serial of the Methodist Student Movement, which connected American Methodist college students across a variety of campuses, both public and private.[1] Each of the forum's authors discussed the current disposition toward sex and tried to better understand sexuality for the impending 1940s. The forum began with a statement of the problem: society was obsessed with sex and yet "sex [was] still taboo." Sex and society were evolving from a Victorian code that portrayed sex as sinful, immoral, and dirty, to an acceptable private act between two persons (of the opposite sex) and an acceptable topic of public discussion. If sex could be understood as a Christian doctrine and as a celebration of God-given energy, then sex could be understood as "the most delightful, the happiest, and the most truly representative adult experience that [one] enjoys."[2] But how did one change the way sex was perceived? In the 1940s, *motive* tried to show that Protestant churches could and should be the place where those who wanted to know more about sex turned.

In this chapter, I will show how, by 1940, Methodist ministers in urban pulpits, Methodists at the administrative level of the Methodist Church, and Methodist college students used publications to develop a new sexual ethic, which

---

1   *motive* magazine never capitalizes its *m*, and this convention will be followed. The paper had just over twelve thousand subscribers in 1950. By 1967, they had around forty-five thousand subscribers ("Motive Circulation Figures," Folder Title: Motive, Folder Number: 2642-5-2:07, Box Title: Campus Ministry, GCAH). The Methodist Student Movement was a movement within the Methodist Episcopal Church in 1937, and had its peak in the Methodist Church, which was formed in 1939 by the unification of the Methodist Episcopal Church, the Methodist Episcopal Church South, and the Methodist Protestants.

2   Unknown author, "I Am Related: Why and How—and for What Purpose?" *motive* 2, no. 4 (December 1941): 9–10.

included non-procreative sex and the use of artificial contraception as, not only common, but *responsible* Christian practice within the marital bond. Through premarital counseling and an emerging emphasis on sex education, Methodists created a new form of healthy sexuality. Methodists, from those in the pew to those in the administrative ranks of the general agencies, worked together to rearticulate their sexual ethic in order to accommodate social and sexual change.

This chapter overlaps contextually with the next chapter. The two together conclude with the creation of a new sexual ethic, which reconstructed healthy sexuality to include the responsible use of birth control and the reality of divorce as natural parts of Christian marriage. The birth-control movement runs parallel to the women's suffrage movement and is thus categorized as the first sexual revolution in America. Note that even though this revolution threatened white, male power, it cannot be viewed in the same light as the revolutions of the 1960s. The revolutions of the early nineteenth century into the 1920s were more palatable to white men because they liberated mainly white, married women. In both chapters 1 and 2, the subjects analyzed are mainly white, middle- and upper-class members of the Methodist Episcopal Church (MEC) and the Methodist Church (MC), with brief references to the Methodist Episcopal Church South (MECS), the Church of the United Brethren in Christ (UBC), and the Evangelical United Brethren (EUB).

This chapter will look at a small piece of sexuality's history, the birth-control movement, and how it reshaped sexuality on a social level by challenging conventional notions of reproduction, family life, and women's "proper" place. It will argue that in order to harness women's newfound sexuality, Methodists created a new sexual ethic that embraced this sexuality within the confines of heterosexual, Christian marriage. The primary sources employed are the *Discipline* (the law book of the denominations), pamphlets created by the Methodist Committee on Family Life, and *motive* magazine. First, I will describe the changes in sexuality that led to the birth-control movement in America and how the movement changed sexuality. I will then show how and when the Methodist Episcopal Church and the Methodist Church responded to this first sexual revolution. This chapter will conclude with a look at the new sexual ethic as exemplified through *motive*.[3]

---

3   The term *Methodist* is the most frequently used noun to describe the members, both clergy and lay, of the various denominations that make up the current United Methodist Church. For the purposes of this

THE FIRST SEXUAL REVOLUTION IN AMERICA, 1880–1900

The birth-control movement in America officially began in the 1910s, but sexuality was already undergoing a revolution. It is hard to pinpoint the beginning of any revolution, especially one involving sex, an act that is usually performed and discussed in private. Over the last half of the nineteenth century, scientists, specifically sexologists such as the influential Richard von Krafft-Ebing, discussed sex and sexuality as directly connected to psychology and biology.[4] In the 1940s, sexologist Alfred Kinsey continued this rhetoric and separated sex from its historically religious, that is, moral, context.[5] Between 1880 and 1940, scientists became the experts in sex, replacing clergy as *the* persons to turn to for information and guidance. As ministers' sexual authority was threatened, they learned that in order maintain control of congregational morality, they, too, would have to learn the scientific approach to sex, one that looked at the brute facts of sex separate from moral connotation.

Historically, Christianity, specifically its clergy, was concerned, at times obsessed, with women's sexuality. According to science, sexual acts, on their own, have no moral meaning. Morality has to be assigned, and religious authorities were quick to assign morality to all aspects of sexuality. Historian Tom Davis describes men as jealous of women's ability to bear children, and they considered this act sacred. Men, unable to bear children, found another means to acquire a sacred standing in childbearing—religion. As clerics and priests, men took sexual power away from women by assigning sexual acts a moral or immoral connotation. Davis argued that "while women could continue to have the children, it was the priest who would decide the conditions under which that process was moral or immoral, whether the woman was clean or unclean, whether the child was legitimate or illegitimate."[6]

---

chapter, when the term *Methodist* is used, it is describing members of the Methodist Episcopal Church or the Methodist Church. When discussing members of the smaller denominations (the Methodist Episcopal Church, South; Methodist Protestants: or the Evangelical United Brethren), a differentiation will be made. The best way to determine if *Methodist* refers to a member of the MEC or TMC is the date: pre-1939 refers to members of the MEC; post-1939 refers to members of TMC.

4   Richard von Krafft-ebing, *Psychopathia Sexualis*, F. J. Rebman, trans. (New York: Rebman, 1906).

5   Amanda H. Littauer, *Bad Girls: Young Women, Sex, and Rebellion before the Sixties* (Chapel Hill, NC: University of North Carolina Press, 2015); John D'Emilio and Estelle B. Freedman, *Intimate Matters: A History of Sexuality in America*, 3rd ed. (Chicago: University of Chicago Press, 2012); and Marie Griffith, "The Religious Encounters of Alfred Kinsey," *Journal of American History* (September 2008): 349–77.

6   Tom Davis, *Sacred Work: Planned Parenthood and Its Clergy Alliances* (New Brunswick, NJ: Rutgers University Press, 2005), 10.

Over the last third of the nineteenth century, a plethora of events affected the role of women, their sexuality, and thus male authority. The Industrial Revolution created new, nondomestic professional opportunities for women; women increasingly sought college-level education; the rise of urban living provided social and spatial freedom for women; the debut of the motion picture celebrated sexually liberated woman; Darwinian science provided women with a non-Eve creation story through which they might be seen as equals of men; the emergence of "masculine Christianity" reinforced the gender binary in a new way; the increase in immigration to America and its accompanying new religions and cultures provided new examples of how women could live; and a variety of innovations, such as the bicycle and car, forever changed courtship by giving couples privacy and mobility. All of these culminated to influence sexuality and gender at the turn of the century, and whenever women's sexuality changed, men's authority was threatened. Davis argues that the birth-control movement was "engaged in a form of sacred work," because it focused on women's reproductive justice and sought to undo the centuries-old power-hungry acts of papal and clerical authority.[7] This section will focus on two events, from roughly 1850 to 1930, that challenged conventional urban, white, middle-class Christian notions of wifely submission and female chastity and set the stage for the birth-control movement.

The Purity Movement

First, just after the American Civil War, the infamous Anthony Comstock and others began the purity movement. These white, Protestant men sought to eradicate what they deemed "obscene" from the streets of urban middle- and upper-class America.[8] To ensure that a white moral Christian mentality was perpetuated throughout their lineages, no "book, pamphlet, paper, writing, advertisement, circular, print, picture, drawing, or other representation, figure, or image on or of paper or other material, or any cast, instrument, or other article of an immoral nature, or any drug or medicine, or any article whatever for the prevention of conception" was to be discussed, sold, or marketed under the Comstock laws.[9] Within state lines, "baby Comstock laws" established a com-

---

7   Davis, 6.
8   Foster, *Moral Reconstruction,* 48–50; Nicola Beisel, *Imperiled Innocents: Anthony Comstock and Family Reproduction in Victorian America* (Princeton, NJ: Princeton University Press, 1998).
9   Andrea Tone, "Contraceptive Consumers: Gender and the Political Economy of Birth Control in the 1930s," *Journal of Social History* 29, no. 3 (Spring 1996): 488.

plete ban on the sale and use of contraceptives, including the sale of information that taught "do it yourself" methods.[10] Because of such laws, "American women in the early twentieth century were far more ignorant about contraception than their foremothers were in 1850," a problem that, as chapter 4 will show, created the need for abortion rights in the 1950s and 1960s.[11]

The promotion of purity was in response to an increase in the use and availability of a wide variety of artificial contraceptives and an increase in immigration. According to historian Andrea Tone, "Douching powders and astringents, dissolving suppositories, and vaginal pessaries had supplemented male withdrawal and abstinence as mainstays of birth-control practice in pre-industrial America" and were "increasingly available from commercial vendors." In fact, "by the 1870s, condoms, douching syringes, douching solutions, vaginal sponges, and cervical caps could be purchased from mail-order houses, wholesale drug-supply houses, and pharmacies."[12] Their availability in commercial outlets parallels the scientific introduction of sex into public discourse. Contraceptives, like sex, made their way into the public eye and ear, and consequently, a purity movement pushed back and put an end to the public discourse of sexuality.

Race was also a major contributor to the rise of the purity movement. Immigration to America was at an all-time high during the last third of the nineteenth century; and the influx of new ethnicities, cultures, and religions threatened white, Christian, middle- and upper-class morality, especially since many European immigrants passed as "white." Comstock and his supporters upheld what David Sehat called *the moral establishment*, "a religiously derived morality, enforceable by law, [which] was essential to the health of the state."[13] The moral establishment combined with evangelical theology and "demand[ed] the intervention of believers into public life in an attempt to shape the world according to the dictates of their conscience."[14] Only evangelical Protestants—a category that did not include European immigrants—who adhered to a narrow sense of

---

10 Davis. *Sacred Work*, 23.

11 Davis, 24.

12 Tone, "Contraceptive Consumers," 489.

13 Abolition in the 1860s and Prohibition in the 1920s were two of the best examples of how the moral establishment worked within the federal government. David Sehat, *The Myth of American Religious Freedom* (New York: Oxford University Press, 2011): 5.

14 Sehat, 6.

morality based in biblical literalism, temperance, chastity, and submission to God could *correctly* contribute to society as American citizens. The purity movement was an enforcement of the moral establishment. Fear of immigrants, because they were different and yet appeared white, shaped the foundation of Comstock's desire to eliminate contraception within the middle and upper classes of American Protestantism, forcing them to reproduce. The purity movement was an example of how one narrow, evangelical Protestant definition of morality, which George Marsden would call fundamentalist, was enforced through federal law, limiting sexual expression and dissemination of information, and forcing thousands of women to find alternative and dangerous methods for unwanted pregnancies.[15]

On the surface, it seems that the purity movement did not change women's sexuality, but upheld a specific type of women's sexuality—chaste and incorruptible—as a moral compass. However, as evidenced by the increase in contraceptive sales and use, women's sexuality evolved despite Comstock's attempts. Women chose whether or not to conceive children, and, with technological advances such as cervical caps and diaphragms, women had that choice without the consent or even knowledge of their husbands. The purity movement and Comstock laws did not stop the use of contraceptives; but they did create an underground countermovement that relied on marketing what was euphemistically called "feminine hygiene." Most important, it created a gap between the middle- and upper-class white women, who could afford black-market contraceptives and could find the rare booklet on contraception, and lower-class women, usually immigrants and African Americans, who were left with abstinence-only methods and tried to balance marital intimacy with the prevention of conception.

The New Woman

Second, and in conjuncture with the purity movement, women of the late nineteenth century sought professions aside from motherhood. The *new woman* sought education and economic independence above all else, and thus "she threatened men in ways her mother never did."[16] She went to wom-

---

15 Marsden, *Fundamentalism and American Culture*, 26, 222.
16 Carroll Smith-Rosenberg, *Disorderly Conduct: Visions of Gender in Victorian America* (New York: Oxford University Press, 1986), 245.

en's colleges, and once male universities opened their doors, coeducational universities offered her the opportunity to gain an education for life beyond the home. She demanded not only equal but identical education to that of her male peers. Her mother believed that a college education would make her a better wife; but the new woman saw college as an opportunity to achieve independence outside of the patriarchal family. She eschewed motherhood and marriage, viewing them as outdated institutions that prevented women from living into their full potential as contributors to society. After college, she entered the professional workforce, often working in a settlement house where "women spun out a delicate web of interlocking social-justice organizations led and staffed by militant (and, often, single) New Women."[17] Settlement houses gave these women social authority and a portal through which to enact real social change.

Within these types of reform-oriented environments, women used familiar rhetoric that emphasized their purity and natural ability to care for others, to fight for social justice for all. Their mothers had taken on a similar task when they organized women-only social-reform organizations such as the Young Women's Christian Association and the Women's Christian Temperance Union. However, while their mothers still identified primarily as mothers and wives, new women identified as economically independent, educated, and single women. In reality, new women, as Smith-Rosenberg argued, were liminal figures, existing outside of the conventional domestic realm, which women of their mother's generation occupied, and not yet allowed into the professional, political, and public world of men—at least that was the case for the first generation of new women (ca. 1880–1910).

Over the course of the early twentieth century, the next generation of new women (ca. 1920–1930) left the settlement house to fight directly within the public forum, demanding suffrage and better health care for women. These second-generation women sought to better their own health through sex education; and they questioned, not only gendered conventions of women in the home, but sexual conventions of women that upheld women as passive, asexual, and pure.[18] Historian Amanda H. Littauer described the various changes in women's sexuality in between the world wars:

---

17   Smith-Rosenberg, 255.
18   Smith-Rosenberg, 284.

In the early twentieth century, immigrant and working-class young women explored the amusements and commercial opportunities of city life, often on the arms of young men who paid their way in exchange for sex. . . . The rise of dating practices eroded parental and community control, and prostitution lost ground to taxi dancing, stripping, and erotic dancing. . . . The rise of urban life and commercial amusements in the late nineteenth and early twentieth centuries contributed to "a new spectrum of women's [hetero]sexual activities," including treating as well as dramatically higher rates of premarital sex; these practices, in turn, facilitated the decline of prostitution. Major cities hosted thriving sexual subcultures for men who had sex with men and also for heterosexual couples seeking cross-racial encounters, sexual spectatorship, and performances of queer sexuality. Lesbian communities also formed within educational and reform circles. Intellectual developments—such as the popularization of Freud's critique of sexual repression and trans-Atlantic advocacy for freedom of sexual speech—encouraged sexual expression.[19]

New women, of both generations and of middle and upper classes, embraced self-determination. Leaving home for education, for economic opportunities, or to escape parental control, these women took advantage of their newly found freedom. They openly expressed their sexuality and, as Smith-Rosenberg argued, the second generation sought to undo conventional mores by questioning the very idea of gender: "Gender conventions lay at the heart of the confining traditions," that is, the sexually pure, domestically bound wife and mother, which "they, as modernists, fought against."[20] These women turned to androgyny, cutting their hair and donning pants. If they could show that gender could be as easily changed as changing one's dress, then they could show that the institutions, values, and behaviors built upon the authority of men could also be changed.[21]

The first two generations of new women had one goal: to prove that women are equal to men. The first generation turned to education and challenged men in the classroom by demanding identical education. The second generation turned to the very foundation of male authority—their maleness—and showed

---

19 Littauer, *Bad Girls*, 3.
20 Smith-Rosenberg, *Disorderly Conduct,* 288.
21 Smith-Rosenberg, 289.

men that women, too, could be educated, articulate, sexual, and political. For this reason, Smith-Rosenberg argued:

> Loving and living with other women, within the separatist environment of women's colleges, settlement houses, and reform organizations, dedicating their lives to the advancement of other women, the New Women amassed greater political power and visibility than any other group of women in American experience.[22]

These two generations of women set the stage for the political, social, and sexual reforms that accompanied the birth-control movement.

THE BIRTH-CONTROL MOVEMENT IN AMERICA, 1910–1940

With the changes in the social and sexual world of women and the failure of the purity movement, Protestant clergy reformulated their notions of sexuality in order to harness women's sexuality. Thus, they created a new ideology of healthy sexuality that allowed for the full expression of women's sexuality within the confines of heterosexual Christian marriage. Protestants were slow to address sexual change, with a majority of denominational legislative assemblies waiting until the 1930s to make public proclamations. However, some actions prior to 1930 evidenced that clergy and laypersons active in these denominations were well aware of the changes occurring around them. There to help move them along was Margaret Sanger, the founder of the official birth-control movement and of the organization that would come to be called Planned Parenthood. Sanger appealed to Protestant churches for support, because she understood that social change was bound to happen and would directly affect Protestant denominations, especially in the context of the Social Gospel and the reform efforts of some liberal Protestants. Protestant denominational support of the legalization of birth control could help birth control become an accepted and respected norm.

Margaret Sanger and Reproductive Justice

Margaret Sanger, a nurse in the lower-east side of Manhattan, along with a host of other brave women and men, sought to educate the women of 1915 about how to control reproduction in an effective way without risking marital

---

22 Smith-Rosenberg, 256.

intimacy. Sanger, after she witnessed her own mother have eighteen pregnancies and herself having delivered hundreds of babies to low-income immigrant women, set her sights on what historian Tom Davis called "sacred work, the work, that is, of securing reproductive justice for women."[23] Davis framed the birth-control movement as a justice-oriented movement and not a rights movement, because Christian organizations, especially during the period of the Social Gospel movement, were more inclined to be involved with justice issues due to their moral undertone. If birth control could be portrayed as a moral obligation that would improve marital life, familial life, and the health of women and children, then Protestant churches would have little choice but to publicly and positively address the movement.[24]

Sanger's efforts began in 1913, when she spent six months researching contraception in the United States' largest libraries, including the Library of Congress. Unable to find any information on contraception, she went to Europe to learn from contraception advocates, including Marie Stopes.[25] She returned in 1914 and began to write and publish *The Woman Rebel*, a paper whose aim was to "stimulate working women to think for themselves and to build up a conscious fighting character."[26] After a grueling critique of the status of American sex education in 1914, Sanger stated that the paper would be a forum "to advocate the prevention of conception and to impart such knowledge in [its] columns."[27] Because she was willing to provide such information, the New York Post Office informed her:

> In accordance with the advice from the Assistant Attorney General for the Post Office Department . . . the publication entitled "The Woman Rebel," for March 1914, is unmailable under the provisions of Section 211 of the Criminal Code.[28]

---

23 Davis, *Sacred Work*, 6–7.

24 Davis, 6–14.

25 Marie Stopes was a feminist in the United Kingdom who founded the first birth-control movement in Britain. In 1921, she opened her first birth-control clinic and received more than one thousand letters each week from women seeking information. Her other works include *Contraception: Its Theory, History and Practice* (1923), *The Truth about Venereal Disease* (1921), *Sex and the Young* (1926), and *Sex and Religion* (1929).

26 Margaret Sanger, *The Woman Rebel* 1, no. 1 (March 1914): 1. Sanger coined the phrase "birth control" in the July 1914 edition of *Woman Rebel*.

27 Sanger, 1.

28 Robin Pokorski, "The Origins of the Woman Rebel," Margaret Sanger Papers Project, October 25, 2013, https://sangerpapers.wordpress.com/2013/10/25/the-origins-of-the-woman-rebel/.

In other words, the Comstock Act blocked the paper's distribution. After an indictment and dropped charges, Sanger toured the country, taught women about controlling conception, and handed out pamphlets with such titles as "Family Limitation." In 1916, she opened her first birth-control clinic, and it remained open for ten days before being shut down for, again, violating the Comstock law. This time she was imprisoned for thirty days, thirty days that brought her cause into the social and political limelight.[29] Finally, people began to talk about birth control in public. But talking was not enough; to start making actual legislative change, Sanger knew that she had to get the churches on her side, for

> what will finally win this fight, take away legal restrictions, develop new methods, educate people of all classes to an understanding of the meaning and use of Birth Control, is a positive belief in the idea that sex is fine and holy, that the body and the spirit are not enemies, but one.[30]

Most Protestants were concerned with the moral status of their social environment, from the sexually charged to the overworked poor. Mainline Protestant denominations began their social reform efforts with the less controversial, the overworked poor. They officially aligned to take positive action on general social reform in 1908, when the Federal Council of Churches of Christ in America (FCC) adopted, with revisions, the Methodist Episcopal Church's Social Creed. Written by the Methodist Federation for Social Service (MFSS), the Social Creed of the Churches focused on economic and labor reform.[31]

Denominations' official agencies and legislative conferences responded differently to the Social Creed and the FCC's endorsement of it based on their individual history, geography, theology, and size. The members of the Methodist Episcopal Church, South, were leery of asking the federal government to make pronouncements on social morality based on the denomination's geography and historical support of slavery. Its members were mostly evangelical-leaning Methodists who believed that conversion was the best means to improve society, for a converted Christian would naturally embrace

---

29 Davis, *Sacred Work*, 29–30.
30 Margaret Sanger, "Editorial," in "The Churches and Birth Control: A Symposium," *Birth Control Review* 14, no. 5 (May 1930): 131.
31 *MEA*, vol.1, 322, 324–25.

Christian morality. Its General Conference did, however, endorse the Social Creed in 1914.

The Methodist Protestant Church and the United Brethren were smaller in size, more rural, and emphasized personal holiness over social holiness, leading them to create their own version of a social creed for their respective denominations. Methodist ethicist Darryl W. Stephens used these facts to argue that "of The UMC's predecessors, only the MEC General Conference consistently addressed issues of public policy," a statement that this book upholds. This was due to a majority of liberal-leaning Methodists working at the administrative level.[32] Protestant liberalism drastically challenged two main tenets of evangelicalism: *activism* and *crucicentrism*. Activism, for progressives, was no longer evangelism; activism was now social action, bettering society through social reform, which included working with the poor, advocating for better working conditions, and pursuing better family life for all. Crucicentrism, understanding Christ's sacrifice on the cross as a reflection of God's love, was replaced with Borden Parker Bowne's personalism, the idea that one's active role in bettering society was the best reflection of God's love. Seminary-trained liberal Methodists created a new theology for the MEC, one that was built on a desire for active social reform, the undoing of systemic oppression, and improving society for the glory of God.[33] Whether or not denominations agreed with the FCC, their constituents were aware of economic burdens on families due to harsh working conditions, low pay, and long hours, and were sensitive to other issues that added to familial stress, such as the size and quality of a family. The first necessary step toward accepting birth control was a willingness to intervene in society and admit that economic stress affected family life.

If Sanger was successful in any rhetoric, it was convincing the world, and particularly the clergy, that pregnant women and mothers suffered. Performing sacred work meant taking action, not preaching "theology or anemic intellectualism."[34] Sanger knew about women's suffering because they wrote to her, told her their stories, and asked her for information. In fact, "throughout the 1920s,

---

32 Darryl W. Stephens, *Methodist Morals: Social Principles in the Public Church's Witness* (Knoxville, TN: University of Tennessee Press, 2016), 25.

33 Spann, "Evangelicalism in Modern American Methodism," 259, 308–12.

34 Davis, *Sacred Work,* 37.

Sanger received more than 250,000 letters filled with questions and pleas for help from families without access to proper birth control."[35] One letter pleaded:

> Directly after the birth of a child I go insane for about three or four months. The doctor said I should stop giving birth to children, but will not tell me how. If you will please help me, I will be blessed and free from suffering.[36]

Another cried:

> When my second youngest was born I had kidney or uremic poisoning. . . . I was blind and had convulsions and since, I'm not well at all. . . . The doctor said if I had anymore I couldn't live thru it, but he will not tell what to do to prevent from getting any more.[37]

Women wrote to her admitting that they had prayed for children at one point in their lives and now they "pray just for the opposite that I shall never bring any crippled children in to the world to suffer, as that I think is the greatest sin I can ever commit."[38] A selection of these letters was published in 1928, in *Motherhood in Bondage*. Women described their multiple pregnancies, their children's disabilities, their own disabilities and physical demise, their poverty, their miscarriages, their loss of older children, their marital problems due to their fear of sex, their attempts to self-abort, and their guilt over not wanting another child. They begged for information on how to live a better life with fewer children. Sanger took their stories and shared them with clergy.

Rethinking Marriage

Due to changes in sexuality, espoused by the first and second generations of new women, Protestants needed to rethink the purpose of marriage; was it an intimate partnership based on companionship, or an institution for the continuation of the species? Historian Christina Simmons explores the history of marriage revisionists, those who advocated for a new institution of marriage that existed somewhere between the lax sex radicals and the conservative purity reformers.

---

35 Jess Kluge, "Motherhood in Bondage: The Ultimate Horror Story," Margaret Sanger Papers Project, October 16, 2013, https://sangerpapers.wordpress.com/tag/motherhood-in-bondage/.

36 "Newsletter #6: Motherhood in Bondage" (Winter 1993/1994), https://www.nyu.edu/projects/sanger/articles/motherhood_in_bondage.php.

37 "Newsletter #6: Motherhood in Bondage."

38 Margaret Sanger, *Motherhood in Bondage* (New York: Brentano's, 1928), 138; as quoted in "Newsletter #6: Motherhood in Bondage."

Marriage revisionists sought to uphold the authority of science, which portrayed sex as the glue of a happy marriage, allowed the freedom of youth to explore their sexuality (with limits), and supported the full equality of women within the marital institution. While all of this seemed radical for the time, marriage revisionists believed that the best way for society to progress was through monogamous, heterosexual, Christian marriage, and advocated against premarital sex.[39] However, they knew that certain limitations within marriage had to respond to cultural change.

By the late 1920s, in an almost complete reversal of the conservative evangelical Protestant ideology of sexual intimacy of the 1870s, sex was viewed by an increasing majority of Protestants as a good act that should be enjoyed within the confines of heterosexual, Christian marriage without the worry of conception. In order to encourage newly liberated women who were coming to understand their gender and sexuality on new levels, marriage had to emphasize the pleasure experienced and the bond forged during sex. Motherhood, while still valued, was no longer the sole goal of married women, who, after the passage of the Nineteenth Amendment, now believed themselves more equal to men in the eyes of the law. For marriage (and the family) to remain the foundation of society, it had to evolve to a more companionate model, one that valued sexual intimacy without the worry of conception, and one that equally valued men's and women's role in the institution. By the end of the 1920s, a new, healthy sexuality linked sexual intimacy and sexual satisfaction to marital happiness. This new sexual ethic was a necessary step for the modernization of Protestantism. However, by the 1960s, it normalized heterosexuality and sex within marriage, thus demonizing homosexuality and extramarital sex. While radical and necessary changes occurred within Protestant sexual ethics, these changes had unforeseeable consequences for American Protestantism and especially American Methodism.[40]

Protestants created a new framework for healthy sexuality, one centered on the goodness of heterosexual, nonreproductive sex. One of the first Protestant discussions of contraception in the twentieth century was during the 1908 Lambeth Conference, a periodic gathering of Anglican bishops and leaders

---

39 Christina Simmons, *Making Marriage Modern: Women's Sexuality from the Progressive Era to World War II* (New York: Oxford University Press, 2009).

40 Simmons, 105–37.

who directed the Anglican denomination on social, theological, and cultural questions. They sought to determine the difference between *control*, that is, the use of contraception, and *restraint*, that is, abstinence.[41] These actions both had the same motive: the prevention of conception. Did one do more harm to the amount of intimacy experienced between husband and wife than the other?

As early as 1908, Anglicans had not been ready to condone the use of contraception due to its association with increased moral laxity, material greed, and health risks. In 1920, The Lambeth Conference again refused to endorse birth control, but the vote was a close 70–69. While this discussion was taking place in England, not in the United States, it brought the Protestant discussion of birth control to the mainstage, or the main-pulpit, by deeming it worthy of discussion in a religious setting.

The Catholic Church soon chimed in. In 1921, Margaret Sanger organized a conference in New York City for the celebration of the American Birth Control League's founding. At the closing session of the conference, police refused to let Sanger speak, influenced by the authority of Monsignor Dineen, secretary to Archbishop Hayes of the Catholic Church. Predictably, conflict ensued, and Sanger was arrested. The following day, the *New York Times'* headline was "Birth Control Raid Made by Police on Archbishop's Orders."[42] Catholicism taught that contraception was immoral, abnormal, and injurious to marriage; and these beliefs applied to all people, not just Catholics. Therefore, Catholics felt it their duty to enforce "true" morality by preventing any and all public discussion of birth control by any means necessary. The debate between Sanger and Catholics on the front page of the *New York Times* invited the public to join in. Protestants, continuing to distinguish themselves from Catholics, took a serious second look at the purpose of marriage and the place of birth control in it.

Responding to these events, in 1927, the Federal Council of Churches of Christ in America (FCC) created the Committee on Marriage and the Home, which was dedicated to the improvement of the American (read: white, middle-class, Protestant) family. It was composed of twenty-eight members,

---

41 *Britannica Academic*, s.v. "Lambeth Conference," accessed July 25, 2016, http://academic.eb.com.ezproxy .drew.edu/levels/collegiate/article/46948.

42 Davis, *Sacred Work*, 32–33.

three of whom were ministers of the Methodist Episcopal Church: Dr. John W. Langdale, Dr. William S. Mitchell, and Dr. Worth M. Tippy.[43] In 1929, the committee published a tract entitled "The Ideals of Love and Marriage," which defined marriage foremost as a "vision of devoted loyalty and life-long companionship," not as an institution with solely procreative purposes.[44] The committee recognized that man and wife should experience different types of emotional and physical intimacy without the worry of conception. While intimacy was important, they further asserted that a marriage was expected to progress to the creation of a family by the introduction of children. While the main purpose of a marriage remained the production of a family via offspring to ensure the continuation of "good moral Christian" families, having too many children was problematic. The committee recognized that the current "overstrain of the family income" was a result of "too many children."[45] Therefore, the purpose of marriage remained the creation of a family—with *family* defined as a married man and woman and their children—but due to financial strain, necessary measures to prevent conception were allowed.

EARLY PROTESTANT AND METHODIST RESPONSES: 1924–1936

From 1929 to 1937, three changes overturned parts of the prohibitive Comstock Act and subsequently led to an increased use and acceptance of birth control. The first was a police raid at the Clinical Research Bureau (CRB), Margaret Sanger's main birth-control clinic and research lab in New York City. In 1929, officers arrested doctors and nurses at the CRB for providing birth control to married patients for non–disease preventative measures.[46] To clarify, in 1918, Judge Crane of the New York Appeals Court legalized the distribution of contraception to married couples for the prevention of disease—specifically venereal disease—as many infected World War I veterans returned home. Doctors of the CRB argued that "disease" included any threat to a woman's health, and listed pregnancy as a major threat. In other words, the Crane decision argued for the prevention of what was believed to be a male disease, but the CRB

---

43   "The Federal Council on Birth Control," *Christian Advocate*, April 2, 1931, 4.
44   Rev. Dr. Worth M. Tippy. "The Protestant View of Sex, Love, and Marriage," *Current History* 29, no. 5 (February 1929): 1, 4–5.
45   Tippy, "The Protestant View," 6–7, 8.
46   Peter C. Engelman, *A History of the Birth Control Movement in America* (New York: Praeger, 2011) 157.

extended Crane's decision to include pregnancy. In 1929, after a two-day trial, charges against the doctors were dismissed, and it was ruled that doctors were "absolved . . . if they act in good faith in instructing a married woman in the use of contraceptives." Here, "good faith" was "the belief by the physician that the prevention of conception is necessary for the patient's health and physical welfare."[47] This decision was monumental because it extended the legal pre-scription of contraception to married women and broadened the term *disease* to include any threat to anyone's health or physical welfare. Since the improper spacing of children was proved to threaten a family's lifestyle and health, it was now legal to prescribe contraception to married couples for the proper spacing of children.

Second, two legal cases dismantled portions of the restrictive Comstock law. In 1930, *Youngs v. C. I. Lee*, a trademark suit between two condom manu-facturers, determined that condom manufacturing was "a legal enterprise and therefore entitled to trademark protection."[48] Prior to this decision, it was ille-gal to manufacture condoms in the United States. *Youngs* not only legalized the manufacturing of condoms; it made it legal for magazines to advertise contra-ceptives if they had a non-contraceptive use. Thus, contraceptives advertised as "feminine hygiene" were not in violation of the Comstock law.[49]

The commercial industry relied heavily on euphemisms to give women ac-cess to contraception without a prescription: vaginal jellies, douche powders, and suppositories were all sold under the guise of "feminine hygiene" that of-fered "protection," "security," and "dependability" from "the fear of a major crisis."[50] In 1930, coitus interruptus and condoms were the two most popu-lar forms of contraception, and were used by 60 percent of white married women. In 1940, the main form of contraception was the antiseptic douche, one of the most unreliable and dangerous forms of commercial contraception.[51] The douche was available at any local department store and was affordable for women of all classes.[52] If the local store did not have douches, one could order them through the mail or buy them from a female door-to-door sales

---

47 Engelman, 158.
48 Engelman, 166.
49 Tone, "Contraceptive Consumers," 491.
50 Tone, 485–86.
51 Tone, 487.
52 Tone, 492.

representative.[53] In 1938, the commercial birth-control industry exceeded $250 million annually (not including the price of prescription-based contraception), and a *Ladies' Home Journal* poll reported: "79 percent of its readers favored the legalization of birth control."[54]

The *Youngs* case and the commercial market's response peaked, and by 1940, "the size of the female contraceptive market was three times that of the 1935 market."[55] For this reason, *Fortune* magazine called the birth-control industry "one of the most prosperous new businesses of the decade."[56] *Youngs* revolutionized the commercial contraceptive market, forcing the question of birth control, once again, to the forefront, where churches would have to realize that their congregants now had access to a whole host of contraceptive options, but were without moral guidance from the clergy.

In 1935, *U.S. v. One Package of Japanese Pessaries* legalized the import of foreign contraception by proving that, if sent to a doctor, these items would not be used illegally, since doctors could legally prescribe birth control to married women.[57] In June 1937, after the *One Package* ruling, the American Medical Association deemed birth control "proper medical practice."[58] Physicians across the nation could once again legally write and publish information on birth control and would now know how to use, prescribe, and inform the public. With these three changes, by 1938, prescription-based contraceptive sales were estimated to be over $2.5 million per year with more than six hundred brands of female contraceptives available at more than three hundred nonprofit birth-control clinics across the nation. Perhaps Margaret Sanger's reaction to the changes of the 1930s is best: "The birth control movement is *free*."[59] By the end of the 1930s, birth control was readily accepted and used by a healthy majority of couples, and it was now socially acceptable, if not necessary, for Protestants and the Methodist Church to show support.

By the end of the 1930s, most Protestant denominations and a large majority of Americans accepted and used birth control, as will be shown in the

---

53   Tone, 498; Jean H. Baker, *Margaret Sanger, A Life of Passion* (New York: Hill & Wang, 2011), 240.
54   Tone, "Contraceptive Consumers," 485.
55   Tone, 499.
56   Tone, 485.
57   Baker, *Margaret Sanger*, 239–42.
58   Engelman, *A History of the Birth Control Movement in America,* 169.
59   Engelman, 169, emphasis in original.

following paragraphs.[60] This was true within Protestantism by March 1931, when the Federal Council of Churches' (FCC) Committee on Marriage and the Home, which included three MEC pastors, approved the use of birth control. In 1927, they had recognized an economic disadvantage to having large families and gave a "guarded approval of birth control" to married couples. They believed that "some form of effective control of the size of the family and spacing of children" was necessary in order to prevent poverty."[61] Approval was limited to heterosexual married couples because the FCC feared that an overall approval would increase premarital sex and, therefore, the current sexual laxity of youth. Within a marriage, however, they recognized that birth control was necessary, because sex had two purposes, procreation and "an expression of mutual affection." Until 1931, while most Protestants denominations supported companionate marriage, none had publicly recognized that sex could be for enjoyment alone. While the FCC did not speak for individual denominations, every mainline Protestant denomination was represented and had a voice. Their "guarded approval" arguably changed the way Protestant churches viewed sex and birth control by forcing them to stand alongside the FCC or find a reason to stand against them.

The guarded approval of contraception created a religious uproar with Baptists, Presbyterians, and certain Congregationalist denominations, who took a stance against the approval of birth control. The Methodist Episcopal Church, however, did not denounce the decision, and it is unknown how the three Methodist ministers on the committee voted. "The Moral Aspects of Birth Control," the Federal Council of Churches' tract that granted approval, was reprinted in the New York Christian Advocate, one of the primary periodicals of the Methodist Episcopal Church, in early April 1931. The Advocate concluded, "The entire report should be read and thought over, with reference to one's own personal experience and observation of the sex-life of others, and the spirit and letter of the Scriptures," a very Methodist way to opine. Here, one was encouraged to think about contraception in reference to one's own beliefs and lifestyle while referring to Scripture for specific answers.

The article emphasized that the Methodist Episcopal Church had not faced the birth-control issue at its General Conference, but expected that when it did,

60 Tone, "Contraceptive Consumers," 485–98.
61 "The Churches and Birth Control," Federal Council Bulletin 14, no. 4 (April 1931): 19.

the opinion would be "divided, not so much as to the basic morality of birth control, as to the dangers flowing from the general dissemination of information regarding the use of contraceptives."[62] This suggests that the stance of the MEC was not morally against birth control because it prevented conception within marriage; it was concerned that approval would lead to an increase in the sexual laxity of unmarried couples. This was a common fear. It was, in theory, avoided by the FCC when they approved birth control use by married couples only; nonetheless, they concluded that the benefits of birth control used within a marriage outweighed the dangers of birth control use outside of marriage. By 1931, a few individual conferences of the Methodist Episcopal Church and the Federal Council of Churches had approved the use of birth control within a marriage.

During the early twentieth century, the Methodist Episcopal Church (along with the Methodist Episcopal Church, South, and the United Brethren) focused their moral reform efforts on Prohibition, an effort promulgated by Methodists who believed that Christian morality necessitated abstention from all alcohol. Once Prohibition passed in 1920, they shifted their focus to lowering the divorce rate, advocating for uniform marriage and divorce laws, and supporting the eugenic platform of required medical exams prior to marriage, all of which hinged on a new sexual ethic, suggesting that an endorsement of birth control was not too far off.[63] Local endorsement within the MEC began in 1930 at the annual conference level and made its way to the Methodist Church's (MC) General Conference by 1940. It began when urban clergy noticed that their congregations were hungry for information on how to better their own family lives through the spacing and prevention of children. Congregants sought information from pastors; pastors sought information from annual conferences; and annual conferences asked the General Conference to provide the denomination with a way forward.

The Reverend Joseph F. Michael, a Methodist minister in Texas, observed "the plight of hundreds of homes" and became convinced that Margaret Sanger's birth-control movement was a "God-sent movement," for it was a movement that sought to better the family. Reverend Michael supported the legalization of contraception and its use within a monogamous heterosexual Christian marriage

---

62   "The Federal Council on Birth Control," 4.
63   Kathleen A. Tobin, *The American Religious Debate over Birth Control* (New York: McFarland, 2001), 59.

for the sake of the wife's health, the congeniality of the home, the social and religious adjustment in the community life, a fair and impartial opportunity for each child . . . and to help lift . . . part of the burden from the shoulders of father and husband.

He believed that "every baby" should come into this world as a "welcome guest."[64] Birth control improved the livelihood and health of each member of the family, and since it improved the family, Reverend Michael believed it improved society. In line with the claims of Reverend Michael, Margaret Sanger believed that birth control would allow "each child to have proper food, warmth, sunlight and fresh air, devotion and love."[65] Sanger and Reverend Michael witnessed the birth of children into broken homes, homes that could not afford them, and homes that did not want them. They concluded that these children were not given opportunities that families with fewer children could offer. The proper use of contraception alleviated this problem by allowing parents to plan for the most opportune time to conceive a child and prevented them from having unwanted children or children that could not be cared for properly.

At first, it seemed that the General Conference of the MEC agreed with Reverend Michael and with Sanger, and the MEC seemed ahead of the game. Its 1928 General Conference asked

> our Board of Education to prepare Courses of Study setting forth the practical and spiritual values of marriage; such courses to be designed for use among young people in all our Church schools, colleges, and universities. . . . We urge our young people to seek parental, medical, and pastoral advice before entering upon a relationship so vital to the maintenance of the home, the State, and the Church.[66]

Similarly, the United Brethren's 1933 General Conference called for pastors "to counsel with candidates for matrimony on 'eugenic mating, home ideals, sex regulations, rearing of children and personal adjustments.'"[67] It also created a new social advocacy agency, the Social Service Commission, which was "to study social life and lead the church forward in the advancement of social

---

64   "The Churches and Birth Control," 140.
65   Engelman, *A History of the Birth Control Movement in America,* 147. Quote taken from Margaret Sanger's radio broadcast in 1924.
66   *BOD*, 1928, ¶69, 4.
67   J. Bruce Behney, Paul H. Eller, and Kenneth W. Krueger, eds., *History of the Evangelical United Brethren Church* (Nashville, TN: Abingdon Press, 1979), 272.

justice."[68] The United Brethren's Home Missions continued this work through their programs dedicated to family health and welfare, prenatal and postnatal clinics, and instruction in "practical" nursing.[69] Even in the more rural South, The Methodist Episcopal Church, South, asked for "instruction in preparation for marriage" in their 1934 Social Creed.

Unfortunately, many of the courses that sought to educate young persons and young married couples on sexuality were never developed. A statement from the New York East Conference of the Methodist Episcopal Church in 1930 suggested as much:

> We inquire whether our Board of Education has complied with the request of the General Conference to 1928. . . . We assume that such courses, when prepared, will meet the real needs of our young people, giving them such sex education as will lift the entire subject into the realm of spiritual values.[70]

The lack of courses was problematic, especially since the denomination had promised their creation in 1928.

In the same statement, New York East became the first MEC annual conference to declare publicly its support of the birth-control movement. They believed it was the "clear duty of the churches to offer to their young people an opportunity to consult some qualified advisor" on the "fundamental principles of sex morality" and to receive "rational advice" on the subject. "Rational advice" meant "practical courses" and designated the current advice provided to young people as irrational. These types of changes in the language surrounding the discussion of premarital counseling and sex education were vital to understanding Methodism's early support of contraception, for they recognized an error in the way sex was approached, and sought to correct that error. In case their support was unclear, the New York East Conference continued by advocating for "such changes of the law . . . as will remove the existing restrictions upon the communication by physicians to their patients of important medical information on Birth Control."[71] It was no longer solely the duty of the churches to

---

68   Behney, Eller, and Krueger, 272.
69   Behney, Eller, and Krueger, 259.
70   "Religion and Home Life," *Journal of the New York East Annual Conference of the Methodist Episcopal Church* (1930): 250.
71   "Religion and Home Life," 250; reprinted in *Birth Control Review* 14, no. 5: 149.

inform young couples of the technology available to them. It was also the duty of the state. The New York East Conference called for legislative action to be taken so that their youth could legally receive rational advice, practical courses, and information on birth control from their clergy and physicians.

Other Methodist Episcopal conferences followed the example set by New York East. By November 1930, it was recorded that the Rock River Conference (Chicago, IL) recognized certain "economic difficulties" in marriage. They recommended "education for marriage" and "endorse[d] the principle of voluntary parenthood."[72] Once again, a need for "education for marriage" echoed calls for change via "practical courses" and "rational advice." Pastors realized that young couples needed information on how to safely use contraception, and as pastors, they were not fully qualified to provide this information.[73] To clarify, pastors realized that they, too, needed to be educated in regard to contraception, so that they could properly offer "rational" and "practical" advice to their congregants. To support this claim, the Northeast Ohio Conference and the Pittsburgh Conference requested that the General Conference of the MEC "make a study of the question of birth control" so that a "frank discussion" could occur.[74] A frank discussion of the new sexual ethic was necessary; without it, clergy and congregations suffered.

Theological Split

But once again, these courses and studies were never created. Over the course of the late nineteenth and early twentieth century, Methodist theology split into those who maintained biblical literalism and others who adopted biblical criticism. This theological division was seen across all Protestant denominations and led to some institutional splits. However, the Methodists did not divide over this theological disagreement. In fact, in 1939, the Methodist Episcopal Church, the Methodist Episcopal Church, South, and the Methodist Protestant Church united, and did so without confronting their theological differences.

Those Methodists who did not support biblical criticism, or as they called it "modernism," pushed back by preventing the creation of courses and the endorsement of birth control within the official ranks of the denomination.

---

72   "Home Birth Control," *Social Service Bulletin* 20, no. 18 (November 15, 1930): 2.
73   Davis, *Sacred Work*, 57.
74   "Home Birth Control," 2.

Instead, these Methodists shifted the focus to the ongoing battle over the Course of Study, the books that guided the theological development of seminarians. This effort was led by the Methodist League for Faith and Life (MLFL), an early evangelical caucus group within the MEC, founded by Henry Paul Sloan in 1925. The MLFL was not alone. Since the creation of the World Christian Fundamentals Association in 1919, fundamentalist Protestants had been trying to rid Protestantism of liberalism, and they believed the seedbed of modernism was the seminary.[75]

Sloan railed against modernism, which he believed was being promoted within the MEC through the Course of Study. In 1908, when the Social Creed was written and endorsed by the MEC, the ethics of Jesus were actively applied in a social setting so as to better the horrid conditions of modern life, a main tenet of liberal Protestantism. In 1912, "the commission on Courses of Study added several texts bearing on social Christianity," and thus began a backlash campaign for their elimination.[76] Sloan focused on the invasion of modernism in the Methodist faith by "insisting upon a Course of Study in full agreement with our doctrinal standards . . . [and] insisting that all teachings in our Theological Seminaries and Colleges, especially the courses in Bible, shall also conform to our standards."[77] In 1920, Sloan and more than thirty annual conferences petitioned to remove liberal books, such as the writings of Borden Parker Bowne, from the Course of Study, an effort that resulted in the removal of three books. Within two months of the 1924 General Conference, "ultra-conservatives organized themselves into The Methodist League for Faith and Life" with the goal of "bring[ing] the denomination's theological teachings into harmony with the authoritative Articles of Religion."[78] In 1928, the League organized again and brought ten thousand petitions from forty-one different states to General Conference, requesting a special committee to "investigate seminaries, pulpits, and Sunday School literature for flagrant evidences of disloyalty to Methodist doctrinal standards." This commission was appointed but was kept under control by the bishops who preferred to assess seminaries, clergy, and churches by the

---

75 Allan Carlson, *Godly Seed: American Evangelicals Confront Birth Control, 1873–1973* (Pisacataway, NJ: Transactions, 2011), 114.

76 Stewart Grant Cole, *The History of Fundamentalism* (New York: R. R. Smith, 1931), 186–87.

77 *Call to the Colors* (Philadelphia: Methodist League for Faith and Life, November 1926): 134.

78 *Call to the Colors*, 189.

"religious test of holy living" not their ability to maintain doctrinal standards.[79]

What did "holy living" entail? In his weekly radio show, *Dr. Harold Paul Sloan's Radio Hour* on WDAS, Sloan had an answer. In a segment entitled "Which Way America?" he pitted communist principles against American principles. He warned that America's principles are reversed from what they should be in order to have a properly functioning moral society:

> The hierarchy of interests among average modern Americans is not God, people, truth, property, pleasure. Instead it is the reverse of this . . . [a]nd this misarrangement of our interests is largely responsible for our contemporary confusion.

In his serial, *Call to the Colors,* whose title was an overt call to revolution and reformation within the denomination—further enhanced by its logo, an image of John Wesley and Martin Luther as Heroes of Faith—Sloan argued that evolution and scientific authority were atheistic and "cannot be taught without endangering public morals." With his disgust for modernism, evolution, and science, Sloan's rhetoric was an endorsement of the 1920s' fundamentalist platform.[80]

In agreement with Sloan, historian Kathleen Tobin suggested that the 1924 and 1928 General Conferences of the MEC upheld the Comstock laws because

> it appeared to Methodists, and to others, that too many couples were increasingly interested in the pleasure of marital sex over its purpose of procreation [and] . . . too many couples seemed to be limiting their family size to improve their economic status, allowing them to accumulate more worldly possessions.[81]

The 1928 *Discipline* was the first to have one section devoted to "Temperance, Prohibition, and Public Morals," which upheld that "the Christian Church must ever be the protector of humanity against those customs and practices which tempt, debase, and destroy." In 1928, the main practice that could destroy society was still alcohol, even though Prohibition had prevented the legal distribution of alcohol in the United States for almost one decade. The MEC

---

79 J. L. Neve, *Churches and Sects of Christendom* (Burlington, IA: Lutheran Literary Board, 1940), 395.

80 *Call to the Colors* (July–August 1925): 60–61. Sloan labeled himself a fundamentalist, admitting that his only problem with the theology was premillennial dispensationalism.

81 Tobin, *The American Religious Debate,* 101.

was now turning its efforts toward international Prohibition. Within this section, however, were overtures against obscenity and materialism:

> We are profoundly concerned about the moral life of our nation. . . . The subtle forces of materialism and irreligion have been increasingly active since the World War. . . . We are convinced that upon Christian citizens devolves the sacred privilege of counteracting that pagan conception of life which puts a low estimate upon personality, fosters the vulgar and the obscene, develops the irreverent and the frivolous, encourages sensuality and vice, and forever tempts mankind to live on the plane of the animal.[82]

The General Conference was against Hollywood films and literature that "offends public decency" and encouraged the closing of theaters to prevent the moral decay of society. If one considers these statements in the context of the second generation of new women who, after World War I, overtly questioned gender, openly expressed their sexuality, and were economically independent, then it was not surprising that the MEC made such pronouncements.

Over the next eight years, the General Conference of the MEC put forth even more conservative statements. In 1932, its delegates made more direct avowals in support of the Comstock Act and devoted an entire section of the *Discipline* to "Public Morals":

> The freedom of utterance, the laxity of moral cleanness, and development of suggestive relations between the sexes is demoralizing and subversive of the high ideals of our Christian religion. . . . Not alone in word but by illustration, sometimes called art, the nude is all too prevalent on billboards and in magazines of various types. . . . We would call upon our public officials to ban the sale of such literature in our municipalities; and urge that every Christian support and sustain such officials in their efforts to suppress these publications and advertisements.[83]

The 1928 and 1932 General Conferences began the confusing and contradictory social proclamations on sexuality that are still rampant in the current *Discipline* of The United Methodist Church. There was the call for support of the

---

82 "Temperance, Prohibition, and Public Morals," *Doctrines and Discipline of the Methodist Episcopal Church* (New York: The Methodist Book Concern, 1928), ¶599.

83 "Public Morals: Personal Purity," *Doctrines and Discipline of the Methodist Episcopal Church* (New York: The Methodist Book Concern, 1932), ¶563, p. 657.

Comstock law, which not only reinforced a specific ideal of Protestant sexuality but went directly against the desires of many MEC members. In contrast, the 1928 and 1932 *Disciplines* called for courses that helped young people prepare for marriage and advanced a new sexual ethic that prioritized marital pleasure over procreation.

Additionally, in 1932, the Social Creed was amended for the first time since its original penning and supported "instruction in sex hygiene and home build-ing," a statement supporting contraceptive use and instruction in both churches and schools.[84] Some Methodists viewed these courses as "a nauseating account of sinful indulgences [and] nothing less than a villainously vulgar performance."[85] If these classes continued to be provided to young minds, some feared a "fright-ful epidemic of immorality and sex abnormality and morbidity" would com-mence.[86] Within the MEC, in 1932, there was simultaneously a cry in the Special Advices and Social Creed for sex education and a call in the Reports and Reso-lutions to suppress such literature. While Sloan's primary targets were seminar-ies, professors, books, and rhetoric that "den[y] the supernatural character of the Bible, the Virgin Birth, Atoning Death, Bodily Resurrection, Ascension, God-hood, or return of Jesus," his fight for a revised Course of Study was the reason that Methodist courses on sex hygiene, planning for parenthood, and marital life were never created.[87]

This evangelical response was amplified in 1936, when the Social Creed was removed from the *Discipline* for the first (and only) time since its creation in 1908. The Methodist Federation for Social Service, in the eyes of evangelical delegates, was too anticapitalist for the denomination to officially endorse its creed. Its 1932 change to advocate for classes on sex hygiene was the tipping point. There was no evidence that the MLFL wrote directly against sex hygiene, but their rhetoric against evolution (and scientific authority of any kind), their stated belief that pleasure and higher standards of living should be the least concerns of modern Christian America, and their worry that modernism was invading the Methodist denomination were against the very idea of education

---

84 *Doctrines and Discipline of the Methodist Episcopal Church* (1932), ¶1561, p. 648.

85 "Sex Hygiene," *Western Recorder* 88, no. 41 (August 14, 1913): 8; as quoted in Betty DeBerg, *Ungodly Women: Gender and the First Wave of American Fundamentalism* (Minneapolis, MN: Augsburg Fortress, 1990), 112.

86 "Undue Emphasis on Sex Problems in the Devil's Snare," *King's Business* 6, no. 6 (June 1915): 466; "In-struction in Sex Hygiene," *Christian Workers Magazine*, January 1916, 348; as quoted in DeBerg, 112.

87 *Call to the Colors* (November 1926): 120.

in sex hygiene and home building. The fundamentalist desire for control over women's sexual selves reiterates Tom Davis's view that religious men of power desired complete control over women's sexuality in order to have some sort of role in reproduction. Once women turned to an alternate authority for knowledge and learned a rational, scientific basis of their sexuality, they felt the freedom to not only express this sexuality but to be proud of it, to have power over it, and to control it.

The removal of the Social Creed was a direct attack on women's sexuality and occurred due to the efforts of the Methodist League for Faith and Life. At the 1936 General Conference, Sloan and Clarence True Wilson of the Board of Temperance, Prohibition, and Public Morals lobbied intensely for the removal of the Social Creed from the *Discipline*, and they won. That year, "Methodism reached a low point in social advocacy" by removing the Social Creed and replacing it with "a statement on 'the Spiritual Life of the Church' drafted by the evangelical caucus," who called for "a revival of the enthusiasm for conversion that characterized our earlier history" and had no mention of social justice or reform.[88] Sloan and the MLFL enjoyed a decade-long tenure within the MEC. Contributors to his journal, *Call to the Colors*, were mostly non-Methodist fundamentalists, suggesting that, while he may have had a decent following, Methodists were not willing to contribute their own ideas to his platform.[89] Sloan's MLFL was not appealing to most, because Sloan was highly militant in his approach to change. Other Methodist ministers, who might have agreed with some of his beliefs, agreed more with the connectional nature of the denomination, respecting the views of district superintendents and bishops over another local pastor.[90]

Due partly to Sloan's and other evangelical efforts, the MEC in the 1920s and early 1930s did not officially progress toward accepting contraception, evident by the nonexistent premarital and postmarital courses requested by the 1928 General Conference and the removal of the Social Creed in 1936. The MLFL might not have been successful in completely revising the Course of Study, and it did not have much effect after the unification in 1939, but its rhetoric

---

88 *MEA*, vol. 1, 326. "The Spiritual Life of the Church," ¶1462; *Doctrines and Discipline of the Methodist Episcopal Church* (New York: Methodist Publishing House, 1936), 652–53.

89 The periodical was later changed to *The Essentialist* (1927–1931) and *Christian Faith and Life* (1931–1939); see Marsden, *Fundamentalism and American Culture.*

90 Spann, "Evangelicalism in Modern American Methodism," 46.

made its mark on the history of the MEC. However, the birth-control movement soon would rebrand itself to be more "respectable," causing many to take another look.

LATER METHODIST RESPONSES: 1940 ONWARD

Fundamentalists outside of Methodism did not confront birth control publicly until the 1940s and 1950s; and by then, they had rebranded themselves as conservative evangelicals through the founding of the National Association of Evangelicals. These conservative evangelicals were different from their fundamentalist forebears. Instead of trying to drive out modernism from the mainline, they worked both within and outside the mainline to advocate a theology based heavily in biblical literalism, Christ's sacrifice on the cross, and the conversion of people as the best way to improve the world. In regard to birth control, conservatives believed birth control was a sin and a threat to the "race," that is, white, middle- and upper-class, Christian America, and as limiting the expansion of Comstock's chosen people.[91] Billy Sunday, one of the more prominent conservative evangelicals of this era, found birth-control activists deplorable, calling them "the devil's mouthpiece."[92] Contraception not only went against God's desires that God's people be fruitful and multiply; fundamentalists believed that it limited "native" families and allowed "the higher birthrate of the foreign-born, black, and lower-class segments of the population."[93]

New changes in the public rhetoric surrounding birth control made it more "respectable." This and the growing popularity of the new Protestant sexual ethic meant that all Protestants could endorse birth control fully as a responsible part of Christian marriage. In 1937, as mentioned above, the American Medical Association included birth control on the list of responsible medical practices. Also in 1937, Margaret Sanger created the Birth Control Council of America (BCCA), which was renamed the Birth Control Federation of America in 1939, as an umbrella organization for her medical and research clinics. The BCCA was rebranded by Kenneth D. Rose, its new CEO, in two key ways. First, they began using the phrase "family planning" in place of "birth control," hoping that this change in rhetoric would dismiss any association with women's rights and

91 DeBerg, *Ungodly Women*, 114–15.
92 DeBerg, 115.
93 DeBerg, 115

directly associate the council with family improvement, not with preventing life. Second, they brought in male leadership, who, according to Rose, would have more political clout with "federal and state legislatures, hospital boards, public health boards, etc."[94]

They rebranded again in 1942, with a new name, Planned Parenthood Federation of America, removing "birth control" from their organization entirely, and emphasizing that Planned Parenthood "did *not* mean smaller families but, rather, *planned* families—and therefore healthier children."[95] While there were not actual changes in the day-to-day practices of the medical and research clinics, the changes in rhetoric alone made it appropriate for conservative evangelicals to accept contraception, because it was no longer associated with women's rights, it no longer focused on limiting families, and it no longer used "obscene" language. Furthermore, by 1959, leading conservative evangelicals and ethicists such as Alfred Martin Rehwinkel, professor of Christian ethics and church history at Concordia Seminary, admitted that there was "nowhere" in Scripture where "a clear and definite statement on . . . which a positive law or rule making the use of contraceptives in marriage a sinful procedure could be established." Rehwinkel continued arguing that birth control "is not sinful in its very nature, nor can birth control as such be declared as a sinful violation of God's creation order."[96] While conservative evangelical Protestants were a couple of decades behind their progressive mainline contemporaries (discussed below) in the acceptance of birth control, they nevertheless came around and saw birth control, or "planned parenthood," as a benefit to the family.

The Christian Home

In 1939, the Methodist Episcopal Church; the Methodist Episcopal Church, South; and the Methodist Protestant church merged to form the Methodist Church, and with this merger, many changes occurred. One of these changes was, as historian Tom Davis claims, that "by the end of the 1930s, the Methodist Church had officially endorsed birth control."[97] The Methodist endorse-

---

94 Carlson, *Godly Seed*, 119.

95 David M. Kennedy, *Birth Control in America: The Career of Margaret Sanger* (New Haven, CT: Yale University Press, 1970), 256–57; as quoted in Carlson, 119, emphasis original.

96 Alfred Martin Rehwinkel, *Planned Parenthood and Birth Control in Light of Christian Ethics* (St. Louis: Concordia, 1959), 3–5.

97 Davis, *Sacred Work*, 43.

ment was found in the 1940 *Discipline*, specifically in the Social Creed and a new resolution entitled "The Christian Home." The revised Social Creed called for "the protection of both the individual and the family by the single standard of purity; for education for marriage, parenthood, and home-building."[98] First of all, the family was to be protected by the church. Second, the church was to take responsibility in educating young couples on issues involving marriage and parenthood. Education for marriage and for parenthood reflects earlier statements by the Methodist Episcopal Church for practical courses that offered rational advice and used less controversial language than 1932's direct call for "instruction in sex hygiene." This chapter has shown how these courses reflected a need for the distribution of contraceptive information to clergy and congregants. This language was again found in the Social Creed and emphasized marriage preparation and sex education as a vital issue for the Methodist Church, this time without rebuttal from evangelicals.

In addition, the 1940 *Discipline* had a new resolution entitled "The Christian Home," which defined the Methodist ideal of the American Christian family. Some of its more pro-contraception claims concerned children, giving them the "birthright" to an emotionally stable home with two parents who provide the child with the opportunity to develop emotionally, spiritually, and intellectually—reflecting earlier claims made by both Rev. Joseph F. Michael of Texas and Margaret Sanger. From this, one can conclude that children should not be born into homes where they were not wanted, for these homes stunted them emotionally and prevented their proper development. Therefore, the proper planning and spacing of children was necessary for proper development and the success of the family.

The resolution continued and discussed sex education and premarital counseling. Children had "the right to know before adolescence the facts regarding the origin of life and the nature of their personality as it relates to sex." Children should not be afraid of sex. Sex was natural and should be taught from a young age so that a child became an adult who was comfortable with sex. Youth needed to be educated on the "Christian ideal of love, courtship, and marriage." To clarify, youth and engaged couples should be taught to wait for marriage to engage in intercourse, but they should not be ashamed of sexual

---

98 "Our Social Creed," *Doctrines and Discipline of The Methodist Church* (New York: Methodist Publishing House, 1940), ¶1712, pp. 766–70.

desires. The resolution recommended certain "scientific" literature and information for engaged couples. *Scientific* implied medical, and with the American Medical Association's approval of birth control, medical publications discussed contraception as a legitimate medical practice.

The denomination's endorsement of scientific authority over religious authority showed a willingness on behalf of the clergy to forgo their authority over women's sexuality and a victory over fundamentalist rhetoric (at least for the time being). Furthermore, "courses of instruction for young married couples on home building, income budgeting, child training, [and] life adjustments" were recommended; and this time were actually created and taught at Methodist and non-Methodist colleges and universities, along with "pre-marital and post-marital counseling."[99] The stress on "home-building" and "income budgeting" referenced Reverend Michael's and the Federal Council of Churches' concern of the financial strain of large families. To properly build a home, couples had to understand the cost of having children. The adjustments of the Social Creed along with statements concerning premarital education supported an endorsement of contraception in 1940. Birth control was still new and still growing in acceptance. The Methodist Church wanted it to be clear to young heterosexual married Methodist couples that if they wanted to space children for economic reasons, the statements in the *Discipline* would not prohibit such actions.

All of this was further substantiated by the involvement of Methodist clergy in the Planned Parenthood Federation of America (PPFA) and the increased discussion of birth control within Methodist publications after 1940. In March 1941, Margaret Sanger, seven clergy, and five members of the Birth Control Federation of America (the predecessor to Planned Parenthood) created the National Clergymen's Advisory Council (NCAC), a group that was "to be the spokesman for the Federation on the moral and religious values of planned parenthood."[100] In other words, instead of stressing a woman's right to control her reproductive system, the NCAC reflected the Methodist stance on contraception, as a relief measure, a solution to certain health issues, and a benefit to the institution of the family. An example of their work was the institution of National Family Week, an annual event that focused on family education, planning,

99 "The Christian Home," *Doctrines and Discipline of The Methodist Church* (1940), ¶1713, pp. 770–72.
100 Davis, *Sacred Work*, 55.

and celebration. By 1948, the Methodist *Discipline* encouraged all churches to observe National Family Week, a direct connection between congregations and the programming efforts of Planned Parenthood.[101]

This was not the only connection between the Methodist Church and Planned Parenthood. Methodist bishop G. Bromley Oxnam became a member of the NCAC in 1941 and is remembered as "one of the boldest and most controversial Protestant leaders of the post–World War II period," more for his socialist leaning than his support of Planned Parenthood.[102] Bishop Oxnam was one of two speakers at the twenty-fifth anniversary celebration of Planned Parenthood in 1946. In his speech, he declared that "the love between a husband and wife is sacred. Those who insist there shall be no expression of that love except for the purpose of procreation are not defenders of the family."[103] Oxnam's speech was mostly a direct attack on the Catholic Church's stance that the prevention of conception during sex was sinful. However, his speech also showed that as a Methodist bishop he supported Planned Parenthood, the right to enjoy sex without procreation, and the idea that birth control enhanced, or to put it more strongly, *defended* family life.

One of the goals of the NCAC was to rid ministers of their ignorance and misinformation concerning contraception. In 1944, two of its members, Rev. L. Foster Wood and Dr. Abraham Stone, published a pamphlet entitled "Marriage Counsel in Relation to Planned Parenthood: An Outline for Clergymen." The pamphlet was written in question-and-answer format and reflected the conversation between a pastor and an engaged coupled enrolled in premarital counseling. Remember: the 1940 *Discipline* emphasized the need for premarital counseling, and this pamphlet provided a glimpse of what was discussed and most likely what had been discussed for years during such counseling. The goal of this pamphlet was to provide ministers with "practical and specific" information on family planning and types of contraception for these were "a normal part of married life."[104]

Married couples were not the only ones in need of practical and rational

---

101 "The Local Church," *Doctrines and Discipline of The Methodist Church* (New York: Methodist Publishing House, 1948), ¶198, p. 72.

102 Davis, *Sacred Work*, 55.

103 Davis, 60.

104 L. Foster Wood and Abraham Stone, "Marriage Counsel in Relation to Planned Parenthood: An Outline for Clergymen" (New York: Planned Parenthood Federation of America, 1944), 7.

advice. Pastors needed it, too, for they were middlemen between doctors and congregants. In order to provide their congregants with reliable advice on a medical topic, they needed practical information. What this pamphlet presented as abnormal was relying on a supposed "safe period," which was a "risk," and on continence, which "cannot be advocated or advised as a general practice."[105] According to the pamphlet, not enough was known about female menstruation to fully rely on the safe period. Continence was "not feasible" and could actually damage a marriage.[106] In fact, it was healthy for married people to engage in sex for pleasure's sake. The act increased intimacy and a more intimate family for a healthier family. In the end, this pamphlet argued that most couples would want to have children, for children fulfill a marriage, but it also emphasized the need to plan for marriage and for parenthood.[107]

motive Magazine

These types of pamphlets were now necessary. As birth control increased in popularity, Methodist congregants, especially students, discussed and asked questions about contraception and sex. *Motive* magazine, the periodical of the Methodist Student Movement, hosted a forum in December 1941 and discussed the separation of sex from Christian doctrine. The authors included a campus minister (James S. Chubb), a professor of law (Harriett S Daggett), the dean of men and the head of the Department of Home Life (William H. Morgan and Mildred Inskeep Morgan), a Wesley Foundation director (C. W. Hall), a popular campus lecturer (Grace Sloan Overton), a male graduate student (Robert Rathburn), and a female college senior (Marjorie Charles). Together, they tried, in a variety of ways, to reinvent the Christian view of sex to make it more apt for young adults in the 1940s. None of the authors denigrated sex. Sex was consistently upheld as a positive, divinely inspired good that was best experienced between two heterosexual persons who had mutual respect and love for each other. However, the authors were split on whether or not this meant that the two persons should be married. Four believed that the sexual relationship was best when the two persons were married, and three admitted that the

---

105 Wood and Stone, 12, 30.
106 Wood and Stone, 30.
107 Wood and Stone, 41.

social context of war complicated matters and thus premarital relations could be accepted.

In a 1941 article entitled "There Is Nothing the Matter with Marriage," professor of law Harriet S. Daggett discussed the changes in marriage since the Civil War. In the 1940s, people married at a later age and married people with whom their families were unacquainted. Divorce was on the rise. Recently married couples were no longer promised an inheritance or dowry as part of a marital contract and were thus left to establish themselves economically. Professor Daggett argued that in the early 1940s, parents, college students, and college administrators hoped that students graduated college prior to marrying. Most approached marriage knowing that divorce provided them with a way out if they were unhappy. She argued that the problem with marriage was that "there has been so much 'viewing with alarm'—so many doubts have been cast— that thoughtful young people may justly wonder if the marriage institution had any elements of safety at all." In her views, it was not that marriage itself had changed; it was the rhetoric about marriage that had changed.

Adding to this tension, Professor Daggett argued that the rhetoric surrounding sex had not helped: "We have come from a period of ignorance and 'hush-hush' about many important matters of marriage to an era of too much talk, too much discussion, to bad taste and some forms of exhibitionism." Sex, which was "ignored or whispered about" a decade earlier, "has now assumed a place out of proportion to its importance . . . as a factor in marriage." Professor Daggett argued that while sex was important in marriage and in life, it had been given too much attention by too many fields and should simply be left to science, where it would be treated factually instead of discussed in classrooms, in churches, and in community centers, where emotions often overrode facts. If a scientific approach to sex became more popular, then marriage would be evaluated economically and rationally instead of based in a purely emotional response to love or lust.[108] Supporting her argument was the fact that America was about to enter World War II, and thousands of eligible men were leaving for war again. Emotions were heightened, and couples rushed into relationships. Historian Amanda H. Littauer described all of the reasons for these rushed courtships:

108 Harriet S Daggett, "There Is Nothing the Matter with Marriage! A Professor of Law Makes Some Judicial Suggestions." *motive*, December 1941, 13–15.

Fearing death and seeking companionship, soldiers rushed girlfriends to the altar before shipping out; short periods of leave replaced drawn-out courtships; popular culture eroticized the man in uniform. War work generated economic independence and social opportunity as it lessened parental supervision over teens. Young women who left their home communities could rationalize their travels and adventures as contributions to the war effort, and thousands of married teen girls followed their new husbands to training facilities across the country only to find themselves desperate for money and company after the men went overseas. Young women and men in the military encountered new places, people, and possibilities for sexual self-discovery, including homosexuality. A wide range of teenage girls and adult women rushed to meet the sexual 'needs' of GIs on furlough, blurring lines between commercial and casual sex.[109]

Littauer argues that the context of wartime did not change sexual mores but provided a reasonable, even patriotic, excuse for women to more publicly proclaim their existing sexual desires. Instead of setting the stage for later sexual revolutions of the 1960s and 1970s, the wartime sexual assertion of "victory girls" was a continuation of a sexual revolution begun by the new woman, and one that would continue to intensify in the postwar years.

In Professor Daggett's eyes, rushed courtship was not the rational move. Marriage should be based on "true friendship," and wartime was not appropriate for such a drastic, life-altering decision. Adding to Professor Daggett's arguments, C. W. Hall, a Wesley Foundation director, argued that "each of us wants a virgin for a wife, but under the present conditions," that is, another world war, "we do not feel that we can expect this." Most of his article discussed a recent survey of married couples, 760 husbands and 777 wives, and their experiences prior to being married. The survey showed that "the trend toward premarital sex experience is proceeding with extraordinary rapidity." Hall argued that while the statistics supported this conclusion, those who had premarital relationships still wanted to get married and have children, evidenced by the increase in those taking home-building and family-planning courses on college campuses.[110]

Finally, Robert Rathburn, the male graduate student, and Marjorie Charles,

---

109 Littauer, *Bad Girls*, 3–4.
110 C. W. Hall, "Rears Its Ugly Head! A Wesley Foundation Director Faces a Dilemma," *motive*, December 1941, 18–19.

the female college senior, reflected on their experiences. These were the most poignant articles, because they were written by those experiencing premarital and early postmarital life, not professors or ministers observing the changes. Robert Rathburn discussed how personal displays of physical affection had become more public on college campuses as "war psychology" increased the "what the hell attitude" on campuses. Physical displays of love were generally accepted because war changed what was socially acceptable. War forced young adults to become adults, and when faced with grave uncertainty about the future, those who argued for sexual restraint quickly lost "because Bill goes to the army in February and two and a half years is a long time." Rathburn argued that premarital relations were more accepted than student marriage. What was "a greater problem now than two years ago" was student marriage: "This group of happily married students, is still inconsiderable in comparison with the great unwashed of the single, who finds outlets in intermediate physical love manifestations and other sublimations." Rathburn did not provide much reasoning for this statement, but his colleague, Marjorie Charles, offered further insights.

Marjorie Charles agreed that love was manifesting in a variety of ways. She argued that premarital sexual relations were a fact on college campuses. Where there was "a system of tolerance" when it came to those who "steal a sacred bit of their future before the minister has stamped his seal of approval," promiscuity was unacceptable in all situations. Premarital sex, however, by "the couple, deeply in love, who are faced with long years of waiting for what they both most want—marriage" was largely accepted by the student body. The basis of her argument was that the age of marriage was constantly delayed due to the demand that those who entered the workforce needed a college degree to be competitive and maintain a higher standard of living brought on by an ever-increasing advertising and material culture. Yet the proper "mating age" remained the same, making premarital relationships inevitable. Further complicating the fact that sex occurred outside of marriage, and in agreement with Professor Daggett, Charles stated, "As has been done too many times, [sex education] should not be approached from an emotion[al] angle (which causes a great percentage of the difficulty in the home), but rather from a scientific angle."[111]

---

[111] Marjorie Charles, "Love, The New Security: A College Senior Writes on Truth as Motivation for Relationships," *motive*, December 1941, 25, 28.

When approached as a whole, this forum uncovered the sexual tension and changes by 1941. First, sex had been separated from Christian doctrine, and this was supported by the lack of discussion about religion in a majority of the articles, especially those written by students. Instead of directly discussing Christianity, Rathburn and Charles discussed social change and used words with vague religious connotations, such as *virtue*. Even the director of the Wesley Foundation did not mention Christianity in his article; instead he focused on statistics of premarital relations and the overall desire to still marry. The trend observed from these articles is that premarital sexual relations between committed couples increased and were largely accepted by college students because the age of marriage was delayed by the need for a college degree, by the need to afford a comfortable lifestyle for your family, and by World War II. Throughout these articles, there is a consistent reference to the need for a *scientific* approach to sex. "Scientific approach to sex," as has been shown, was a euphemism for information regarding birth control. College students, college advisors, and clergy advocated for the dissemination of knowledge that supported sex-for-pleasure that hopefully avoided conception.

In 1944, *motive* published another article, "The A.B.C.'s of Getting Married," written by a twenty-two-year-old woman who was recently married. She answered an inquiry that asked, "What do you wish you would have known before getting married?" She replied, "I wish I might have had more satisfactory education in the area of sex."[112] She admitted writing to the "Birth Control Clinic requesting information with regards to their services in marriage counseling and medical advice," a statement that shows that, at the time, it was common to go to birth-control clinics prior to marriage.[113] She also repeated the type of language surrounding birth control. While willing to admit that she wrote to a "Birth Control Clinic," she was not willing to admit that she wanted information on birth control. Instead, she used language similar to that of the 1940 Methodist *Discipline*, "marriage counseling and medical advice." While Methodist campuses did not get their requested courses in 1928, they did have those courses by 1941, when there is proof that lectures on birth control and family planning were taught at the university level and were frequently advertised and discussed by Methodist students.

---

112 "The A, B, C's of Getting Married," *motive*, November 1944, 17.
113 "Now That We Are Married," *motive*, November 1944, 15–18.

These student opinions were heightened by a new frankness surrounding sex in the 1950s, after Alfred C. Kinsey published *Sexual Behavior in the Human Male* (1948) and *Sexual Behavior in the Human Female* (1953). People had talked openly and written about sex since the 1920s, as this book shows, but Kinsey shook society with his alarming statistics about unmarried couples and homosexual experience. Previously, sex was okay to discuss as long as it was in reference to married heterosexual couples; unmarried couples were an entirely different story. It was widely known that premarital sex was occurring, as was evident in *motive*, but publicly acknowledging its occurrence was another story, proving that *motive* was quite a radical magazine. Historian R. Marie Griffith argues that Kinsey sought support and information from clergy.[114]

According to Griffith, Methodist ministers were open and willing to support Kinsey's studies. In 1953, Rev. Lawrence K. Whitefield, in a Sunday sermon, thanked Kinsey for forcing Christians to realize "the imperativeness of rethinking our whole philosophy of sex relations."[115] After Kinsey's revelations, Methodists did not necessarily change their stance on birth control; Methodists simply made their pro-contraception stance more explicit.

Methodist Pamphlets

In the mid-1950s, the Methodist Church's publishing house directly advertised the denomination's pro-contraception stance. One pamphlet, entitled "Now You Are Engaged," encouraged young couples to think about children prior to marriage, for "the spacing of children will involve some method of timing conception." Couples should also visit the local "Planned Parenthood Clinic" to "take advantage of the opportunity it provides."[116] This pamphlet recommended "scientific literature," such as Dr. Hannah Stone's *A Marriage Manual*, which "emphasized . . . the problems of birth control," because "reliable contraceptive information is essential for a well-adjusted and satisfactory marital union."[117] The Methodists no longer suggested an approval of birth control; instead, they openly encouraged young couples to visit Planned Parenthood for

---

114 R. Marie Griffith, "The Religious Encounters of Alfred C. Kinsey," *Journal of American History* 95, no. 2 (September 2008): 349–77.

115 Griffith, 368.

116 Oliver M. Butterfield, "Now You Are Engaged" (Nashville: Methodist Publishing House, 1955), 5, 7.

117 Hannah Stone, "Foreword to the First Edition," *A Marriage Manual* (New York: Simon and Schuster, 1935), x. Dr. Stone was the head physician and researcher of the CRB in the late 1920s and early 1930s, and was one of the doctors arrested in the April 1929 raid on the CRB.

advice on child spacing, and they recommended materials that openly discussed different types of contraception. Another pamphlet thanked Kinsey for alerting the church to the "extent that sex was a concern" and to how "sexual practices were changing."[118] It declared that the church was "pushing ahead in a restudy of the Judeo-Christian tradition regarding sex, love, and marriage" and believed that "the church must provide realistic guidance, direction, and counsel."[119]

The Methodist Church was not the only denomination putting forth literature and making pro-contraception stances. Members of the Evangelical United Brethren (EUB), after 1950, began to rethink marriage and parenthood. Clergy were advised to continue to counsel young couples preparing for marriage, a tradition carried over from the United Brethren. Postmarital counseling was encouraged to help "planning at long range of the family they hope to establish." The 1950 EUB *Discipline* was the first in its history that explicitly affirmed as "ethically and morally right to properly use methods and techniques medically approved for the purpose of achieving planned and responsible parenthood."[120]

For the first time since 1940, despite minor changes to support uniform adoption laws, the 1956 *Discipline* amended the resolution on the Christian home. It still advocated preparation for marriage via educational courses and premarital counseling, but it also included a statement on *planned parenthood*, a phrase that emphasized family more than reproductive rights. It stated, "We believe that planned parenthood, practiced in Christian conscience, may fulfill rather than violate the will of God."[121] Instead of supporting the use of birth control, which implied a women's rights issue, the *Discipline* supported "planned parenthood," which centered the issue on concerns for the family. Such parenthood must be practiced with a "Christian conscience." In other words, it must be between one man and one woman who have united in Christian marriage. This practice fulfilled the will of God by welcoming children into the world who would be loved and given ample opportunities for social, spiritual, and intellectual growth.

After 1956, the MC continued to produce materials that encouraged the use of contraception. In 1964, a pamphlet entitled "Responsible Parenthood

---

118 "The Christian Family and Rapid Social Change" (Nashville: Methodist Publishing House, 1962).
119 "The Christian Family and Rapid Social Change."
120 Quoted in Behney, Eller, and Krueger, *History of the Evangelical United Brethren*, 378.
121 "The Christian Home," *Doctrines and Discipline of The Methodist Church* (New York: Methodist Publishing House, 1956), ¶2021, pp. 707–12.

from a Christian Perspective" claimed that "married couples are free, within rather broad limits, to use the gifts of science, whether to foster conception or avert it."[122] The Federal Drug Administration approved the use of an oral contraceptive pill in 1960, which can and should be classified as one of these "gifts of science" supported by the Methodist Church. By 1968, The United Methodist Church issued a resolution on the Christian Family, which echoed the stance of the Methodist Episcopal Church in 1940 and the Methodist Church in 1956, calling for responsible family planning as a Christian means of raising a family.[123] The 2012 *Discipline* called for the marital use of all forms of contraception as part of "responsible parenthood."[124] Thus, even in the twenty-first century, for The United Methodist Church to fully support the use of contraception, it must maintain the connection between birth control and the improvement of the family.

CONCLUSION

Purity reformers, new women, birth-control advocates, and fundamentalist Christians all influenced the Protestant and Methodist approval of contraceptive use within marriage over the course of the first half of the twentieth century. Methodist clergy and laypersons asked for a new sexual ethic in 1928, when the General Conference of the Methodist Episcopal Church requested courses on education for marriage and parenthood. They knew that the church needed to provide guidance in the areas of sex, love, and marriage ever since the New York East Conference challenged the denomination in 1930. Furthermore, since 1940, the Methodist Church, as a denomination, consistently supported birth control through resolutions in the *Discipline*, clergy involvement in Planned Parenthood, articles written by their constituents, and the distribution of accurate information regarding birth control. Approval was gained through a grassroots movement, requests for basic information, and responses at the denominational level to real changes in sexuality. Congregants, clergy, and annual conferences worked together to lobby the General Conference of the Methodist Episcopal Church for information, for action, and for eventual endorsement

---

122 Richard M. Fagley, "Responsible Parenthood from a Christian Perspective" (Nashville: Methodist Publishing House, 1964).

123 "The Church and the Family" (Nashville: Methodist Publishing House, 1968).

124 "Social Principles: Responsible Parenthood," *The Book of Resolutions of The United Methodist Church* (Nashville: United Methodist Publishing House, 2004), ¶161, hereafter *BOR* with the year following.

by the Methodist Church. Though met with pushback in the 1920s and early 1930s from the Methodist League for Faith and Life, Methodists were successful in implementing necessary changes to the Methodist sexual ethic because the denomination could no longer ignore changes in society around them.

When it comes to changes in sexuality, Methodists (of all of the denominations that currently make up The UMC) are cautious people. A majority will assert themselves in the public and political realm for the sake of bettering society with little hesitation, but when it comes to amending the *Discipline*, putting those actions into words, they tend to take a step back. In 1932, after the FCC gave a guarded approval of birth control within marriage, the *Christian Advocate* stated that when the question of contraception reached the General Conference floor, its members would be "divided" due to contraception's association with sexual laxity. In 1940, the Methodist Church's stance was not by any means radical. It implied the use of contraception within the confines of Christian marriage, and it was not until 1956 that an overt support of planned parenthood was made. Methodists have always maintained a strong stance against premarital sex, one that would become more explicit toward the end of the twentieth century. For the sake of the family, the Methodist Church recognized that there needed to be some wiggle room for couples who needed to limit the number of children for the betterment of their marriage and their overall well-being. However, these efforts defined the new sexual ethic in terms of heterosexuality and Christian marriage as the norm, thereby categorizing homosexuality and sex outside of marriage as abnormal. However, in order for the new sexual ethic to be relevant in the context of the 1960s' sexual revolutions, Methodists would again reevaluate their sexual ethic.

2

AMERICAN METHODISM AND SEXUAL REVOLUTION

TOGETHERNESS, DIVORCE, AND *PLAYBOY*

I n 1958, *Together* magazine presented the Detweilers to their readers as the "1958 Methodist Family of the Year." The Detweilers lived in Burbank, California. They were "the kind of folk you'd enjoy having as neighbors" and "so well typif[ied] Methodist families the country over who put Christian ideas and ideals into their lives seven days each week." They were, of course, white and middle-class. James and his wife, Dorothy, were happily married for twenty-five years and had three children, Douglas aged seventeen, Jeanette aged fifteen, and Richard aged eleven. James worked for Lockheed Aircraft Corporation. Not only were they active together as a family, but "their church activities [were] numerous." James was a lay leader and Dorothy worked part-time for the church school. Doug and Jeanette were "devoted" to Methodist Youth Fellowship, and Richard was "senior acolyte." They epitomized "outstanding Christion devotion to church, home, community—and to one another."[1] Other Methodist families were to see something of themselves and their families in the lives of the Detweilers; and if they failed to relate to the Detweilers, then they were expected to aspire to be more like them. They were the ideal.

The Methodist Family of the Year was not new in 1958; in fact, the Methodist Church's Committee on Family Life had elected these idealized, even idolized, families since 1954, and continued to do so into the early 1960s. With the revolutionary changes in post–World War II America in regard to social, sexual, and familial life and the new sexual ethic preached within their own clerical ranks, it is not shocking that the Methodist Church's Committee on Family Life felt the need to find a more "traditional" ideal for the denomination's constituents to look up to.

---

1   "Meet: Methodist Family of the Year," *Together*, November 1958, 14–17.

This chapter will discuss the historical notion of the 1950s American family and how the Methodist Church (and in part the Evangelical United Brethren), the National Methodist Committee on Family Life, and *Together* magazine reinforced this ideal. It will argue that Methodists came together during these ten years to promote this picture-perfect image of the family. Methodists idealized, and even idolized, a specific type of family life in order to combat Communism. At the time, the Methodist Church was the largest Protestant denomination in the United States, and as such, its leaders believed that they had a Christian duty to help protect the American family from the Communist threat. The best weapon against Communism was the Christian family, and the best way to protect the Christian family was to create a white, middle-class, heterosexual ideal that all Methodists could look up to. However, this notion of family was "threatened" by more than just Communism. This chapter will conclude with a look at challenges to Methodist marital life, specifically the rise in divorce and the beginning of the sexual revolution, which prompted Methodists to once again reevaluate sexuality and marriage. Unknowingly, these 1950s Methodists allowed American political rhetoric to find a captive audience within the Methodist denomination, providing the framework for the eventual influence of the New Christian Right.

THE FAMILY AS INSTITUTION: VICTORIANS AND METHODISTS IN AMERICA, 1840–1900

Over the course of the nineteenth century, ministers of the Methodist Episcopal Church, both North (MEC) and South (MECS), and ministers of its related denominations, mainly the United Brethren in Christ (UBC), changed in three vital ways in order to embrace family life as necessary to good religion. Alongside Protestantism, Americans embraced family life as a primary source of satisfaction and pleasure after the rise in urbanization and consumerism in the first few decades of the twentieth century. This section will briefly sketch these changes in family life in order set the stage for the 1950s "cult of togetherness."

First, over the course of the early nineteenth century, ministers of these denominations who were circuit riders, "located" in order to establish themselves and their families in society.[2] Ministers were usually single for a large portion of

---

2   *MEA*, vol, 1, 113.

their lives, because itinerancy and the size of their circuits demanded that they travel thousands of miles by horseback within a few months' time to maintain the denomination's "connection." Constant traveling made living a "normal," that is, settled, family life implausible. Ready for a family, these Protestant ministers wanted to stay in one place, marry, raise children, and become the religious authority for one local congregation. The minister's wife would serve as a "subminister" through her efforts "in teaching, in visiting, in comforting the ill and bereaved, in witnessing, in heading missionary societies, in modeling family piety, in interpreting her husband (to women and other preachers), [and] in supporting the ministry."[3]

Second, the polity of the MEC and MECS began to focus less on the individual and more on the family. In the early Methodist movement, Methodists were disgraced as countercultural. Those who joined the movement, women like Hester Ann Roe, often joined despite their family's disapproval.[4] This gave individuals an identity outside of their family and created tension between family members. If one was lucky enough for one's entire family to join the Methodist movement, it was often hard for the entire family to maintain good standing. Initially, the class meeting "defined who was, and who was not, a Methodist."[5] Joining a class meeting was the initial and most important step to becoming a Methodist, and it was through the class meeting that Methodists kept one another in check, spiritually and morally. Only members in good standing were allowed to attend, and "this exclusiveness formed the foundation of Methodist solidarity and communal identity" outside of the nuclear family.[6] Historian John Wigger argues that as the nineteenth century progressed, the class meeting lost its appeal with the rise of urbanization:

> Its artisan-like concepts of intimate self-disclosure and emotionalism simply did not fit in a world of fashionable parlors and measured decorum. . . . Hence, with little formal discussion or doctrinal debate, antebellum American Methodists gradually, almost silently, abandoned the class meeting in search of a more respectable faith.[7]

---

3   *MEA*, vol, 1, 113.
4   Jean Miller Schmidt, *Grace Sufficient: A History of Women in American Methodism, 1760–1939* (Nashville, TN: Abingdon Press, 1999).
5   John Wigger, *Taking Heaven by Storm: Methodism and the Rise of Popular Christianity in America*, repr. ed. (Chicago: University of Illinois Press, 2011), 82.
6   Wigger, 82.
7   Wigger, 87.

As the accountability of the class meeting lost its appeal, Methodists relied on accountability within the nuclear family, and thus the nuclear family replaced the class meeting as the basic unit of the Methodist movement.

Finally, third, closer to the turn of the twentieth century, Methodism, in particular, shifted its theology from bettering the world through evangelism to bettering the world through social intervention. The brain child of Borden Parker Bowne and his successors, *personalism* became "a distinctive modernist Methodist metaphysic" that connected "the sacred personality of each human being in relation to the loving Personality of God." In the 1950s, Methodist clergy considered (hetero)sexuality as a part of one's sacred personality.[8]

By the late nineteenth century, the membership of the MEC and UBC denominations was representative of the nuclear family—largely middle-class, urban, and white. As historian Anna Lawrence argues, Methodists went from "home wreckers to home builders."[9] This shift from circuit riders to local ministers, from class meetings to salon parlors, and from conversion to personalism, represented a more institutional form of Methodism; and other Protestant denominations followed a similar shift, evolving from single, mobile, and individual-focused ministries to married, established, and family-focused ministries.

Methodists were not the only group to become family-focused toward the end of the nineteenth century. Victorian America, circa 1840–1900, eventually evolved into a family-centered ideology. As "America's first leisure class, with the time and money to develop a genteel way of life," those who constituted Victorian America were urban and affluent.[10] By the end of the century, many Methodists were as Victorian as the cities that they occupied—New York, Philadelphia, Washington, and Chicago—became "Methodist Vatican cities." These men and women began reform societies and led the United States to become one of the strongest economies in the world. Historian Elaine Tyler May provides a history of this class in *Great Expectations: Marriage and Divorce in Post-Victorian America*:

> The Victorian formula, set by native-born white Protestant Americans of the middle classes, reflected the spirit of independence and

---

8   *MEA*, vol. 1, 300–301.
9   Anna M. Lawrence, *One Family Under God: Love, Belonging, and Authority in Early Transatlantic Methodism* (Philadelphia, PA: University of Pennsylvania Press, 2011), 185.
10   Elaine Tyler May, *Great Expectations: Marriage and Divorce in Post–Victorian America* (Chicago, IL: University of Chicago Press, 1980), 17.

self-denial that was believed to be the key to progress. Their world view contained very specific prescriptions for individual behavior, especially pertaining to the proper duties and functions of the sexes. . . . The key element was moral autonomy: total control over one's instincts as well as independent pursuit of one's calling.[11]

If one is familiar with early Methodist theology, the quote above should ring a bell, as Methodists were insistent on self-denial, self-assessment, and moral autonomy as a requirement of daily life. Where earlier Methodists were leery of dancing, socializing, and gambling (to name a few); Victorians were leery of urban vice: prostitution, fraternization, alcohol, and materialism. Key to continuing the Victorian moral worldview was the connection between the public realm and the private realm, and through middle-class white Protestant women who "filled the churches, led the reform movements, worked among the poor in their communities, and provided numerous charity and welfare services," they brought their natural sense of morality from the home into the world.[12]

A consequence of this intense look from the home outward was an ideal of marriage based on "duties and sacrifices, not personal satisfaction." Wife and husband were "helpmates—providers and protectors of the home rather than partners in pleasure." The home functioned simply to better society by providing the proper roles through which men and women engaged with society; they experienced pleasure through participation in these proper public roles. Couples looked outward, toward others, for satisfaction through bettering society either economically and entrepreneurially, or reforming society as a moral guardian. For most, the home was not "a self-contained private domain geared toward the personal happiness of individual family members," and the shift inward occurred as a response to urban consumption (discussed below).[13]

This does not mean, however, that people chose their spouses for solely economic purposes. Marriage during the late nineteenth century was slowly evolving from a practical union based on economic or social need—between persons who may or may not know each other—to a union based in romance, beauty, lust, and pleasure. Once individuals moved away from the home and into the city, they were more inclined to associate with members of the opposite

---

11   May, 17.
12   May, 18.
13   May, 47.

sex based on choice, not status or familial relation. However, many Victorians were conflicted; they wanted to maintain a moral life, but they were exposed to new avenues for pleasure. How do you reconcile a desire for pleasure with a desire to be moral?

Elaine Tyler May argues that "after 1900, the communal values of sacrifice, voluntarism, and virtuous domesticity were seriously shaken by the rise of urban culture."[14] Corporate America replaced entrepreneurial America; thus, work for many Americans became monotonous, not creative. This forced people to look somewhere else for personal development, for individual expression, and for pleasure in their lives. Women, too, were involved in the monotonous workday as their out-of-home employment increased drastically in the first few decades of the twentieth century. Working men and women of all classes succumbed to the "new consumer ethic" as higher wages allowed them to indulge in "clothes, personal care, furniture, mechanical appliances, cars, and recreation." May points out that "the amount spent nationally on personal consumption nearly tripled between 1909 and 1929."[15] The availability of these items to all classes threatened the Victorian code that sought to monitor pleasure through self-assessment. The genius of the Victorian response was its promotion of suburbia as the proper release for pleasure. A post-Victorian morality portrayed the city not as dirty but as tiring. People should leave the city, get away from its noise, and go to a home in the suburbs to experience true relaxation and true pleasure. May eloquently narrates this propaganda:

> As cultural reformers, [Victorians] attempted to channel desires for excitement into the private sphere, which would become further isolated and protected from public life. . . . Now the home became one of the primary places where the fruits of production would be consumed. . . . Suburban families became consuming units, absorbing abundance and leisure into the home. In this sense, although the home may have lost some of its previous social functions, it evolved into an even more important institution for satisfying personal desires. . . . With this increasing isolation, the home became a focal point for personal gratification. Accordingly, marriage—the foundation of family life—came to mean something new.[16]

---

14 May, 49.
15 May, 51.
16 May, 58–59.

As sources of pleasure moved from the city to the home, marriage had to change. It had to become a mecca for pleasure, as discussed in chapter 1. Pre-marital sex, however, was still taboo. Youth were allowed to be *sexy,* especially in light of the consumer culture that stressed beauty and body, but they were not allowed to be *sexual.* In a hurry to experience the seemingly endless plea-sures of marital life, young urban men and women of the 1920s rushed to marry (as the previous chapter discussed), setting the stage for the next generation.[17]

METHODIST SEXUALITY EXEMPLIFIED: POST–WORLD WAR II AMERICAN FAMILY LIFE

Today, most Americans know the stereotype of the 1950s American family: white, heterosexual, middle-class, Protestant, happily married, three children, one dog, and a large suburban home complete with a grill, a white picket fence, and a big yard. In the late 1980s and early 1990s, many historians of American culture dedicated their research to deconstructing, complicating, and disprov-ing this stereotype that created the 1950s "cult of togetherness." These works are admirable and necessary to understand *all* of post–World War II America. This chapter does not seek to reconstruct an argument for this stereotype. But it does argue that many Protestant denominations, particularly the Methodist Church—favoring its white, heterosexual, middle-class membership—created propaganda that put forth this stereotype as the healthy norm.

Methodism promulgated the stereotypical ideal Methodist family. The ideal was connected to the health of the nation through its connection to the new eugenics—a post-1930s ideology that was arguably "race-neutral" and advo-cated voluntarily creating "better" families to improve democracy and the safety of the nation.[18] Methodism has a complicated history with eugenics. As shown in chapter 1, it endorsed the use of artificial birth control based on the idea that smaller families meant happier and healthier families. Most Methodists did not overtly support the old eugenics, the forced sterilization of the "unfit" for the betterment of society. However, many did support the new eugenics, as on the surface, its voluntary status seemed less dangerous, less immoral.

This section focuses on publications from sources that overgeneralize and

---

17   May, 62.

18   Amy Laura Hall, *Conceiving Parenthood: American Protestantism and the Spirit of Reproduction* (Grand Rapids, MI: Eerdmans, 2007), 269–72.

whitewash society. It deconstructs the National Methodist Committee on Family Life, specifically, its Methodist Family of the Year and the pages of *Together* magazine as platforms that supported a specific type of Methodist family life—one that was white, heterosexual, monogamous, and middle-class—as best for society.

It is important to note that the 1950s' stereotypical family life was new to the American scene. Many people, including contemporary politicians, specifically argue that "the legendary family of the 1950s . . . was . . . the last gasp of 'traditional' family life with deep roots in the past." Historian Stephanie Coontz, one of the most renowned experts on the history of American family life, argues that the 1950s were not traditional in any sense:

> At the end of the 1940s, all the trends characterizing the rest of the twentieth century suddenly reversed themselves: For the first time in more than one hundred years, the age for marriage and motherhood fell, fertility increased, divorce rates declined, and women's degree of education parity with men dropped sharply.[19]

It was also "the first wholehearted effort to create a home that would fulfill virtually all its members' personal needs through an energized and expressive personal life."[20] The stereotypical family that so many of today's politicians reference as "traditional" was not only a brand-new ideal in American history; it was also "an historical fluke, based on a unique and temporary conjuncture of economic, social, and political factors." Stephanie Coontz sums up the uniqueness of this historical context:

> During the war, Americans had saved at a rate more than three times higher than in the decades before or since. Their buying power was further enhanced by America's extraordinary competitive advantage at the end of the war, when every other industrial power was devastated by the experience. . . . During the 1950s, real wages increased by more than they had in the entire previous half century. The impact of such prosperity on family formation and stability was magnified by the role of government, which could afford to be generous with education benefits, housing loans, highway and sewer construction,

---

19   Stephanie Coontz, *The Way We Never Were: American Families and the Nostalgia Trap* (New York: Basic Books, 1993), 25.

20   Elaine Tyler May, *Homeward Bound: American Families in the Cold War Era* (New York: Basic Books, 2008), 27.

and job training. All this allowed most middle-class Americans, and a large number of working-class ones, to adopt family values and strategies that assumed the availability of cheap energy, low-interest home loans, expanding education, occupational opportunities, and steady employment. These expectations encouraged early marriage, early childbearing, expansion of consumer debt, and residential patterns that required long commutes to work—all patterns that would become highly problematic by the 1970s.[21]

About 60 percent of the American population took advantage of these conditions and subsequently can be categorized as having a middle-class income. By 1960, 76 percent of Americans owned their home, 87 percent owned a television, and 75 percent owned a car.[22] These statistics tell us that economic prosperity was available to a healthy majority. This does not mean that all families who owned a home, television, and car functioned in the same way. However, all families did have one thing in common: the Cold War Era was a time to focus on the family. People of all races, ethnicities, religions, classes, and educational levels married at an earlier age, had more children, and were less likely to get divorced during this era than any other time in the twentieth century.[23]

The focus on the family also had a political overtone. The health of the family was directly connected to the health of the nation. Elaine Tyler May, renowned historian of American family life, describes this Cold War mentality best:

> For in the early years of the Cold War, amid a world of uncertainties brought about by World War II and its aftermath, the home seemed to offer a secure, private nest removed from the dangers of the world. The message was ambivalent, however, for the family also seemed particularly vulnerable. It needed heavy protection against the intrusion of forces outside itself. The self-contained home held out the promise of security in an insecure world. It also offered a vision of abundance and fulfillment. As the Cold War began, young postwar Americans were homeward bound.[24]

Young couples rushed to build families and gain a sense of security. Postwar America saw a surge in the number of young couples getting married and

---

21 Coontz, *The Way We Never Were*, 28–29.
22 Coontz, 25.
23 May, *Homeward Bound*, 3.
24 May, 1.

having children, a statistic that reached beyond racial, religious, and socio-economic lines.[25] One might contribute this factor to any postwar era, but it was unique to post–World War II America when the country was involved in an ideological struggle with the Soviet Union: capitalism versus Communism.

America faced many threats on its own soil, from racial divides to gender inequality, but its leaders—both political and evangelical leaders like Billy Graham—advocated "the American Way of Life." This was the idea that participation in capitalism, as represented by consumerism and an affluent suburban lifestyle, would create a domestic ideal that strengthened American society at home and abroad.[26] May argues, "According to the Cold War ethos of the time, conflict within the United States would harm our image abroad, strengthen the Soviet Union, and weaken the nation, making it look vulnerable to Communism."[27] This argument formed the basis of the Methodist endorsement of the American Way of Life, as will be shown below.

Women's magazines presented the above luxuries and mentality as typical of the average family in the 1950s. One of the more popular women's magazines, *McCall's*, renovated its image in the early 1950s. In May 1954, a letter from the editor, Otis Wiese, asked readers to "live the life of *McCall's*." After describing how *McCall's* "has been striving to widen [women's] horizons, inspire [women] to lead lives of greater satisfaction, help [women] in [their] daily tasks," Wiese claims, "*Today women are not a sheltered sex*." His evidence for this claim is that

> men and women in ever increasing numbers are marrying at an earlier age, having children at an earlier age and rearing larger families. . . . We travel more. We earn more, spend more, save more. . . . We worship more. And in ever greater numbers we enjoy the advantages of a higher education.[28]

This claim supports everything Coontz claims about the 1950s. According to Wiese, what was most impressive about people of the 1950s was the fact that "men, women, and children are achieving it *together*. They are creating this new and warmer way of life not as women *alone* or men *alone*, isolated

---

25 May, 3.
26 May, 8.
27 May, 9.
28 Otis Wiese, "Live the Life of McCall's," *McCall's*, May 1954, 27, emphasis original.

from one another, but as a *family* sharing a common experience."[29] This rhetoric made its way through other magazines, such as *Ladies' Home Journal* and eventually *Together*, and it created "the cult of togetherness," which described, recommended, and idolized new ideas of co-parenting, co-domesticity, and dedicated recreational family time.

However, the rhetoric of togetherness did not originate with *McCall's*. Amy Laura Hall, theological ethicist and author of *Conceiving Parenthood: American Protestantism and the Spirit of Reproduction*, argues:

> Many Methodist women were sufficiently preoccupied with their own families' appearance to stave off a call by Jesus to live outside the suburban box. . . . By the time Methodism was flourishing as the postwar norm for religiosity, there were too few resources to enable the groundbreaking, ecclesial miscegenation for which Methodists should have been infamous.[30]

Hall recalls the multi-denominational aspect of Methodist camp meetings, where both families and single persons gathered together to worship. She argues that this form of nineteenth-century Methodism could not be more different from Methodism of the 1950s. With 8.9 million members in 1950, and 9.8 million members in 1960, 6.5 percent of the American population was Methodist.[31] They were "the quintessential mainline denomination, spanning the country with largely homogenous congregations." These congregations were largely white, middle-class, and attended church regularly, but were more concerned with the state of their own household than they were with helping neighbors. They were the group against which everyone else was deemed an "other."[32]

Methodism, historically, set out to save the world; the means of saving the world changed over time, of course. Originally, Methodism saved the "New World" through conversion. Then it set out on foreign missions to save the rest of the world, again, through conversion. Around the turn of the twentieth century, Methodism sought to save the world by bettering the institutions that shaped society. Its penning of the Social Creed in 1908 was the best example of this shift from conversion-centeredness to social-centeredness. Hall argues that

---

29 Wiese, 27, emphasis original.
30 Hall, *Conceiving Parenthood*, 79–80.
31 David Hempton, *Methodism: Empire of the Spirit* (New Haven, CT: Yale University Press, 2005), 212.
32 Hall, *Conceiving Parenthood*, 80.

in the 1950s, Methodist women, who had historically been highly involved in missionary and social work through the deaconess movement, the temperance movement, and foreign mission work, among others, were now taught to save the world through "the Lysol habit," creating an exceptionally clean, proper home, both physically and morally, which would strengthen the nation by developing equally clean and proper American citizens.

Hall rightly puts forth the notion that Methodism was equated with whiteness and heteronormativity. Methodists were not only a majority white, but whiteness was built into the denomination's structure. For example, the Central Jurisdiction, created in the 1939 merger, segregated black Methodists into a racially based jurisdiction while white Methodists were geographically jurisdictioned. Beyond institutional structure, Hall argues that Methodists reproduced whiteness and heteronormativity in less overt ways, such as through the pages of *Together* magazine and through the Methodist Family of the Year. *Together: The Midmonth Magazine for Methodist Families* was created in 1956, and was "the official organ of the Methodist Church." It was a continuation of the *Christian Advocate*, which had once been "the largest . . . magazine in the world except the *London Times*" and was "conducted on liberal Christian principles . . . an entertaining, instructive, and profitable family visiter [sic];--devoted to the interests of religion, morality, literature, and science."[33] Its founder and managing editor was Charles Keysor, the later founder of the Good News Movement, suggesting a connection between its rhetoric and that of later evangelical Methodists.[34]

THE NATIONAL METHODIST COMMITTEE ON FAMILY LIFE

The following is in conversation with Amy Laura Hall's work in order to deconstruct whiteness and heteronormativity in the Methodist church and relate them to sexual morality. When "threatened" by sexual "others," that is, divorce and the sexual revolution, those who relied on these ideologies for power sought to reassert the white, heterosexual norm as a safe haven for American families.

The white, heterosexual, middle-class, Protestant family was not only a beacon of cleanliness; it was portrayed as America's best weapon in the fight

---

33 "Untitled," *Together*, October 1956, 8.
34 *MEA*, vol. 1, 503.

against outward threats: "Americans hoped that secure home life could stave off the dangers posed by Communism, sexuality, and new technology."[35] Some Methodists, taking their cues from non-Methodist evangelicals like Billy Graham and the National Association of Evangelicals (discussed more in chapter 3), portrayed Methodists families as "the front line of defense" simply by being a "'normal' family" with a "vigilant mother."[36] They used the National Methodist Conference on Family Life to argue that togetherness combated worldliness.

The National Methodist Conference on Family life (NMCFL), composed of representative lay and clergy delegates from around the United States, met five times between 1951 and 1966, with its first gathering on October 12–14, 1951 in Chicago, Illinois. The themes of the various conferences showcased how Methodists saw the Methodist family as the savior of the nation, "the hope of the world." Startled by the rising divorce rate (which did have a short rise immediately after World War II, but lowered again by the early 1950s) and by the rise in juvenile delinquency, bishops G. Bromley Oxnam, Hazen G. Werner, and William C. Martin thought it was necessary to give "a careful and prayerful examination of the whole situation of marriage and family living in America today." The goal of NMCFL was to help "families all over America . . . to live the Christian way."[37] These conferences represent the crux of Methodist cooperation in regard to sexuality. Methodists came together recognizing that society was changing, and its leadership needed to respond to these changes.

The Second NMCFL was held October 8–10, 1954 in Cleveland, Ohio, with 2,644 attendees. Its theme declared "The Christian Family—the Hope of the World." In the opening address, Bishop Werner articulated what Amy Laura Hall calls the "family's salvific role":

> At a time . . . when the general public and Social Agencies of the land are turning to the family as the one hope for the growth of sound persons to make a safe world; . . . at a time when the home that is to be our salvation is itself under threat of the disturbing influence of the new mass media, the mobility of the home, the growing employment of wives and mothers, the tension of a troubled world—the

---

35 Jessica Weiss, *To Have and to Hold: Marriage, The Baby Boom, and Social Change* (Chicago, IL: University of Chicago Press, 2000), 5.

36 Coontz, *The Way We Never Were,* 33.

37 GCAH, Program for the National Methodist Conference on Family Life, Oct. 12–14, 1951 (Administrative records of the General Board of Discipleship, Folder title "National Conference on Family Life—Program, 1951," 2358–3–5:18.

Methodist Church is pressing toward the restoration of the religious
life of the home, summoning the family to its divine vocation.[38]

The Methodist Church was going to save the world by promoting an image of
domestic life that was equally God-centered and family-centered.

The Methodist Family of the Year

This ideology is most clear in the election of the Methodist Family of the Year.
Methodists knew that "its members live in all parts of the world. They are
of every race and class." They considered Methodist diversity as part of "the
greatness of our heritage and denomination" and believed that "all Methodist families need not be alike, nor think alike."[39] Each NMCFL repeatedly talked
about how families were different and praised that fact, and yet they prescribed
ways of living that prioritized an idealized middle-class, white, American lifestyle. This was evident in two ways. First of all, the various NMCFLs had few international families present, and when they were present, they were put into
one group to look for commonalities with the American way of life instead
of spread among various groups to discuss differences. The NMCFL of 1962
praised the presence of international delegates, not for providing the conference with different ways of being family, but for giving the conference "the
appearance of the United Nations."[40] Second, the NMCFL awarded the "Methodist Family of the Year" to one white, middle-class American family at each
of its gatherings, and thus, not only ignored the variety of families, but gave a
physical example of the white, heterosexual, middle-class, American standard.[41]

The Methodist Church strategically linked democracy and family life by asking each Methodist church (within the United States) "to nominate one family
from its congregation" for "the honor" of being named the Methodist Family of the Year. That family would "represent your church" at the next Family

---

38 Hazen G. Werner, "Report of the National Family Life Committee: For the Quadrennium of 1952–1956,"
    Journal of the 1956 General Conference of the Methodist Church (1956): 1855.

39 "Faith, Freedom, and the Family: Study Booklet for the Third National Conference on Family Life of The
    Methodist Church" (Nashville, TN: The Methodist Church, 1958), 32, (Administrative Records of the
    General Board of Discipleship), Folder: "National Conference on Family Life—Bulletins and Programs,
    1958," 2358–3–5:15.

40 "Overseas Areas Send Delegates; Other Denominations Present,' *Methodist Family Life News* 1, no. 1
    (Oct. 19–21, 1962): 2.

41 "Family of the Year Given Warm Reception in Chicago," *Methodist Family Life News* 1, no. 1 (Oct. 19–21,
    1962; see *Together* 6, no. 11 (November 1962): 16–20.

Life Conference. After nomination, "each candidate" was "screened by offi-cial family-life judges at the district, conference, and finally, the national level." Churches could not just nominate any family, however. They had to meet certain criteria to be nominated:

1. Family has parents age 50 or under.
2. Family has two or more children, at least one teenager, baptized and church members or in Sunday school.
3. Family exemplifies inspiring Christian family living.
4. Family applies Christian ethics in business or profession.
5. Family takes a creative role in church and community life.
6. Family members are known as warm, good neighbors.[42]

Accompanying the curious criteria for the 1958 competition, *Together* mag-azine included a photo of a white family of four, exuding togetherness. The teenage daughter tries on a pink dress, presumably for Easter, while the parents look lovingly upon her. Even the younger son is doing his best to be entertained and involved in the family outing. The qualifications necessary to even be con-sidered for Methodist Family of the Year tell us a lot about what the Methodist Church regarded as proper family life. The most peculiar part of the list is the age restrictions for both parents and children—parents had to be fifty or un-der, and one of the children had to be a teenager. This tells us that the General Committee on Family Life believed it best to have multiple children before the age of thirty-two. It also suggests that the General Committee on Family Life was not looking for "empty-nesters." Children had to be present, baptized, and active in the church life. The first two qualifications are really the only ones that could be easily defined. The last four qualifications are rather broad and open to interpretation. There's no definition of "Christian family living" or "Christian ethics"; nor is there any suggestion as to how those are applied in "business or profession." What exactly is a "creative role" in the church, and what makes a "good, warm neighbor"?

Amy Hall discusses this annual competition, and her assessment is rightly critical:

---

42   "It's time for you to help select the Methodist Family of the Year," *Together*, February 1958, 8.

The contest easily represents the worst sort of horizontal rivalry and vertical elbowing that might emanate from the polished promotion of faith, aesthetically normalized beauty, and worldly success.

Even more disturbing to Hall than the "specter of women peering at their neighbors with an eye of appraisal" is "the suggestion that the family chosen would be the norm to which all Methodist families," and even some non-Methodist families, "should aspire." The Methodist Family of the Year, to Hall, was "the new and improved holy family."[43]

While some of the qualifications for the competition were initially vague, it all became clear once the Detweilers were chosen in 1958. The four-page spread announcing the family as "the new normal" included only a few paragraphs of text, which can be easily summed up: "outstanding Christian devotion to church, home, community—and to one another." They "so well typify Methodist families the country over who put Christian ideas and ideals into their lives seven days each week," as is evidenced in the surrounding photographs.[44] The photographs walk us through a day in the life of the Detweilers. Each day begins "when Minnie Poo, the family pet, gets up early to bring in the paper." Dorothy cooks breakfast for her family each morning just like "any one of a million homes." Jim is shown at work "testing motors of hydraulic landing gear systems" for Lockheed Aircraft Corp., where he "earns his daily bread . . . and puts sound Christian ethic to good use." Jeannie, the fifteen-year-old daughter, calls another teenage girl with an "invitation to the church youth meeting." Another photo shows the mother, Dorothy, "playing hostess to one of her church groups, Jim's co-workers, or simply a social gathering of neighbors."

Turn the page and there's a glimpse into the recreational life of the Detweilers, because any good Christian family has the time and the money to be active in the community. Jim is shown donning an apron, chef's hat, and an award-winning smile as he grills the family dinner, "relieving his wife of kitchen chores." Mother and daughter are out shopping together, bonding over the latest styles. The younger son helps his father mow the lawn. The pride and joy of the family, the "Husky Doug Detweiler" is "a champion swimmer," "headed his Hi-Y and MYF groups," and "is a 'do-it-yourselfer' like his father." The final page shows the family active in the church. Dorothy heads the church school.

43 Hall, *Conceiving Parenthood*, 92.
44 *Together*, November 1958, 14.

Jim "usually assists his ministers during the morning worship service." And the final photo is all five of the Detweilers in their Sunday best, looking intently toward the minister with the faint glow of a window behind them creating a halo-like effect. Above this photo is a quote from the minister: "As a family . . . it is their desire to grow in their prayer and devotional life and, with humility of spirit, ever to serve the needs of Christ."[45] The Detweilers represented the tie between church and home; good families had a strong religious grounding, and religion needed good families like the Detweilers.

The Detweilers were not the only Methodist Family of the Year. That "honor" was presented to the Barkers of Boaz, Alabama, in 1954. Mr. Henry Barker was a mail carrier, and Mrs. Martha Barker was a Sunday-school teacher, treasurer, and secretary of the Women's Society for Christian Service. They were praised as "the people for whom churches are built" and deemed "representative of all Methodism." Mother, father, and all ten children were active in their church, and "soon after birth, each child went to Sunday school with his parents." At home, "grace was said at every meal and family worship held each evening." They epitomized everything that the NMCFL asked of families: they were religious at home and active in the local church.[46]

In 1962, the Whites were named the Methodist Family of the Year. They were praised as "generous . . . thoughtful . . . neighborly . . . willing and dedicated church workers. . . . Not just a Sunday religion, but parents and children exemplify it radiantly in their association with friends, neighbors, fellow townsmen, and 'the stranger within the gates.'" The Whites had five children, three girls and two boys, between sixteen and five years of age. The parents taught the value of active church life, including tithing, to all of their children. Mr. White was a physician, and Mrs. White was a mother. They both taught church-school classes, attended services every week with their family, and were active "in the entire program of the church."[47] In the same way that *Together* assured all Methodists that the Detweilers of 1958 were just like them, this article assured the reader that "there are thousands of families like the Whites all over the nation" who "hold Christ at the center of their lives every day of every year."

---

45 "Meet: Methodist Family of the Year," 14–17.
46 "Ralph Edwards Presents the Methodist Family," *The Christian Home: The Hope of the World; Report of the Second National Conference on Family Life* (1954), 12.
47 "1962 Methodist Family of the Year," *Together*, 18–19.

At each NMCFL, a white, middle-class family with teenage children who were active in community and church, worked tirelessly at their jobs, and still found time to spend with one another was named Methodist Family of the Year. This not only glorified a very specific type of family with the financial capabilities to have only one parent work, have multiple children, and afford the luxuries of suburban lifestyle; it also made families who could not live up to this standard an "other," lesser, not worthy. It pitted Methodist families against one another and asked them to judge one another based on a specific list of criteria. It fostered Hall's "Lysol habit," as families were judged on the cleanliness of their homes, their appearance, and their lifestyles. Furthermore, it ignored many Methodist families, including but not limited to those outside of America, those without children, those whose children were no longer at home, single persons, families of other classes and races, and homosexual persons.

The Methodist Family of the Year was deemed an honor and gave Methodists a new holy family against which to analyze their lives. The problem with this ideal is its connection to the new eugenics. If all families could adjust their lifestyles to better fit the ideal Methodist mold, then the Christian vision for a safer, better America might be attained. The idea of a perfect home and the perfect family was a rhetorical tool meant to protect America; however, it was more often used as a way to deem certain families as proper, fit, or contributing best to society and to demonize those who could not adhere to this norm.

The last NMCFL was in 1966, and the Methodist Family of the Year did not survive the merger that created The United Methodist Church in 1968. This is rarely discussed in Methodist history for it clashes with other Methodist efforts combating racism, sexism, and classism. An entire book could be dedicated to deciphering the complicated picture put forth by the NMCFL across its fifteen-year existence (1951–1966) and how its rhetoric changed with the complexities of American family life in the Cold War Era.

The key takeaway from this exploration of the NMCFL is the direct connection of the status of the Methodist family to an ideology of nationhood and the health of the world. It connected a piece of Methodist rhetoric to a worldview, which was promulgated specifically by a growing population of neo-evangelicals throughout the 1950s, and it provided a shining example, through the Methodist Family of the Year, of what a proper Methodist family should look like and how they should act in order to combat Communism.

The Methodist Families of the Year were not the only families presented in the pages of *Together*. This periodical was meant to be a tool to provide families with new ideas to actively engage with one another in fun, wholesome, Christian activities, and, at its peak, reached 1.25 million families each year.[48] Magazines like *Good Housekeeping*, *McCall's*, and *Together* filled their pages with continuous pressure to maintain togetherness along with a woman's other domestic duties, which forms the basis of what Amy Laura Hall calls "the good-housekeeping panopticon," the idea that women judged one another and were judged by society based on their ability to conform to a perfect domesticity.[49]

THE THEME OF TOGETHERNESS

The theme of the first issue of *Together* was, obviously, *togetherness*, and its importance to 1956 Protestant America was that "togetherness expressed the deepest mood of the Christian fellowship and is utterly necessary. It is the triumph of the tiny church and the constant problem of the giant church." Coming together "was an appropriate reminder that the prophetic strength of our faith is founded in fellowship."[50]

The cult of togetherness had a dual emphasis; it focused on both the married couple and the children. Jessica Weiss's *To Have and To Hold* analyzes the records of the Institute of Human Development, which tracked one hundred families over the course of thirty years (1950–1980) to see how their lifestyles changed in post–World War II America. She argues that the ideology of togetherness "provided the solution to the dilemma couples with large young families faced by combining family time and couple time."[51] This dilemma was rooted in changes in marital life over the course of the previous thirty years. Across the beginning of the twentieth century, the gendered spheres of marital life were for the most part unchanged, but marriage became increasingly based on a romantic ideal. With romance as its base, contraception use within marriage increased (as discussed in chapter 1) and created a new, expected sphere of intimacy for the couple. Additionally, regulations on newly corporate America increased leisure time, which meant that husband and wife had ample time for

---

48 *MEA*, vol. 1, 503.
49 Hall, *Conceiving Parenthood*, 79.
50 "Untitled," *Together*, October 1956, 3.
51 Weiss, *To Have and to Hold*, 116.

recreation together. Thus, "as the home became the focus of recreation and relaxation, Americans' expectations for happiness in marriage heightened," which created new pressures and new duties for women. They were now expected to develop new ways to foster intimacy not only between themselves and their husbands but for the entire family, and they were expected to maintain a certain standard of domesticity while still being fun and flirty.[52]

The economic hardships of the 1930s had forced couples to have smaller families, allowing them to focus more on the husband-wife relationship without neglecting parental duties. This expectation carried over into post–World War II America, when the average family size increased and necessitated an increased focus on children, somehow balanced with the same attention given to marital satisfaction. These various expectations of togetherness created unnecessary tensions:

> The tension between a romantic desire for a couple-focused marriage and the reality of child-focused marriage, the sexual division of labor, and the changes over the family cycle challenged couples to measure up to their individual version of the togetherness ideal.[53]

Togetherness left little time for individual expression and individual development. In reality, togetherness was a white suburban phenomenon, a weekend-only activity due to the time constraints of men's employment and the schedule of children's activities. The ideal of togetherness portrayed in the colorful pages of magazines like *Together*, and the contrast of a reality that rarely allowed for enjoyable family time, not only "discouraged couples" but created an undue stress on the family to make time for each other and to enjoy every minute of it.[54]

Togetherness was not only a family ideal presented by other magazines; it was also an ideal of the church and encouraged churches to emphasize the best ways to foster Christian togetherness.[55] *Together* took the cult of togetherness and asked families to give devoted family time a religious bent. It also showcased the ease through which family time could embolden faith, for simply coming

---

52 Weiss, 117.
53 Weiss, 120.
54 Weiss, 138.
55 *Togetherness* was first mentioned as a family-centered idea in *McCall's* in 1954. It was later picked up by the *Ladies' Home Journal*.

together as a family accentuated God's personality, as God designed people to be communitive. Articles encouraged readers to think of togetherness as

> a matter of conceding and not of conniving . . . a product of humility and not of clever assertiveness . . . fostered by respect for the opinions of others and not by patronage or privilege.[56]

Another definition of togetherness had a more direct religious overtone; togetherness is "God's way of working, both in creation and also in bringing salvation." It connects "faith, love, righteousness, service" to togethering.

An article from February 1957 typified the standard *Together* story, portraying the business world as tiring, the home as comforting, and the family as the sole source of happiness. Written by Will Durant, the article is titled, "Why Are Happy People Happy?" The article is an amazing piece of togetherness propaganda. Durant encouraged people to "get out of the city if you can," because cities are full of "fever and filth." Instead, "live in the country, or next best, the suburbs." It encouraged the husband to "relieve" himself for "two hours a day with physical activity" and claimed, "It's a blessing for you if your wife has some work for you to do when you come home." The *Leave It to Beaver* family brings to mind the husband coming home from work at 5:30 p.m., the wife pouring him a Scotch, and the family enjoying a nice, hot, home-cooked meal together before the father enjoys his evening off—after all, he deserves it. But the cult of togetherness actually encouraged fathers to be active parents and co-domestics by marketing specific domestic activities, like mowing the lawn or grilling, as easy ways for men to help around the house.

Durant's article spoke to the men of 1957 and encouraged them to "go out and cut the lawn, root out the weeds, wash the car, paint the fence—and not the town!" Durant polished this story off with a suggestion that helping the wife out around the house could lead to sex. He once saw his own wife washing the car and decided "there was something unmanly in me to let her do all that washing by herself." So, he joined her and "what pleasure there was then." Along with spraying the car, the Durants sprayed each other, engaging in healthy, literally clean, marital fun. These "little acts of solicitude and tenderness each day are never lost." Health, action, and affection were the sources of happiness, and these could only be rightly achieved with "a friend and a mate,

---

56   Roy L. Smith, "The Secret of Togethering," *Together,* October–November 1956, 16.

a husband or a wife." This lovely story that Durant presented was typical of the lifestyles and ethics portrayed in *Together*.

A source of tension for many Methodist families, as evidenced by articles throughout *Together*, was balancing equality of the sexes. The 1950s idea of togetherness emphasized co-domesticity and co-parenting. But reality placed undue pressure on women to balance morality and sexuality, family time and couple time, and domestic work and, if necessary, outside employment. In 1951, the Women's Division of Christian Service held a symposium titled "The Family—A Christian's Concern," which, much like the first NMCFL that would meet a few months later, sought to define the Protestant ideal of family life. According to this symposium, the Christian family was natural, procreative, and monogamous. It upheld equality of the sexes and demonstrated the basic educational unit of society. However, "equality" of the sexes was not the same in 1951 as it is today:

> The meaning of this is that the two adult partners in a family have equal basic rights and equal basic responsibilities, even though the functions they perform as family members are different. . . . [Marriage] is a relationship between two adults, who enhance and complete each other's lives through performing their respective functions, and who, if they have children, assume equal though different responsibilities in rearing them.[57]

Co-parenting and co-domesticity, then, did not mean sharing all of the tasks equally; it meant doing your gender-specific tasks. For women, this was the day-to-day domestic work: laundry, cleaning, child rearing, cooking, and so on. For men, this meant helping in areas that they could: mowing the lawn, grilling, and fixing things around the house. Women did most of the child rearing, but fathers were more and more expected to be intentional role models to their children, active parents, and disciplinarians. A good example of this is found in *Together*, May 1960, in a story called "Half a Gift." The story depicted two boys, eleven and fourteen years old, who wanted to get their mother a Mother's Day gift. They knew that she spent most of her day doing household chores: "She worked all day, cooking and buying and tending to us in illness, and stocking the stove in the kitchen with wood and coal to keep us warm in the winter.

---

57 Women's Division of Christian Service, "The Family—A Christian's Concern, A Symposium," (April 1951), 3–4.

She did her own washings of family clothes in the bathtub." The boys purchased for her "a scrubbing pail," thinking it would bring her happiness, since she spent her days cleaning. When she opened the gift, "her voice almost broke" into sadness. Seeing the mother's disappointment, the father, ever quick on his feet, said, "You did not let Nick finish. . . . Part of his gift was that *he* was going to wash the floor from now on."[58]

This story epitomizes the complexity of co-parenting and co-domesticity. Mother is still in charge of all household chores and "does them silently," because she does not enjoy them. The children, trying earnestly to help, get her a gift that reminds her of daily monotony. Father steps in to co-parent and volunteers the children to help mother out with one task, washing the floor. In 1960, the idea of children helping with chores and the father helping co-parent was radical and needed to be discussed in magazines so that it became a norm for families to do the everyday, mundane activities together.

Other articles zoomed in on couples' marriages to assure readers that any problems they faced in marriage, others faced too; and they faced them head-on with help from their faith. In the article "We Married Young, But . . . ," author Esther Mishler explained how, even though she and her husband married at ages seventeen and nineteen, respectively, they had a successful marriage. Many teenagers during the 1950s were encouraged to wait until they were out of their teens to marry, because many of those teens who rushed to marry right before and right after World War II ended up divorcing due to immaturity. However, this was not the case for Esther. While the two did face financial hardships and had to adjust to not going to parties, they quickly settled into a routine and had children early. Whenever they had a "misunderstanding" they turned to their faith, which "has carried us through circumstances that, at the time, seemed hopeless." Esther's article was short but sweet and exhibited well *Together's* idea of a faith-centered marriage.[59]

Every topic in the glossy pages of *Together,* from marriage, to disarmament, and even advertisements, discussed family and the ideals of togetherness. There were even articles that gave instructions on crafts to do as a family, advice to teenagers on how to deal with crushes or bullies, family devotionals, and movie and book reviews. The purpose of *Together,* as Amy Laura Hall understands it,

---

58   Robert Zacks, "Half a Gift," *Together,* May 1960, 20–21.
59   Esther Mishler, "We Married Young, BUT . . ." *Together,* May 1960, 29–30.

was to "methodically [gather] up the flotsam and jetsam of domestic life, [and order] the home itself with spiritual efficiency," so that "a household might become the epicenter of Hope itself."[60] Its purpose was to create a hopeful family; and the way to create hope in the grim context of Cold War America was to encourage togetherness and faith. With togetherness, "'the Christian Home' would become the crux of the age—the site at the intersection of scientific progress, national security, and blessed, divine providence." The Christian Home, armed with Lysol and a strong faith, was based on a "properly cleansed and situated family" and could "restore every person's confidence in America's power to provide."[61]

THE LIMITS OF TOGETHERNESS

But not all Methodists felt this way. Some Methodist women worked against the insular cult of togetherness. Potential conflicts disrupted the American Way of Life as promoted in magazines like *Together*, and were based within the ideal itself: certain racial groups, socioeconomic classes, and minority identities (such as those persons who remained "in the closet" during this era) were prevented from fully participating in the American Way of Life due to systemic barriers. Furthermore, some women did not embrace the domesticity that accompanied the American Way of Life. These were viewed as potential threats to national security and were thus portrayed as anti-patriotic. However, after a brief stint embracing the ideal Methodist family in order to embrace the new sexual ethic, some Methodists realized the limits of this ethic. They began to disrupt the cult of togetherness through support for the civil rights movement and an acknowledgment of the limits of Christian marriage. These moves, and others discussed in chapter 3, were seen by some Methodists as attacks on family life and gave them a reason to formally organize in the late 1960s into groups such as the Good News Movement.

Race

One of the tension areas between Methodists during the first half of the twentieth century involved race. Why discuss race in a book about sexuality? First, the Methodist construction of the ideal family was white, as discussed throughout

---

60   Hall, *Conceiving Parenthood*, 83.
61   Hall, 84.

this chapter. Second, during the Cold War Era, racial and sexuality minorities were discriminated against by the same groups of persons and for the same reasons: political unrest threatened national security, and movements for the rights of women, African Americans, and LGBTQ persons were a main source of political unrest. Third, Methodist historians, such as Jane Ellen Nickel, argue that race, gender, and sexuality share a similar history of discrimination within twentieth-century Methodism. Race, gender, and sexuality represented threats to the power of the white heterosexual male's ability to maintain control over the vision and mission of the denomination. They based their efforts to maintain power in theology, morality, and practicality in order to discredit marginalized groups who threatened that power.[62] Furthermore, Alice G. Knotts argues that white Methodist women were the first Protestant group to attempt race reconciliation. Her argument is based on the fact that Methodist women, due to their Methodist theology, were allowed "freedom of opinion and dialogue on controversial issues." To them, Methodism "transcend[ed] race, class, and gender," for "spiritual life [was] related to all aspects of life." Some white Methodist women believed that it was their "Christian and civic responsibility" to improve human relations within their communities and nations.[63]

White Methodist women's involvement with the Woman's Christian Temperance Union (WCTU) and the deaconess movement gave them a solid foundation in interracial work. With these relationships, as early as the 1930s, Methodist women organized to combat lynching as well as inequality in education. They based their efforts in personalism, grounding their faith in liberal Protestantism.[64] They sought to change not only individual situations but relationships and the social and legal systems that oppressed African Americans. Many of their more radical actions were performed at the national organizational level. However, at the local level, women worked across racial lines to better their communities, their schools, and their local governments. They did so under the guidance of African American Methodists and non-Methodist women, where "attitude-changing conversations" could occur.[65]

In the 1940s, the Women's Division of Christian Service of the Board of

---

62   Nickel, *We Shall Not Be Moved*, 14.
63   Alice G. Knotts, *Fellowship of Love: Methodist Women Changing American Racial Attitudes, 1920–1968* (Nashville, TN: Abingdon Press, 1996), 18.
64   Knotts, 40.
65   Knotts, 150, 178, 209, 234.

Missions set out "to create a new social order, a world in which people would be treated fairly, where there would be no artificial barriers of race, and where people could live in peace."[66] Using the teachings of Jesus as a moral guide, they believed that "love, justice, human dignity, and equality had priority over racial supremacy, racial purity, and segregation," for God loves all equally and made all in God's image.[67] In 1948, they added to the *Discipline* a statement titled "The Christian Church and Race," which labeled racial discrimination an international problem and called it a "clear violation of the Christian belief in the fatherhood of God, the brotherhood of man, and the Kingdom of God." The statement was the first in the Methodist tradition to officially denounce racial discrimination as "unchristian" and "evil."[68] In 1944, the Women's Division supported the formation of the United Nations, and in 1947, they supported the Universal Declaration of Human Rights.[69]

Women of the Methodist Church were not alone in these endeavors. When the Evangelical Association and the United Brethren united in 1946 to form the Evangelical United Brethren (EUB), they reaffirmed their previously held positions on racial equality: "The Church respects human personality inherent in the people of every race, and protests against social, economic, or political discrimination based merely on racial differences."[70] The EUB's General Christian Social Action Committee supported the Supreme Court's decision that segregation was unconstitutional, and it sought to educate children on race relations through lessons with titles such as "We Are All Alike, Yet We Are Different."[71] The EUB tradition of supporting racial equality emphasized "the value of godly love" over "divisions over social practice," thus giving Methodists and future United Methodists an example of how to live out God's love amid social (and sexual) disagreement.[72]

The Women's Division of the Methodist Church supported boycotts, sit-ins, and the Civil Rights Act, and their own declarations received intense pushback

---

66 Knotts, 139.

67 Knotts, 142.

68 *BOD* (1948), 600–602.

69 Knotts, *Fellowship of Love*, 145–46.

70 Wendy Deichmann, "'True Holiness' as Social Practice in the Evangelical and United Brethren Traditions: A Legacy for Successor Denominations," in J. Steven O'Malley and Jason E. Vickers, *Methodist and Pietist: Retrieving the Evangelical United Brethren Tradition* (Nashville, TN: Kingswood Books, 2011), 186.

71 Deichmann, 186–87.

72 Deichmann, 189.

from some Methodists. The civil rights movement was based on principles of the Social Gospel and human dignity, ideologies professed by Soviet Communism. Some Methodists were quick to label those who fought for human dignity and equality as "Communists." In the context of the American Way of Life, which espoused the white, heterosexual, nuclear family, and togetherness as patriotic, anything that threatened that family was seen as supporting Communism and, therefore, unpatriotic. Along with the Women's Division, the Methodist Federation for Social Action (MFSA) faced the brunt of the attack, mainly by members of the Circuit Riders, Inc., a small evangelical caucus group whose sole purpose was to denounce MFSA. In February 1950, many Methodist organizations, leaders, and bishops were deemed Communist sympathizers in Stanley High's "Methodism's Pink Fringe," an article in *Reader's Digest*.[73] The situation was serious enough to involve the House Un-American Activities Committee, who investigated MFSA and the Women's Division, using their "interracial meetings and civil rights legislation" as evidence that the organizations were Communist.[74]

The Women's Division responded by ensuring that all of their women were registered voters and continued their campaigns for racial reconciliation. They, and women from other denominations, such as the EUB, continued to educate the denomination on race and corrected misinformation. They worked with women from the African Methodist Episcopal Church, the Colored Methodist Episcopal Church, and the African Methodist Episcopal Zion to

> implement inclusive racial policies in boards and agencies of the church and in local churches, and to assist communities in protecting and delivering constitutionally guaranteed civil rights to all citizens.[75]

They even hosted international conferences on race, where women were taught that racial reconciliation was a universal goal. The Women's Division fought against the creation of the Central Jurisdiction, a connectional jurisdiction that segregated African American clergy and bishops, from its creation in 1940 until its undoing in 1968.[76] Their efforts in fighting for racial and gender equality were immense for their time. As Jane Ellen Nickell argues, the pushback

---

73   Stanley High, "Methodism's Pink Fringe," *Reader's Digest* 56, no. 2 (February 1950): 134–38.
74   *MEA*, vol. 1, 419–23; Knotts, *Fellowship of Love*, 179–80.
75   Knotts, *Fellowship of Love*, 228–31.
76   Knotts, 246

they received from some Methodists was out of fear of losing power, a fear that was based in sexual and racial dominance. In the context of the 1950s, the Women's Division was labeled Communist in order to prevent local churches from supporting their efforts. Most problematic, Methodist families were instead presented with a white, middle-class, heterosexual ideal in the Methodist Family of the Year to look up to, one that was guaranteed to be patriotic. The Women's Division, and other liberal Protestant women, such as those within the EUB, sought to break this mold. They fought to break down racial barriers that kept the Methodist Family of the Year unattainable for all Methodists and non-Methodists.

Divorce

Complicating perfect togetherness in the 1950s was a rise in the divorce rate across the decade and into the early 1960s. There was also a new rhetoric about marriage as *work*, accompanied by an increase in premarital and postmarital counseling. Historians Heather R. White, Rebecca L. Davis, and Christina Simmons argue that liberal Protestant clergy's new sexual ethic helped create marital counseling as a profession.[77] Through their innovations in pastoral counseling and their desire to make (hetero)sexuality a good, positive thing, they accidentally created a heterosexual, marital norm that deemed those sexual persons outside of the norm, mainly homosexual persons and persons engaged in sex outside of marriage, abnormal. After a brief synopsis of the changes in divorce laws among Protestant denominations, this section will focus on pamphlets, articles, expert advice, legislation, and personal testimonials, and will argue that alongside the desire to advocate for togetherness, some Methodists sought to change Methodist law to allow for divorce.

As previously mentioned, in the first third of the twentieth century, marriage shifted from an institution based on economics to one based on love. This modern view also provided a new reason for the dissolution of marriage. Previously, spouses in an unloving marriage maintained their commitment for its economic or social benefit. With marriage being voluntary and based on love, if a marriage was emotionally or sexually unsatisfactory, there was little reason to stay. As one of the more popular marriage preparation textbooks stated:

---

77 White, *Reforming Sodom*; Rebecca L. Davis, *More Perfect Unions: The American Search for Marital Bliss* (Cambridge, MA: Harvard University Press, 2010); and Simmons, *Making Marriage Modern*.

> If a culture makes happiness the goal of marriage, it must grant the right of divorce to those who fail in their efforts to find happiness in each other. . . . The right of divorce is important in the new system of marriage values. It recognizes two facts: first, human judgment is fallible, and second, those who fall in love may also fall out of love.[78]

This became even more so when women increasingly became involved in the workplace and became financially independent outside of marriage.

Most American Protestant churches share a similar history in regard to divorce. Around the end of the nineteenth century, these churches were forced to acknowledge divorce as a potential reality in the life of their congregants. By 1920, the national divorce rate was 20 percent.[79] Up to this point, the Protestant stance on divorce was that it was to be granted only in the case of adultery, and the guilty party could not remarry; this was the stance of the Methodist Episcopal Church, the Methodist Episcopal Church, South, the Methodist Protestant Church, the Evangelical Association, and the United Brethren.[80]

In order to allow divorced persons to remarry, Protestant clergy had to reinterpret Scripture, which was, as then interpreted, against divorce and remarriage, and to view Scripture as setting an ideal for marriage, not a prescription for it. By the 1930s, many Protestant denominations decided on the language to relax their divorce laws by redefining infidelity. By 1930, the Presbyterian Church of the U.S.A. expanded their definition of infidelity: "Anything that kills love and deals death to the spirit of the union is infidelity."[81] In 1928, the Methodist Episcopal Church proclaimed that marriages were dissoluble due to adultery "or its full moral equivalent," and remarriage of the innocent party was allowed.[82] By 1932, the MEC was clearer as to other causes: "other vicious conditions which through mental or physical cruelty or physical peril invalidated the marriage vow."[83] In 1948, the Methodist Church had no change regarding its stance on

---

78 Paul H. Landis, *Making the Most of Marriage* (New York: Appleton-Century-Crofts, 1955), 12.

79 Mark A Smith, "Religion, Divorce, and the Missing Culture War in America," *Political Science Quarterly*, 125 (Spring 2010): 69.

80 For MEC, see MEC *Discipline* 1884, ¶46, p. 33; for MPC, see MPC *Discipline* 1888, section "Annual Conference," ¶14, p. 71); for MECS, see MECS *Discipline* 1890, ¶136, p. 87); for EA, see Behney, Eller, and Krueger, *History of the Evangelical United Brethren Church*, 200; for United Brethren, see Behney, Eller, and Krueger, 165.

81 Smith, "Religion, Divorce," 70.

82 MEC *Discipline* 1928, ¶70.

83 Smith, "Religion, Divorce," 71; see also MEC *Discipline* 1932, ¶72, pp. 63–64.

divorce, accepting the 1932 statement of the MEC, but it did add a paragraph encouraging couples to undergo premarital counseling:

> In planning to perform the rite of matrimony the minister is advised to have an unhurried premarital conference with the parties to be married. It is strongly urged that the minster have this conference at least several days before the date of the wedding, and that the minister advise and instruct to the best of his ability to the end that the parties to be married become soberly aware that successful marriage is dependent on those spiritual qualities which are best nurtured and kept alive by a constant sense of loyalty to God and to God's organized Church.[84]

The General Conference of the Methodist Church continued to relax its views on divorce, and by 1960, advocated marital counseling, not only for couples prior to marriage, but "to those under the threat of marriage breakdown in order to explore every possibility of reconstructing the marriage."[85] The Evangelical United Brethren maintained a strict stance on divorce until 1950, when marriage was reevaluated along with many of its stances on family life. In 1950, divorced persons were allowed to remarry if "the divorced persons have sought and received forgiveness and are seeking a genuine Christian relationship not only in marriage, but with God."[86] States followed suit and relaxed their divorce laws beyond adultery to include "cruelty, desertion, prison terms, and two years' separation"; by 1969, California had passed the first no-fault divorce law.[87]

The idea of marriage as work first became popular outside of religious circles. As people moved away from home and into the city, they left their primary source of marital advice and information—their parents. Seeing an economic and professional opportunity, psychological experts branded themselves as marriage experts and began a new field, teaching people how to prepare for marriage, how to maintain a happy marriage, and when to approach divorce.[88] Experts portrayed religious authorities, friends, and parents as ill-equipped to save a marriage because divorce, according to them, was

---

84 MC *Discipline* 1948, ¶355, p. 107.
85 Smith, "Divorce, Religion," 71; see also MC *Discipline* 1960, ¶356, p. 159.
86 Behney, Eller, and Krueger, *The History of the Evangelical United Brethren Church*, 378.
87 Smith, "Divorce, Religion," 72.
88 Kristin Celello, *Making Marriage Work: A History of Marriage and Divorce in the Twentieth-Century United States* (Chapel Hill, NC: University of North Carolina Press, 2012), 32.

a psychological issue, not a moral issue.[89] Most of the preparation for marriage occurred in college classrooms, and by 1937, one-third of colleges in
America offered a class on preparing for marriage. These courses offered "scientific facts and pragmatic advice" on "individual personality assessment, find-
ing a potential mate, and adjusting sexually, economically, and psychologically
to married life." Professors also offered individual, private counseling to students. This "blend of academic and practical subject material paired with therapeutic intentions" led to a "distinctive classroom experience." These courses
were limited to only college-educated and some high school children. Professors thought that their methods would sufficiently reduce divorces based on
the "scientific information given in such courses." Furthermore, "unlike traditional home economics courses, which taught young women how to manage
well-run homes, marriage preparation classes contained strong emotional and
sexual components (which is also why most professors preferred to teach to
sex-segregated classrooms)."[90]

With the onset of World War II, marriage experts were faced with the reality of rushed, young marriages that often ended in divorce. During the war, the
divorce rate doubled; there were more than five hundred thousand divorces in
1946, a historic high.[91] By 1942, the American Association of Marriage Counselors was established. They were successful because they "identif[ied] the war
marriage phenomenon as a problem of national significance and [broadcast]
their desire and ability to mitigate it." With the war, they "made their skills
known to a broad audience beyond the narrow confines of their expert community."[92] War caused difficulties in marriage for a variety of reasons. First,
these marriages were often rushed or pressured. There was pressure to marry
prior to having sex, and many women felt it "unpatriotic" to say no to either
having sex with or marrying a soldier. Second, the husband quickly left after the marriage ceremony, which delayed the adjustment period and allowed
women who remained home to go about their lives as if they were not married. Third, many couples were "disillusioned" by war and later regretted marrying in the first place. Fourth, once their husbands returned home, young

---

89   Celello, 26, 38.
90   Celello, 33–34.
91   Celello, 67–68.
92   Celello, 59.

couples faced financial difficulties that they were not properly prepared to deal with together. And finally, when apart for months or years at a time, many couples were not faithful to each other.[93] With the failure of so many war marriages, magazines opened their columns to marriage experts, whose articles quickly became ubiquitous.[94]

Many marriage experts put the burden of marital happiness on the wife, especially in the 1950s. Universities encouraged women to take courses to learn just how rewarding wifehood could be. They taught that "it takes intelligence to be a modern wife."[95] Articles in magazines, such as "Woman's Finest Role" in *Reader's Digest*, taught that "to be a successful wife is a career in itself, requiring among other things, the qualities of a diplomat, a businesswoman, a good cook, a trained nurse, a school teacher, a politician, and a glamour girl."[96] Wifehood or motherhood was rebranded as a full-time job; and added to her workload was an awareness of the physical, professional, emotional, and psychological needs of all of the members of her family and a special attention to her husband's sexual needs.[97] The idea was that any marriage could be saved if the wife wanted it. The strategy seemed to work. The divorce rate in the 1950s dropped from 10.3 per 1,000 in 1950, to 9.2 per 1,000 in 1960.[98] Wives accepted that saving their marriage was a matter of "accepting one's limitations as well as those of one's husbands," a statement that becomes highly problematic when physical, sexual, or emotional abuse enters the picture.[99]

In the 1950s, Protestant churches reclaimed some authority over marital satisfaction and counseling. In the Methodist Church, this was evident in the sheer number of pamphlets produced by the General Board of Discipleship that encouraged young couples to talk with their pastors or their local Planned Parenthood about how to best plan for marriage and what to do when marital crises occurred. These pamphlets stated that "one needs to learn what to expect, about when to expect it, what not to worry over too much and what to be really concerned about." They almost unanimously taught that "adjustment

93   "The Whys of War Divorces," *New York Times*, 1946. For more on this, see Littauer, *Bad Girls*.
94   Celello, *Making Marriage Work*, 69.
95   Celello, 35.
96   "Woman's Finest Role," *Reader's Digest* (August 1955).
97   Celello, *Making Marriage Work*, 75.
98   Celello, 84.
99   Celello, 98.

to sex is one of the first problems to confront a couple in marriage." They assured young couples that many others experienced the same "unnecessary dissatisfactions" early in their marriages, but it was best to not let sex get in the way of a happy marriage. In this way, sexual adjustment meant an adjustment to heterosexuality.

Many clergy believed, as will be shown in chapter 5, that homosexual desires were often the by-product of sexual maladjustment. These pamphlets also provided young couples with statistics on common problems. For example, "More than 90 percent of divorces in the first year are caused by in-law troubles." Other major issues mentioned are consumption of alcohol, the number of children, the amount of participation in church, financial troubles, and nagging. These pamphlets were incredibly practical. They, of course, promoted, first and foremost, that "anyone seriously concerned about improving his marriage, therefore, should turn first to that church which most promotes a sense of 'we-ness' between him and his mate." They always concluded with a few easy steps to help any marriage:

1. Read the latest literature that reflects the experience of others.
2. Carefully avoid wounding your mate's economic or sex ego, or any other deliberate wounding while dealing with problems.
3. Be big enough to go for outside help to a qualified minister, physician, or counselor when you need to.
4. Do not go to friends and relatives who cannot give objective advice.
5. If confession is involved, as in a triangle situation or infidelity, refuse to unload the burden of your guilt onto your mate, but go instead to your pastor or someone who can handle it without becoming emotionally distraught.
6. Refuse to consider a divorce as justified until at least a year's separation before proceedings are begun. . . . After you have done all that you know how to do and continued marital tensions seem to threaten the physical or emotional health of you, your partner, or children, get the opinion of at least two well-qualified persons. . . .
7. If your partner steadfastly refuses the help available in your community and your physician, pastor, or counselor knows of nothing more that can be done, then you may validly consider the possibility of divorce.

8. If a divorce is obtained, continue with your counseling to minimize the emotional and psychic damages involved in your experience.[100]

The practical advice put forth by these pamphlets occurred at the same time that the NMCFL was putting forth unrealistic ideals of family life. The eight guidelines can be applied to any marriage, not just that of the white middle class.

Another early 1960s pamphlet asked, "Will marriage counseling help?" Husband and wife are seated at breakfast. The wife's elbow is on the table with her face resting in an open palm. She looks beyond distraught. The husband looks at her as if he is waiting for a response. Written by Leon Smith, the pamphlet outlines what to expect and not expect in marriage counseling. Do not expect advice. Do not expect the minister or counselor to take your side. Do not expect your problem to be immediately resolved. Do expect to feel glad that you sought help. Do expect to see improvement if you continuously work at your marriage. Smith defines marriage counseling in the pastoral setting as

> a confidential relationship between the pastor and a couple in which the couple, individually and together, are enabled to talk out their problems with sufficient help and understanding so that they are able to realize the causes of their difficulties and to find within themselves the resources for solving their problems and for developing a more mature and satisfying way of relating to each other.[101]

The pamphlet concludes with this definition and a resounding, "It's worth it!" Again, this pamphlet is incredibly practical, dismantling any foregone expectations and providing a concrete definition of what a counseling session is. It also puts forth a positive attitude that, even though one has come to the conclusion that counseling is needed, it can help. The strict dichotomy between these pamphlets and the overly idealistic work of the NMCFL could not be more apparent.

In 1955, the Board of Education's Department of Christian Family, with cooperation from the Television, Radio, and Film Communication of the Methodist Church, produced a series of filmstrips that sought to "help young people prepare for Christian homemaking." The films were arranged by age group, and each included a leader's guide to help the leader prepare for and answer

---

100 Albert Dale Hagler, "Every Marriage Has Problems," reprinted by the Department of the Christian Family from *The Christian Home* (1956).
101 Leon Smith, "Will Marriage Counseling Help," reprinted by the Division of the Local Church from *The Christian Home* (1963).

questions. The first film, "Junior-Hi Friendships," was intended to "assist intermediates in forming standards for the selection of friends." The second, "How about a Date?" was to help "intermediates and seniors learn greater skills in dating." Older adolescents learned to "make wise choices in friendships which might lead to marriage" with "Is This One for Me?" Finally, "The Meaning of Engagement" taught "the significance of engagement as a time of preparation for marriage."[102]

These film strips epitomize the new Methodist sexual ethic in the 1950s. They create a fear that "going steady" and engaging in "petting" too early will lead one to miss out on other fun activities. They encourage young persons to wait to marry until after military service is complete and to wait until marriage to have sex. They emphasize the importance of talking with a counselor and working out all known and unknown problems before marrying. Perhaps most problematic, they encourage young persons to date people who go to their same church (which one can infer means the same class and race), because it provides a better understanding of the other person's faith, church habits, and a common Christian basis for creating a life together. This rhetoric is found throughout marriage preparation textbooks, pamphlets, manuals, and in counseling transcripts.

Miscegenation, marriage between two persons of different races, was illegal until the 1967 Supreme Court case *Loving vs. Virginia,* which legalized interracial marriage.[103] Prior to this, interracial and interfaith marriage was discouraged by "marriage educators, counselors, and clergymen" because it was viewed as a "threat to white status and identity."[104] Films, pamphlets, sermons, and textbooks that advised restricting marriage to "people of the same background" were prevalent during this time period and sought to protect white, middle-class, Protestant America—which was the barometer of nationhood—from being tainted by the working-class, African Americans, immigrants, Catholics, or anything that did not fit into the perfect suburban brick home.

In order for these promises to be actualities, ministers needed training about how to counsel with couples. In the late 1950s, a Committee on Education for

---

102 "Preparation for Marriage Filmstrips: A Leader's Guide," the Television, Radio, and Film Commission of The Methodist Church (GCAH, 1955).

103 Fay Botham, *Almighty God Created the Races: Christianity, Interracial Marriage, and American Law* (Chapel Hill: University of North Carolina, 2009).

104 Celello, *Making Marriage Work,* 90.

Marriage and Marriage Counseling was formed by the Methodist Church. Its goal was to travel to annual conferences and host "one-day district meetings for ministers concerned with preparation for marriage and pre-marital counseling." By 1960, they had been to eleven annual conferences across the United States and would continue on to reach more annual conferences by end of the year.

Preparation for marriage was intended to reduce the divorce rate. Asking young couples to go to premarital counseling gave them a safe space to work out major problems prior to marriage and showed them how helpful counseling could be if needed in the future. While the Methodist Church tried to avoid divorce at all costs, it was forced to face the truth that divorce was a reality for many congregants, and thus divorce and pastoral counseling became an important part of the new sexual ethic. By 1960, the Methodist Church relaxed its laws to allow for the remarriage of divorced persons and to encourage those having troubles to seek counseling. It recognized that not all marriages were salvable. By the early 1980s, one in every two marriages ended in divorce, a statistic that few persons of the 1950s could have predicted or prepared for. In less than fifty years, Americans went from restricting divorce to only cases of adultery and the occasional case of abuse to the full support of no-fault divorce laws.[105] As the divorce rate increased over the mid-twentieth century, many people wanted to study it and attempted to fix it. Everyone from marriage counselors, to college professors, to clergy wanted their chance to better marital life for the average American. By the 1980s, divorce had evolved from a matter of "shame" or a "closely guarded secret" to "a matter of general knowledge, sympathy, and discussion."[106]

Playboy Magazine

You cannot talk about family life and sexuality in the 1950s without talking about *Playboy*. At a time when the Methodist Church's Committee on Family Life worked diligently to paint a scene of pristine togetherness, *Playboy* promoted an ideal of urban bachelorhood and sexual self-expression. Methodists continued to condemn publications such as this, calling them pornography and labeling them obscene and un-Christian. In 1960, after the growing popularity of *Playboy* and the increased rhetoric of the sexual revolution, the *Discipline* included a new resolution, "Exploitation of Sex," which reads:

---

105 Riley B. Case, *Evangelical and Methodist: A Popular History* (Nashville, TN: Abingdon Press, 2014), 156.
106 Case, 181.

The recent deluge of "glamor" magazines and motion pictures which overemphasize sex to pornographic extremes reveals a growing and dangerous sickness in society. We urge our churches to institute courses of study for young people regarding Christian attitudes towards sex and personality growth. We call upon our members to encourage and participate in community action to eliminate the distribution and sale of pornographic literature, films, and amusements through voluntary and, where necessary, legislative means.[107]

This resolution is not unlike previous resolutions of the 1930s, which also called for community action to help ban obscene magazines. However, it is unlike the resolution of 1948, which states simply that "papers, magazines, and books which offend common decency are on the increase" and asks Methodists to be an "example" of "the sacredness of the human body" to "youth as they face life in a changing world."[108] In 1960, the use of the word "glamor" specifically calls out *Playboy*. Its call to action contrasts starkly with that of 1948, showing nervousness about this new, blatant sexuality. This section will focus on a Methodist-produced radio show, *Night Call*, and its discussion of *Playboy*. It's a unique primary source in that it combines a Methodist seminary professor with the voices of everyday laypersons who present varying degrees of comfort with the magazine.

Playboy was begun by Hugh Hefner in 1953 and promoted an image of manhood directly opposed to the image of family in *Together* magazine. While *Together* and other magazines, like *McCall's* and *Ladies' Home Journal*, encouraged co-parenting and co-domesticity, *Playboy* put forth "an image of the young, affluent, urban bachelor—a man in pursuit of temporary female companionship and a good time, without the customary obligations of marriage and fatherhood."[109] Hefner, in a similar vein to that of the NMCFL, saw his magazine as providing the solution to the stress of the Atomic Age by providing a few extra laughs and diverting male attention away from the era's stresses.[110]

Historian Elizabeth Fraterrigo discusses "the good life," which she calls "an abstract concept encompassing the apparent comfort, security, and abundance

---

107 *Doctrines and Discipline of the Methodist Church* (Nashville: Methodist Publishing House, 1960), 698.
108 *Doctrines and Discipline*, 589.
109 Elizabeth Fraterrigo, Playboy *and the Making of the Good Life in Modern America* (New York: Oxford University Press, 2009), 1.
110 Fraterrigo, 1.

made possible by postwar prosperity." It was a product of white, middle-class "leisure and consumption," and showcased "national achievement."[111] The NMCFL and *Together* magazine promoted togetherness as the good life. Hugh Hefner had a different idea. According to Fraterrigo, Hefner "positioned his magazine as a challenge to the wholesale acceptance of postwar domestic ideology. . . . [It] allowed readers to envision an upscale, masculine identity based on tasteful consumption and sexual pleasure."[112] Where *Together* offered family devotionals, crafts, marriage advice, mission stories, and stories meant to drive families toward one another, the church, and community, *Playboy* offered "fashionable attire, gourmet food, sports cars, and exotic vacations" along with "luxurious bachelor pads," "well-stocked liquor cabinets," "the latest hi-fi equipment," "and "abstract art and jazz collections."[113]

Fraterrigo argues that *Playboy* began a men's revolution where "men took umbrage at the constraints of breadwinning and challenged the family ideal." These men "joined a broader chorus of anxiety and dissatisfaction voiced by both men and women over so-called traditional gender arrangements and idealized suburban life."[114] However, ever the clever man, Hefner believed that making space for young men (and young women) to enjoy the good life and delaying true adult responsibility (mainly marriage and children) would eventually lead to stronger marriages. Allowing young men to self-express would help them regain a sense of their masculinity, which many men felt was threatened by over-civilization in the 1950s.

The "over-civilized" white man was a unique product of post–World War II America. Modern work, which was the main culprit of over-civilization for corporate America, undermined individualism by forcing men to work in groups and follow corporate rules. Consumerism encouraged not only shopping but a well-kept look that required work and beauty products. At home, men experienced a decline in patriarchal authority as marriage was slowly becoming a more equal institution, with women making a majority of the day-to-day decisions and with men being asked to co-parent and co-domesticate. Outside of the home, women were increasingly present in the workforce, invading the

---

111 Fraterrigo, 2–3.
112 Fraterrigo, 3.
113 Fraterrigo, 3.
114 Fraterrigo, 4.

typical male sphere. From every corner of society, many men believed that their well-being was threatened.[115] *Playboy* provided these threatened white middle- and upper-class men with a forum and a lifestyle that sought to reassert their social status. It gave them a temporary outlet for self-expression before they moved to the suburbs to marry and start a family.

Playboy was so revolutionary that Protestant churches could not ignore it as just another obscene magazine. In 1965, *Night Call*, one of the first call-in, na- tional radio shows produced by the Television, Radio, and Film Commission of the Methodist Church, took on *Playboy*. Its goal as a radio show was to "build understanding and reconciliation through conversation."[116] One of its earlier shows, "Playboyism: A New Religious Alternative," was radical for its day, tack- ling the sexual revolution and the popularity of *Playboy*. It will be discussed in full in the following few pages, because it is one of the few tools, besides *mo- tive* magazine, available to Methodist historians that explores the sexual revolu- tion in an honest way and creates space for the voices of everyday Methodists. The host was Russ Gibb, and his guest on this episode was Dr. Allan Moore, pro- fessor of church and society at Claremont School of Theology whose specialty was young persons and urbanization. Dr. Moore was a self-proclaimed "social theologian," which he defined as someone who is "concerned with the events in society and the cultural forums which we have today." As a social theologian, it was his job to "reflect on these cultural forums to see what is being asked or what clarification is needed from the church in terms of its message." As a social observer who worked with the institutional church to help it respond to changes in society, Dr. Moore should be understood as trying to expand the new sexual ethic beyond heterosexuality and beyond the confines of Christian marriage. His work with sex education efforts around the same time as this ra- dio show (which will be discussed in chapter 3) prove that here, Dr. Moore, ar- gued for a Methodist embrace of the "new morality."

The show began with a brief interview of Dr. Moore. Gibb asked: "Why all the fuss about *Playboy* magazine?" Dr. Moore responded with a few statis- tics, such as the astounding popularity of *Playboy*, with over three million is- sues in circulation in just ten years, calling the magazine a "fantastic success."

---

115 Fraterrigo, 10.
116 "Night Call," ReThink Church, accessed 1/23/2017, http://www.rethinkchurch.org/articles/conversations -on-race/night-call. After a brief hiatus (1967–1968), the show came back on air and dealt with race re- lations in a new, radical, and nonviolent way.

Dr. Moore was most fascinated with *Playboy*'s philosophy of life: "*Playboy* has become a way of life for many young men and women, and challenges the church, especially in terms of the kind of orientations which we've generally given to young people, as to how life should be lived."[117] Asked to clarify, Dr. Moore continued:

> The church has not really taken seriously the urban revolution which we're in. Thousands of young men and women are growing up in a new world of materialism, of wealth, of a world in which sex is much more open, and *Playboy* has taken seriously this world in a much more realistic way than the church has in the past.[118]

Within the first two and a half minutes, this Methodist-produced and -funded radio show challenged the church to be more like *Playboy* and to actually pay attention to the realities of life. Thinking back to *Together* magazine, the NMCFL, and the Preparation for Marriage films, it is obvious that the views of the Methodist Church stand in a strict dichotomy to *Playboy*. And yet, here was a professor of church and society at a Methodist seminary stating bluntly that the Methodist Church was the one that needed to change, the one that needed to come to the realization that young people were looking for different advice and a new way to live. While he did not represent the denomination as a whole, for him, if the church wanted to be impactful in young lives, it needed to accept the fullness of teenage life.

Continuing, the two discussed the new morality. Gibb asked Dr. Moore if *Playboy*'s philosophy of life was the new morality. "The new morality means many different things," Dr. Moore responded. Hefner has his own sense of new morality based in a "greater sense of sexual freedom." Dr. Moore contrasted this with the new morality as seen on college campuses, where "[sex] is generally thought of in terms of love makes it right." Opposed to this, theologians discussed the new morality, "meaning we need to think through what is right today and certainly think through the things we've said have been wrong."[119] In regard to race, divorce, and the sexual revolution, Dr. Moore's words are apt. Some Methodists realized the limits of their sexual ethic, which supported a

---

117 "Playboyism, A New Religious Alternative," *Night Call* (September 29, 1969), 2:01–2:17, accessed 1/23/2017, http://catalog.gcah.org/DigitalArchives/NightCall/Dr_Moore_DA_1067.mp3.

118 "Playboyism," 2:27–2:49.

119 "Playboyism," 2:5–3:30.

biblically grounded and rules-based ethic. These Methodists, as will be shown throughout chapter 3, slowly turned to the new morality for answers and for new ways of talking about sex. For Dr. Moore, the new morality embodied race, divorce, and the sexual revolution. It was a culmination of situational ethics, sexual freedom, premarital sex, and the church's response to those.

Moore recognized that the mid-1960s was "an age of transition, between the old and new world," when traditional mores had been "broken down" and young persons were "trying to find some new answers for this new world."[120] To do this, they turned to many avenues: peers, television, movies, music, the church, and, yes, *Playboy*. The particular appeal of *Playboy* was that "Hefner gives these answers much clearer and with more frankness than we tend to do in the church sometimes."[121] Dr. Moore added that young adulthood was a time to search for one's true identity, and *Playboy* offered a packaged identity, one branded as "the good life." If the church wanted to remain relevant in these changing times, it, too, had to offer a packaged sexual ethic that could embrace all the varieties of sexuality in the 1960s and do so from a unique, Christian perspective. For Dr. Moore, such an ethic was the new morality.

Here, Moore differentiated between young adult women and young adult men. To him, *Playboy* appealed only to young adult men. Other magazines "have always served as a guidebook for the young women." *Playboy* is that for men. It is a men's fashion magazine, with fashion defined in a "broad sense" to "include style of life, shape of existence." Furthermore, "It tells young men what to wear, what to eat, best places to go, how to talk with a girl, and of course . . . ethics" and the "orientation of life."[122] Gibb asked for a bit of a history lesson here to see what void *Playboy* was filling in shaping young men. Dr. Moore answered him with what most modern American historian would say: "In a simpler society, pre–World War II, there were ready-made models. The young person grew up at home; he worked alongside his parents; he didn't travel too far from his community." Back then, "the church was a much stronger influence in his life." After World War II, young people settled away from the homes in which they were raised. They left home after high school graduation to go to college. They settled down in urban areas. In other words, "They don't have the

---

120 "Playboyism," 7:00–7:18.
121 "Playboyism," 7:19–7:28.
122 "Playboyism," 7:55–8:38.

models of family life to set their eyes upon."[123] In this new, urban setting, did religion have a place? With *religion* defined as that which is "concerned with those ultimate meanings of life," Dr. Moore believed that, yes, "the young adult is very much concerned with his life meaning and destiny." But, "he's not sure that the organized church he knew back in the small town or community can answer these questions."[124]

Again, the institutional church was directly challenged to stop idealizing families as beacons of domestic bliss and togetherness, to stop ignoring the sexual realities of American teenagers in the 1960s, and to provide a space for young adults to carve their own identities while maintaining a sound Christian faith. With this statement, Dr. Moore agreed that "today the church is doing a great deal" in regard to accepting sex as a positive, natural thing in life, specifically, in its willingness to produce courses for "junior high, senior high, and college students where any question goes and adults try to be honest with young people about sex."[125]

The show concluded with Dr. Moore stating that *Playboy* was not becoming a religion but was answering a need in a way that the church was not. However, it was taking on many characteristics of a religion. It provided a philosophy to follow in much the same way the church did. It provided meeting places for its followers to gather (*Playboy* clubs), and it provided symbols for its followers to idolize (the rabbit).[126] Young people turned to *Playboy* and its philosophy, because it was more open and more welcoming of the realities of the sexualized young adult. Throughout this discussion, Dr. Moore challenged the church to live into the new morality and to reevaluate its present sexual ethic.

Night Call was a radical show, often openly discussing topics that the institutional church rarely would: sex, race, and class to name a few. While not representative of the entire church, Gibb, as host, and Dr. Moore, as guest, challenged the Methodist Church in this particular episode to be more understanding of sexualized young persons and to create space for them to find needed answers away from the glossy pages of *Playboy*. Dr. Moore declared himself at the beginning of the episode to be a social theologian, one concerned with how

---

123 "Playboyism," 9:30–10:20.
124 "Playboyism," 14:00–14:33.
125 "Playboyism," 17:54–18:25.
126 "Playboyism," 51:13–51:40.

the denomination approached social change. He was open to discussing sexuality and new ways of life. His main concern was that the denomination was not doing enough to educate persons on matters of sexuality, thus making the church irrelevant. The callers, willing to discuss a taboo topic on a national radio show, conveyed the courage and curiosity of the Methodist people when it came to sex.

The older-sounding callers showcased mostly shock or disapproval of *Playboy*. Yet, they were willing to discuss sex, historicize the sexual revolution, and recognize that the church was lacking in keeping up with sexual and social change. The younger callers echoed the need for the institutional church to create space for their generation and provided evidence for why *Playboy* was appealing to young persons. It gave them answers and acceptance when few people or places would.

Night Call began in 1965 and hosted 230 programs, all of which discussed various social issues, bringing together experts in their fields, clergy, and average Methodist laypersons. The show took a hiatus from 1966 to 1968; and after its reboot, it focused on race reconciliation. It received attention from *Time* magazine for bringing together persons of all races to converse with and learn from one another in a new, nonviolent platform.[127] It is unknown how most Methodists responded to the show and its willingness to take on such controversial topics. More research needs to be conducted on this radio show, its impact on the average layperson within the Methodist Church and other Protestant denominations, and its willingness to address radical social issues such as sex and race.

CONCLUSION

American family life in the 1950s has been the topic of many well-researched and well-known historical works. More recently, the 1950s family has been idolized in contemporary American politics as the "traditional" family, as "the standard" against which all families should be judged today. Jessica Weiss argues that this is because "to contemporary Americans, the 1950s represent the quiet before the storm of social, sexual, and gender role changes that rocked the nation over the next four decades." It was a "placid, static view of happy nuclear families composed of breadwinning husbands, homemaking wives, and

---

127 "Night Call."

their requisite three children ensconced in an affluent suburban home." While politicians today may find this ideal comforting, it ignores the complexity of the 1950s, specifically, how the gender, racial, and sexual revolutions took root during the decade.

Heather R. White argues that liberal Protestant clergy's concern to help Christian families find a healthy, Christian sexual life through advice texts and pastoral counseling forced clergy to take new psychological insights and morph them into a Christian ideology of sexuality, which "prized sexual health and normalcy as an expression of actualized spirituality." This is the foundation of the new Methodist sexual ethic. White calls the increase in pastoral counseling a kind of *therapeutic* orthodoxy, which, as will be shown, "yielded unintended consequences" through the creation of "abnormal" sexualities.[128]

As Christians continued to work on their heterosexual marriages through pastoral counseling and premarital courses, they created a place where sexual licentiousness was permitted—within heterosexual, Christian marriage. When sex within these confines proved unsatisfactory, many desired to leave these marriages without giving up their sexuality. If their healthy sexuality existed outside of the bonds of marriage, what was to prevent those who had never married from being sexual? Thus, the new sexual ethic created by liberal Protestant clergy to harness women's newfound sexuality in the 1920s, backfired in the 1950s and 1960s when all persons used the rhetoric that sexuality was good and part of one's God-given personhood, to embrace sexuality in all of its forms and in any context. White concludes, "Thus, even as many Christians—conservative and liberal—lamented sexual permissiveness and moral decline that they feared might threaten the stability of the family, they also championed views about healthy sexuality that rested on the same therapeutic foundations."[129]

This chapter has hinted at the beginning of these revolutions. It shows how the family became the central and primary place to find pleasure and satisfaction in one's life. This white, middle-class, heterosexual ideal was doomed by its own pressure to be perfect and its limitation of who could participate. Racial inequality, an increase in marriage counseling and divorce, and a desire to look elsewhere for pleasure and information—somewhere such as *Playboy*—threatened this ideal. The Methodist Church tried to reinforce the nuclear family with

---

128 White, *Reforming Sodom*, 5.
129 White, 10.

five National Methodist Conferences on Family Life between 1951 and 1966. It centered the family as "the hope of the world," and taught how to better the world by increasing the number and the quality of Christian family life. Every few years, it recognized a Methodist Family of the Year, providing the denomination's constituents with a patriotic family that would help them adhere to the American Way of Life.

Methodism during the 1950s allowed American political rhetoric, in the form of anti-Communism, to find a comfortable home within the denomination's highest rankings. Furthermore, Methodism during this era began a campaign to protect a specific notion of family life, one that would become increasingly threatened by sexual and social change, causing the future denomination to divide on how to best respond to those sexual and social changes. Finally, with the publication of *Together* magazine, Christian families learned "the cult of togetherness" from the comfort of their own home. With these various rhetorical tools, a heavy demand was placed on the average Methodist family to be more like a white, middle-class, heterosexual, suburban ideal. The stress of "keeping up with the Joneses" (or the Detweilers) created more tension than comfort for many families. This was evident in the increased racial tension within the denomination, and in the general culture by the rising divorce rate by the end of the 1950s and early 1960s.

The Women's Division of the Methodist Church fought to undo racial tension and create reconciliation through education and relationship building. The General Conference of the Methodist Church faced the rising divorce rate, relaxing its statements against divorce and encouraging marital counseling. While the church was willing to accept failed marriages as a part of natural life, it had yet come to terms with premarital sex as a part of natural life. Attempts, such as that by *Night Call,* to challenge the church to adjust its theology, polity, and social awareness to be more open to the idea of a multitude of healthy sexualities, resulted in a brief endorsement of the new morality by a small group of Methodists in the 1960s.

The purpose of this chapter was to highlight the Methodist family. Methodists put forth a specific, limited ideal through the pages of *Together* magazine. Simultaneously, this ideal was complicated through efforts to break down racial barriers, create a new theology of divorce, advocate for marital counseling, and willingly acknowledge the sexual revolution.

Similar to current American politicians, current right-wing United Methodist

political caucus groups focus on 1950s white, middle-class families like the Detweilers as the utopic Methodist family, a family that preexisted the new morality, and a family that they believe has been threatened by an increasingly socially
concerned (as opposed to scripturally concerned) United Methodism. The next
few chapters will further complicate the sexual ethic as the denomination approaches sex education, abortion, and homosexuality.

THE POLITICAL TURN

AMERICAN METHODISTS, THE NEW MORALITY, AND SEX EDUCATION

I n 1962, from the top of Mount Sequoyah in Fayetteville, Arkansas, Methodist youth, parents, schoolteachers, and clergy gathered together for an experiment in sex education, a "sex lab" called *Sex and the Whole Person*, whose purpose was a frank discussion about sexuality. The Methodist Boards of Education and of Social Concern set out to reconstruct the Methodist sexual ethic in a way that was more apt for the revolutionary climate of the 1960s. Attendees gave their testimony of the lab. Lee Vance recalled:

> Until now, the church has done little except to put out some Pharisee-like rules and regulations that say only one thing to a teen-ager—Don't. It seems to me that Christ, with understanding and love, would consider all of the facts and circumstances involved, to decide what was right in any particular situation. Now, at least, the Methodist Church is trying precisely that approach—a sensible, practical, and realistic approach to sex.[1]

Phillip Royal stated:

> The Methodist Church has taken a small step, but an important one, in the right direction. For many years, we have preached, taught, and discussed the matter of making men whole. We have proclaimed that the gospel makes men whole; yet we have neglected one important phase of the wholeness—sex. Now, however, a small voice can be heard saying, "Sex is an important part of life. We must learn to approach it with a Christian attitude if we are to be 'whole persons.'"[2]

---

1   "Guidelines for Using *Sex and the Whole Person: A Christian View*," 2; administrative records of the General Board of Discipleship, "Sex Education Resource Packet," 2355-6-1:36, GCAH.

2   "Guidelines for Using *Sex and the Whole Person*," 3.

From these two testimonies, it is clear that the two agencies were at the forefront of revising the Methodist sexual ethic in order to be more than a rules-based morality enforced solely in the light of Scripture. Their board members concluded that a rules-based ethic was not relevant to the changing society of the 1960s, and if the church was going to have any claim over morality, it needed a new framework. What they developed was a revised sexual ethic, which combined "biblical, psychological, and physiological information on sexuality" into a "new morality."[3] They used the previous ethic's basis that God created all persons in God's image and that a vital part of this image was sexuality. Thus, sexuality was good because sexuality was of God.

They removed the previous ethic's rules-based framework, which deemed certain acts good or moral and others bad or immoral. In its place, they advocated what ethicists called *situational ethics*, giving persons the full moral authority to decide for themselves what to do in a given situation that would best honor their sexual selves. They believed that in honoring one's sexual self, one, in turn, honored God. This new ethic did not *forbid* sexual expression in any situation; although it did still *encourage* waiting until marriage to engage in sexual intercourse. Most important, it placed the decision to be sexual in the hands of a well-informed individual.

This chapter will explore the creation of the new morality and its consequences. Until the 1960s, Methodists cooperated in order to adjust to sexual change. They allowed for the use of artificial contraception within the confines of Christian marriage and recognized that some marriages must end in divorce. However, once sexual morality began to involve persons not married, Methodists were divided. The division began with sex education. American politicians and American Methodists disagreed on how best to teach teenagers about sex. Do you strictly follow what Scripture dictates? Do you provide a list of "dos" and "don'ts" or moral and immoral acts? Or do you provide space for a frank discussion of sexuality? Do you allow informed people to choose for themselves what is moral and immoral?

Beginning with disagreements over sex education, Methodists have become increasingly divided on matters of sexuality since the mid-1960s. Since 1968, The United Methodist Church has witnessed an increase in political caucus

---

3   "Guidelines for Using *Sex and the Whole Person*," 1.

groups, groups that unite and divide Methodists along political lines. Methodist historians Russell E. Richey, Kenneth E. Rowe, and Jean Miller Schmidt argue that "caucuses pledged themselves to the renewal of United Methodism but in many instances found common interest and sometimes collaborative effort with counterparts across denominational lines."[4] In the 1960s, *evangelical* Methodists begin to self-identify as such, and they promote themselves as distinct from *progressive* Methodists through their commitment to biblical morality.

This chapter will trace the increase in power of an ideology, which has proclaimed itself to be "evangelical" or "orthodox" Methodism from the 1940s to the 1970s. It will argue that as neo-evangelicalism became institutionalized in American politics through the formation of the New Christian Right, evangelicals organized within the Methodist denomination through caucus groups such as the Good News Movement, the Confessing Movement, and eventually the Wesleyan Covenant Association.

This chapter will begin with an overview of American evangelicalism in the 1940s through the 1960s, specifically, the rise of the "neo-evangelical." Before proceeding to a discussion of sex education, it will, necessarily, look at the corresponding rise in organized evangelicalism within the Methodist Church. When it comes to sex education, evangelical Methodist rhetoric can be directly tied to the political rhetoric of popular American evangelicals, with both fearing that a frank and scientifically informed discussion of sexuality would threaten the stability of the white, heterosexual family. This chapter will show that from the 1940s to the 1970s—for reasons already explored in previous chapters and for reasons to be presented in the next few pages—Methodists grew increasingly polarized, particularly over sex education and the new morality.

THE NEO-EVANGELICAL AND THE RISE OF THE NEW CHRISTIAN RIGHT

In the 1940s, "post-fundamentalist evangelicals," as Axel Schafer calls them, desired to regain influence in mainstream society, to make evangelicalism relevant again, and to provide a counterpoint to the liberal Protestant message of mainline denominations. They wanted to "reassert the spirit of revivalism, establish a broad interdenominational basis, and create a network of

---

4   *MEA*, vol. 1, 449.

evangelical institutions," and they did just that.[5] They called themselves "neo-evangelicals" and counted among their ranks Billy Graham, Carl F. H. Henry, and Harold John Ockenga. In 1942, they formed the National Association of Evangelicals. By 1947, they had built a seminary, Fuller Seminary; and by 1956, they were publishing a popular periodical, *Christianity Today*. Schafer argues that in order to understand the context in which neo-evangelicals regained power, one must look at both the theology of evangelicalism, which binds the variegated group together, and its engagement with and adjustment to political aspirations.[6]

American Evangelicals Organize

First and foremost, evangelicalism is a theological construct. In terms of evangelical Methodism, it is an adherence to Bebbington's quadrilateral: activism, crucicentrism, biblicism, and conversionism.[7] For neo-evangelicals, Bebbington's quadrilateral holds true. However, theology cannot exist in a vacuum. It is constantly challenged by social and political forces, sometimes necessitating adjustment. The forces that challenged evangelical theology from the 1950s to the 1970s concerned family life. This chapter will explore the role of the family, the school, and the church in sex education.

Before evangelicals could have broad effect, they had to organize. They reached out to the conservatives within the mainline denominations and to the moderates of fundamentalism to build their massive network. The end goal of this was to make evangelical theology a respectable voice within Protestantism, and they did this through ecumenical efforts that their fundamentalist forebears refused to do. As a result of these networks, parachurch organizations spread like wildfire in the mid-1940s through the mid-1950s: most notably, the Christian Crusade and the National Association of Evangelicals. These organizations belonged somewhere on the scale between liberal evangelical and conservative fundamentalist, but they were willing to work together to spread the movement. Evangelicals hosted radio and television shows, built hospitals and social agencies, were educated at their own seminaries and colleges, created political think tanks, and engaged in their own mission work. They strategically merged

---

5   Schafer, *Countercultural Conservatives*, 42.
6   Schafer, 43.
7   Bebbington, *Evangelicalism in Modern Britain*, 2–17.

"ecumenism and orthodoxy . . . a traditional message with a modern image," which is why they were so successful.[8]

In 1942, the National Association of Evangelicals (NAE) was created as a political lobbying group to protect evangelical broadcasting rights, uphold restrictions on liquor advertisements, and limit the political influence of Catholicism. It readopted *evangelical* instead of *fundamentalist* as a sign that this group was different, more respectable than their militant 1920s counterparts, and more willing to work with Protestantism at large in order to be more politically influential.[9] In post–World War II America, fighting Communism was their priority, and anything that resembled socialist aspirations—specifically secularism (defined as the prioritization of worldly things over godly things and the separation of the two)—was a threat to the nation and the American family. Evangelicals proclaimed, "America . . . was a chosen nation that had experienced a moral lapse. The nation needed a spiritual revival in order to become a beacon of light and a leader in the fight against Communism." They epitomized "the American Way of Life," defined as the Christian support of American capitalism and democracy, and connected the health of the family to that of the nation; so any threat—including divorce, pornography, juvenile delinquency, and secularism in the schools—threatened not only the family but the nation.[10] The Methodist version of this rhetoric was evident in chapter 2, represented in *Together* magazine and through the Methodist Family of the Year. By 1945, twenty denominations, all of them small, were affiliated with the NAE. Overall, it was not a very successful organization in terms of uniting evangelicals, because evangelicals could not agree on doctrine or on the necessary degree of social and political involvement.[11] However, the NAE created a multitude of affiliate organizations and agencies, all of which made their own stamp on American history: "National Religious Broadcasters (1944), the Evangelical Foreign Missions Association (1945), the National Sunday School Association (1945), the National Association of Christian Schools (1947) . . . the Commission on Evangelism (1942), the Office of Public Affairs (1943), the War Relief Commission (1944), and the Commission on Social Action (1951)."[12] It created networks with

---

8   Schafer, *Countercultural Conservatives*, 50.
9   Williams, *God's Own Party*, 4.
10   Williams, 23.
11   Schafer, *Countercultural Conservatives*, 62.
12   Schafer, 57–60.

mainline Protestants, persons of other faiths, and other evangelicals that proved invaluable for later political aspirations.[13] The NAE is most well-known, however, for organizing Billy Graham's revivals and sponsoring the contents of *Christianity Today*.

Billy Graham was a celebrity. Schafer claims, "From the Wheaton College revival in 1950, which gave broad-based exposure to the neo-evangelical message to the Madison Square Garden revival in 1957, which marked the break with separatist fundamentalism, Graham succeeded not only in 'saving souls' but also in popularizing the evangelical worldview within mainstream American culture."[14] Graham's revivals drew people from all varieties of religious experience, including Methodists. According to Riley B. Case, a Methodist minister who attended multiple Graham revivals during his seminary years, Methodists "made up a considerable percentage of those who flocked to Billy Graham crusades and Youth for Christ rallies and read journals such as *Christianity Today, Eternity,* and *Moody Monthly.*"[15] For many, including Methodists, his message was one that had not been heard for decades. His revival-style preaching spoke directly to "you," empowering you to change yourself and America. He held in-person revivals, went on television shows, and hosted radio shows—utilizing all forms of modern communication to deliver the neo-evangelical message. Graham spoke about every major social or political issues of his time. During the mid-1960s sexual revolution, his sermon titles included, "A Nation Rocked by Crime," "Victory over Despair," "Students in Revolt," "Conquering Teenage Rebellion," and "Obsession with Sex." All of these warned America that it was in trouble, and each evangelical in the crowd could relate.[16] He spoke in favor of Eisenhower, thus bringing neo-evangelicals solidly into the political realm and giving them an identity as a united voting bloc: "The Christian people of America are going to vote as a bloc for the man with the strongest moral and spiritual platform, regardless of his views on other matters."[17] He was featured not only in *Christianity Today* but in *Time* and *Life*, thus solidifying his celebrity status.

Christianity Today was the NAE's other claim to fame. Funded by J. Howard

---

13   Schafer, 56.
14   Schafer, 51.
15   Case, *Evangelical and Methodist*, 29.
16   Williams, *God's Own Party*, 81.
17   Williams, 25.

Pew, a conservative oil tycoon, "it was designed to give the liberal *Christian Century* 'a run for its biases.'"[18] Through the already established evangelical network of the NAE, it had a massive subscription base and printed its glossy pages from its headquarters in Washington, DC. Articles on theology, Communism, philosophy, and national and international news occupied its pages, all seen through an evangelical lens.[19] The evangelical message presented by Graham and through the pages of *Christianity Today* spoke to people. After 1965, many mainline denominations lost membership while evangelical denominations increased exponentially so that "by the late eighties a third of Americans belonged to evangelical churches."[20]

From the mid-1940s through mid-1960s, the goal of evangelicals was not only to counter liberal Protestants, but to redeem American society and politics from the effects of liberal theology. Neo-evangelicals believed "the theological pitfalls of liberalism could not be separated from its political shortcomings."[21] In the context of the Cold War Era, with Communism lurking at every corner, evangelicals believed that they had a spiritual duty to intervene and save American families by confronting liberal Protestantism and what they believed to be its accompanying ideology of secularism. The rhetoric employed in this tactic was discussed in chapter 2, and thus will not be analyzed here. Add to anti-Communism, the cultural revolutions of the 1960s and 1970s, and more Americans bought into the idea that America was in moral decay. Prior to the 1970s, evangelicals were not convinced that intervening in politics was the best strategy to change the nation. Their strategy of evangelism, revivals, radio shows, and periodicals had been successful. However, the moral issues of the 1960s and 1970s, specifically sex education in public schools, the rights of women and persons who identified as homosexual, and the legalization of abortion, threatened the nation and the family on a new level, one that required political activism.[22]

Historians take both sides of the "who approached whom" debate when it comes to the development of the New Christian Right. Robert O. Self argues that the New Right needed evangelicals, as the New Right was "fused

---

18   Schafer, *Countercultural Conservatives*, 52.
19   Schafer, 52–53.
20   Self, *All in the Family*, 340.
21   Schafer, *Countercultural Conservatives*, 46.
22   Self, *All in the Family*, 340.

from disparate constituencies and conservative sensibilities, including anti-Communism, free-market individualism, and moral traditionalism." Evangelicalism held these three together and gave them an "organizing potential" and "political muscle" that supported the "conventional heterosexual breadwinner nuclear family."[23]

Daniel K. Williams argues that "a rapidly rising divorce rate, the public acceptance of sex outside of marriage, and the national legalization of abortion convinced evangelicals that the two-parent family was endangered." Their political campaign focused on saving the American family, an idea that "appealed to a far larger number of Americans than politicians and pundits had imagined."[24] Both sides are accurate. Neo-evangelicals and the New Right needed each other, which is why they were successful once they joined forces. Evangelicals appealed to their massive networks, held voting registration events, mailed out voting guides, and lobbied for candidates. The New Right used its platform to preach the neo-evangelical message of saving the American family through moral legislation: that is, anti–Equal Rights Amendment, antiabortion, anti-homosexuality, and anti–sex education in public schools. The moment that solidified the relationship between the New Right (the GOP) and the neo-evangelicals was when Billy Graham endorsed Richard Nixon for president, a move that Graham would later regret, but one that symbolized the willingness of evangelicals to fully commit to the GOP's platform.[25] The relationship between the two groups would continue to rise to power through the election of Ronald Reagan and culminating in the election of George W. Bush in 2000. For our purposes, consider that the relationship has been established; we will shift to looking at the rise of Methodist evangelicalism.

A New Evangelical Voice: "Fighting Bob" Schuler

Glen Spann, professor of history at Asbury University, argues in his 1994 book that evangelical Methodists made up the majority of the "great deep" of the denomination, basing this claim on the idea that 55 percent of Methodists in 1952 were members of small, rural churches with fewer than six hundred mem-

---

23 Self, 341.
24 Williams, *God's Own Party*, 105–6.
25 Williams, 99.

bers, and by 1960, 47 percent of American Methodists lived in the American South, an increase of 14 percent since 1900.[26] He uses this data to argue that "this largely rural-small town, small church, and moderate income identity of 'typical' Methodism was not necessarily reflected in the decision-making bodies of the church," an argument that pits "typical" Methodists against the Methodists at the administrative rank. There is some truth to this statement. The argument that Methodists at the administrative level increasingly pushed the denomination in a progressive direction of which many "typical" Methodists were unaware and with which they would not agree is a common evangelical argument, being stated as recently as October 2016 at the formation of the Wesleyan Covenant Association (more on this group later).

At the local church level, the programmatic life of the general church is rarely discussed. Most local churches focus on their communities and local mission work, leaving congregants unaware of the actions of general boards and agencies. The problem with Spann's conclusion is that he uses statistics to reach ideological conclusions based on uncited percentages alone. In order to make these types of conclusions, he would have to have thousands of personal testaments from both rural and urban Methodists, asking them if they agree with the actions, mission, and vision of general church agencies. However, Spann and other self-identified evangelical Methodists believe that there are two Methodisms within United Methodism, and this chapter will delve further into the truth of this argument.

For Spann, the Methodists who provided the denomination with an evangelical voice during these three decades was Robert Pierce Schuler, pastor of Trinity Methodist in Los Angeles, California. Schuler was born in 1880 and converted during an old-school Methodist revival in Virginia. As a licensed preacher during his teenage years, he never trained at the graduate seminary level. Schuler enjoyed great ministerial success, serving in Texas and in California within the MECS, and political success outside of the denomination as a proponent for public morality, earning him the nickname "Fighting Bob."[27] After the unification that created the Methodist Church in 1939, Schuler turned his attention away from public morality and toward giving the new denomination an

26   Spann, "Evangelicalism in Modern American Methodism," 261.
27   Spann, 265–67.

evangelical voice. He chose to do so through a new periodical, the *Methodist Challenge*, whose goal was the following:

> My desire in launching this publication is to give the remaining years of my life to a strong and vigorous defense of genuine Methodism. I believe I know what Methodism is. I believe I understand the motives and processes of those forces that in subtle manner seek today to destroy this movement that I know came from God. Kindly, but firmly, I shall proceed.[28]

In a separate article, he continued:

> The one and only reason for such a publication as this one is the fact that the truce must never be declared until the battle is won . . . For militant Methodism, this is not time for either truce or armistice. . . . We shall firmly meet infidelity and scoffing skepticism in cap and gown or robed in vestments, nor shall we offer or ask for mercy.[29]

Schuler argues that there are two versions of Methodism existing within the Methodist Church: one espouses liberal Protestantism, social action, and is less focused on doctrine; the other professes "genuine Methodism," stresses conversion, and is focused on bringing back the old Methodist revivals. He preached, "There is a breach in Methodism," one between "modernism and evangelicalism" that made the two "incompatible and antagonistic," statements that this book upholds.[30] Schuler, while overtly militant in his cause, reclaimed an evangelical voice within the new denomination, and he believed that the majority of the denomination agreed with him. His periodical peaked in 1948 with around twenty-thousand subscribers, a substantial audience.[31]

Joining the ranks of other American evangelicals and social conservatives, Schuler feared the Communist infiltration of American society and particularly the Methodist Church:

> The swing of Methodism toward socialism and away from the American way of life, known and loved by the fathers is closely knit into the liberalism that has infested our communion. As our church swings away from the orthodox position in theology and doctrine, she finds

---

28 Bob Schuler, "The Personal Word," *Methodist Challenge* (November 1943): 1; as quoted in Spann, 270.
29 Bob Schuler, "Why Re-Enter?" *Methodist Challenge* (November 1943): 3; as quoted in Spann, 270–71.
30 Spann, "Evangelicalism in Modern American Methodism," 273–74.
31 Spann, 271.

herself more and more entwined into those dissipating and sub-versive movements, such as pacifism, socialism, Communism, and foreignism.[32]

Holding such views, Schuler was a staunch critic of the Methodist Feder-ation for Social Action (MFSA) and the Women's Division, which were both suspected of Communist sympathizing. Portraying liberalism as an infestation further stressed his distaste for social action and his belief in an ever-growing Methodist fissure. With a substantial audience, his editorials were effective. However, local pastors wrote to Schuler, complaining that his rhetoric was creating dissension in the local churches, which Schuler considered a sign of success. Schuler's following may have agreed with him to an extent, but his attempts at official organization failed. Despite Schuler's attacks on Method-ist seminaries, Sunday school literature, and social activism; Spann argues that Sloan's militancy, West Coast location, and the willingness of many evangelical and liberal Methodists to work together throughout the 1940s and 1950s to avoid conflict prevented Schuler from organizing an official evangelical Meth-odist effort.[33]

Without Schuler's leadership, evangelical Methodists did organize, in small numbers, to combat the Methodist Federal for Social Action, specifically their use of the name "Methodist." The Circuit Riders formed in 1951 and included many top lay leaders of the denomination. Leading up to the General Confer-ence of 1952, they lobbied for an official denouncement of MFSA and were successful. Their efforts resulted in MFSA vacating their office location at the Methodist Building in New York City, and an official request to remove "Meth-odist" from their name was made, a request that was ignored.[34]

Another small organization, the Committee for the Preservation of Meth-odism, tried to revitalize Methodist orthodoxy and questioned the theological legitimacy of the Social Creed. These organizations were short-lived and had lit-tle impact on the denomination as a whole. Their efforts did force MFSA off of Methodist property, but did not affect MFSA's agenda, existence, or name. The

---

32 Robert Schuler, "Methodists Go Socialist," *Methodist Challenge* (December 1944): 8; as quoted in Spann, 311.

33 Spann, "Evangelicalism in Modern American Methodism," 275–76. For more on West Coast evangeli-cals, see Darren Dochuk, *From Bible Belt to Sun Belt: Plain-Folk Religion, Grassroots Politics, and the Rise of Evangelical Conservatism* (New York: W. W. Norton, 2010).

34 Spann, 317.

small win for evangelical Methodists at the General Conference of 1952 was overshadowed by a larger victory for progressive Methodists when an official Methodist agency was created to direct Methodist action for social reform, the Board of Social and Economic Relations, predecessor to the General Board of Church and Society.

In 1953, Schuler retired, and his periodical turned toward social and political issues, causing him to lose a majority of his following who were more concerned with theology. He ceased publication in 1960.[35] Methodist historians have not given much credence to Schuler. His name does not appear in *The Methodist Experience in America*, the historical compendium of American Methodism. The only mention of him found was in Glen Spann's book and in Riley B. Case's *Evangelical and Methodist: A Popular History*; and both refer to him as rather ineffectual. While he was unsuccessful in organizing the evangelical Methodists, he did provide them with a voice during a period in which they did not have one, and he was an early proponent of the idea of two Methodisms existing in one denomination.

Slowly, other voices came to the forefront for brief snippets of time; many of these voices would be heard loud and clear after the formation of the Good News Movement in 1967. Methodists were not overly active in parachurch organizations like the National Association of Evangelicals, although they were known to attend the occasional Billy Graham revival and to read *Christianity Today*. They were staunch Methodists, however, unwilling to desert their denomination, believing it was their duty to bring back what they believed to be true Methodism. However, they did keep up with the NAE and penned a few articles for *Christianity Today*. Edmund W. Robb, later chairman of the board of Good News and founder of the Institute on Religion and Democracy (IRD), wrote "The Predicament of Methodism" in October 1963, calling for "Methodism . . . to examine itself."[36]

For Robb, the problem was fourfold. First, Methodism had placed its Wesleyan concern for "social righteousness" at the forefront and forgotten the Wesleyan concern for "personal righteousness." He claimed, "The church has become so preoccupied with social concerns that she is failing in her quest for personal righteousness. . . . We are seeking to reform the world rather than

---

35   Spann, 321.
36   Edmund W. Robb, "The Predicament of Methodism," *Christianity Today*, October 1963, 3.

convert the individual." Second was a theological crisis; Robb argued that until World War II, Methodism was dominated by "classical liberalism" or Protestant liberalism. Differing from others, however, he claimed that after World War II, neo-orthodoxy resumed its place in Methodist seminaries and "Methodist theologians began to study their Bibles seriously." This intense Bible study led not to a permanent resurgence of orthodoxy but instead to "left-wing existentialism" which "lack[ed] . . . authority and objectivity [and] worsened the theological predicament of Methodism" by declaring historical Christianity superior to the virgin birth and the Resurrection.[37] Third, Robb argued that the appointment system of the Methodist Church, which guarantees all pastors a church, encourages "inefficiency," "favoritism," "limits personal freedom," and "stifles free speech."[38] Fourth, Robb believed that the church was experiencing a liturgical crisis, that it had become too concerned with "proper anthems," sermons on "social concerns," "divided chancels," and "vestments and clerical collars," all signs of "formal, ritualistic, liturgical worship." Robb was an advocate of old-school Methodist revivals, whose "spirit-filled singing and great gospel preaching" would bring back "the common man." Letters in response to Robb's article affirmed that evangelical Methodists agreed with his basic arguments.

Robb's final point on revivals was one of the more common arguments among evangelical Methodists. In the nineteenth century, Methodism grew rapidly, arguably because of its revivals. They were spirit-filled, emotional, conversion-focused, multi-week events that hosted preachers from a variety of Protestantism and brought together men and women, both slaves and free. During these events, all were equal, for all were seen through the eyes of God. As the nineteenth century progressed, Methodists held fewer and fewer revivals as their membership increased in urban areas and as their constituents became more educated, more settled, and more middle-class. This is typically called the institutionalization of Methodism, the point of Methodist decline according to evangelical Methodists. In the 1950s, amid the stardom of Billy Graham and his massive revivals, evangelical Methodists began to call again for the "old-fashioned, devil-fighting, sin-killing, hanky-waving, amen-shouting, foot-stomping, Methodist Holy Ghost revival[s]."[39]

---

37   Robb, 9.
38   Robb, 10.
39   Case, *Evangelical and Methodist*, 7, 29.

Riley B. Case, an ordained minister in the Indiana Conference, board member of the United Methodist Action (of the Institute on Religion and Democracy), and associate director of the Confessing Movement, wrote a popular history of evangelical Methodists. In his introduction, he described his attendance at a Methodist revival at Union Chapel Methodist Church in Indiana in 1956, confirming Robb's belief that these types of revivals still did exist within Methodism. An ordination candidate at Garrett Biblical Institute (later Garrett-Evangelical Theological Seminary), Case was asked about these revivals and his time at this small, rural church during his ordination interview. The Board of Ministerial Training informed him that these revival-hosting, small, rural churches "are not really Methodist churches, you know?"[40] This evidences the discrepancy between small rural churches and even the lower ranks of administration at the annual conference level. While these revival-style churches were not common, and their status as Methodist was debatable, they did exist under the Methodist name.

AMERICAN EVANGELICALS CONFRONT THE PUBLIC SCHOOLS

In *God's Own Party: The Making of the New Christian Right*, Daniel K. Williams argues that American evangelicalism rose to political power in two stages. The first, 1940–1960, was when white evangelicals began to identify with the GOP due to the anti-communist efforts of the party. This was the era of Billy Graham and evangelical respectability described previously. The second was 1960 onward, when white evangelicals fully identified with the GOP due to their fear of secularism and the influence of what has come to be called the Culture Wars.[41] Dominated by televangelists, parachurch organizations, which lobbied Washington, DC, and rhetoric that focused on family values, this era was led by charismatic white men who were more willing to be divisive, critical, and political for the sake of "God, family, and country."[42] These men included Oral Roberts, Jerry Falwell, Pat Robertson, Robert Schuller, Tim LaHaye, James Robison, and a few women—Anita Bryant and Phyllis Schlafly.[43] This section will continue to sketch the politics of white evangelicals and their increasing concern with

---

40 Case, 11.
41 Williams, *God's Own Party,* 3–4; Andrew Hartman, *A War for the Soul of America: A History of the Culture Wars* (Chicago, IL: University of Chicago Press, 2016), 6–7, 73–80, 86–87.
42 Self, *All in the Family,* 347.
43 Self, 340.

sexuality, a fight that continued to use anti-Communist rhetoric and the new rhetoric of "family values" to combat secular humanism.

In previous decades, white evangelicals believed that a focus on evangelism would help save Americans from the horrors of Communism. However, the late 1960s brought massive cultural change in America, from race riots, to feminism, to gay rights, easy access to pornography, and sex-education reform. All of this altered sexual mores and, evangelicals believed, threatened the American family. Premarital sex was more common; and thanks to the oral birth-control pill, it was accepted and performed without the threat of pregnancy. Colleges allowed coed visitation after hours. Books like *Sex and the Single Girl* praised women's sexual selves, and movies like *Deep Throat* were playing in theaters across America.[44] Neo-evangelicals feared that evangelism alone could no longer save America. In the early 1970s, "Christian leaders grew convinced that *only* political activism could save both souls and the country."[45]

With massive congregations, evangelical leaders related to their audience through moral outrage and provided conservative politicians with an attentive and concerned constituency in every district in the country. The new conservative evangelical rhetoric based in pro-family morality and legislation united blue-collar workers in the Sun Belt and Rust Belt with upper-class families of the Northeast. These groups united in fear of the American

> descent into the moral ambiguity of a new gender and sexual order, which displaced men from the center of economic production and public life and weakened women's moral authority within the family and in society at large.[46]

The only way to make America moral again was to reassert Protestant morality in government life. Secular humanism, a value system based not in theology but in humanity's innate ability to be moral and act in moral ways, along with a faith in science and technology over Scripture and God, was believed by white evangelicals to be a state-sponsored religion taught in public schools, thus endangering American children.[47]

---

44 Hartman, *A War for the Soul of America*.
45 Self, *All in the Family*, 340, emphasis original.
46 Self, 342.
47 *New Oxford American Dictionary*, s.v. "secular humanism," accessed November 20, 2016, http://www.oxfordreference.com/view/10.1093/acref/9780195392883.001.0001/m_en_us1288480; Self, *All in the Family*, 344.

A good way to understand the basis of white evangelical fear is by under-standing their concept of family life. For them, the family was the basic social unit. It was a delicately balanced and divinely inspired system with father as head-of-household, disciplinarian, and breadwinner, and mother as spiritual authority, subordinate, and nurturer. They believed that these roles were fixed throughout history and produced moral individuals and societies. This is why white evangelicals uphold 1950s America as the time when America was truly exceptional, for, as we have seen, media, politicians, and religious leaders came together to propel this ideal as the American Way of Life. However, as explained in the pre-vious chapter, 1950s America was a historical fluke, and the values of American suburbia were unattainable for many nonwhite, non–middle-class Americans. The sexual politics of the 1960s and 1970s shook the foundation of the white evangelical family. To them, "abortion, homosexuality, and feminist demands for equality symbolized the fallacy of secular attempts to alter the family's divine structure."[48] Ensuring the "traditional" foundation of gender and sexuality be-came top priority for white evangelicals. Thus, beginning in the 1970s, and con-tinuing today, white evangelicals joined with white conservatives of the GOP to reclaim Christian morality, not just for white evangelicals, but for all American people. More and more white evangelicals abandoned the Democratic Party due to its endorsement of civil rights, racial reform, feminism, and homosexuality.[49]

Advocating a platform based on moral reform and family values was a eu-phemistic, catchall way to fight *all* threats to the white evangelical family.[50] Using grassroots efforts, they combated secular humanism through local and national campaigns against sex education in public schools, the Equal Rights Amendment, legalized abortion, and gay rights.

The fight against secular humanism began with two Supreme Court rulings that sought to limit religious activity in public schools.[51] Supreme Court rulings involving public schools were already a sensitive issue for white evangelicals

---

48 Self, 348.

49 The following statistics are taken from Williams, *God's Own Party*: In 1948, 38 percent of evangelicals voted for the GOP (p. 20). In 1952 and 1956, 60 percent of evangelicals voted for the GOP nominee, Dwight Eisenhower (p. 28). In 1972, 84 percent of evangelicals voted for the GOP nominee, Richard Nixon (p. 102). In 1984, 80 percent of evangelicals voted for the GOP nominee, Ronald Reagan (p. 206). In 2004, 78 percent of evangelicals and 52 percent of Catholics voted for the GOP nominee, George W. Bush (p. 261). "By 1992, only 21 percent of churchgoing evangelicals were democrats, a decline from 55 percent in 1960" (p. 232).

50 Self, *All in the Family*, 357.

51 Williams, *God's Own Party*, 134.

due to the 1954 and 1955 decision of *Brown v. Board of Education,* which in-tegrated public schools. The first Supreme Court ruling that sought to limit reli-gion in public schools was *Engel v. Vitale*, and it concluded that no school could recite a state-composed prayer in a public school. State-composed prayers were interfaith and, according to neo-evangelicals, "reflected a nondenominational, Judeo-Christian consensus that Americans had promoted as a bulwark against 'godless Communism.'" In 1962, 79 percent of Americans supported prayer in school; therefore, both Democrats and Republicans were angered by the Su-preme Court's decision. However, white evangelicals originally favored the de-cision. They did not like the interfaith doctrine of the state-written prayers, believing that it favored Catholic doctrine. Furthermore, they believed that the best prayers in school were spontaneous, which were conveniently not ruled unconstitutional.[52]

With the second Supreme Court decision, most white evangelicals, again, were originally neutral. In 1963, with *Abington v. Schempp*, Bible reading in public schools was deemed unconstitutional.[53] Moderate white evangelicals, as revealed in *Christianity Today* and *Eternity*, accepted the Supreme Court deci-sions, because they believed that the average school would continue to both pray and read Scripture. It was not until the formation of the Sexuality Informa-tion and Education Council of the United States (SIECUS) that they began to un-derstand these rulings as threats of secular humanism.

In 1961, the National Council of Churches and the Canadian Council of Churches gathered for the Green Lakes conference of the Christian family. It "convened ministers, counselors, and medical experts in human sexuality for a discussion focused on the 'stresses and strains' facing modern families." Discus-sion included the problems of "unmarried pregnancy, masturbation, homosex-uality, infidelity, abortion, and sin." Historian Heather R. White argues that out of this conference, which concluded that science and religion were both neces-sary to "illumine the troubling challenge that confronted families," the "most notable offshoot" was the Sexuality Information and Education Council of the United States (SIECUS).[54]

Officially created in 1964, SIECUS was the brainchild of by Dr. Mary

---

52 Williams, 62–63.
53 Williams, 64–65.
54 White, *Reforming Sodom*, 116–17.

Calderone, medical director of Planned Parenthood and advocate for family planning and abortion rights, formed as the nation's first comprehensive sex-education program.[55] Its goal was "to give students a scientifically accurate perspective on sex that avoided moralizing and helped students draw on their personal values to make informed choices about sexual behavior."[56] The conference developed an ethic for sex education, which promoted "authentic selfhood" instead of scriptural commandments. Since social and sexual norms were challenged by the sexual revolution, the "churches needed to develop ways to talk about sex and sexual decision making that would empower youth and young adults—as well as their parents—to make choices that expressed their own moral commitments." The application of the new morality in sex education was the first time Methodists, and other Protestants, employed the radical, and quite controversial, ethic. The *only* ethical norm that Christians should follow" was "love."[57] Methodists in attendance took the new morality and created *Sex and the Whole Person*, a sex education curriculum designed to provide persons with the information necessary to empower individuals with the ability to make their own moral and sexual decisions.

Historian Donald T. Critchlow argues that an unstated goal of SIECUS was "an attempt to change American sexual mores and cultural attitudes toward gender roles and homosexuality," an argument that, when considered in light of the new morality, held true and fed into the fears of white evangelicals.[58] Over half of the public schools in the U.S. had a sex-education program by 1968. Evangelicals, Catholics, social conservatives, fundamentalist Protestants, right-wing organizations, and conservative legislators came together in "an unprecedented showing of political and religious ecumenism" to fight SIECUS.[59] Their main argument against sex education in public schools was that it usurped parental authority and interfered with their roles as moral arbiters. All of these changes contributed to the rise of secular humanism, but it was sex education in public schools that white evangelicals rallied behind.

---

55 Donald T. Critchlow, *Intended Consequences: Birth Control, Abortion, and the Federal Government in Modern America* (New York: Oxford University Press, 1999), 194. Daniel K. Williams, *Defenders of the Unborn: The Pro-Life Movement before* Roe v. Wade (New York: Oxford University Press, 2016), 51.

56 Williams, *God's Own Party*, 82.

57 White, *Reforming Sodom*, 117–18, emphasis original.

58 Critchlow, *Intended Consequences*, 11.

59 Williams, *God's Own Party*, 83.

Believing they could save America from its sexually liberated self, radical groups designed to combat changes in sexuality sprang up in the mid-1960s. Tim LaHaye and Richard Barnes, a Methodist minister, founded the California League Enlisting Action Now, or CLEAN, to lobby the California state government to limit the availability of pornography. After these efforts failed, CLEAN turned their efforts toward combating sex education. The John Birch Society, a right-wing organization founded in 1958 to combat the spread of Communism, created the Movement to Restore Decency to fight sex education, believing its invasion of public schools was "a product of a communist plot."[60] The Christian Crusade, created in 1957 by Billy James Hargis to "enlarge his anti-Communist ministry," coordinated a national campaign against sex education in 1968, and recruited Gordon Drake who authored *Is the Schoolhouse the Proper Place to Teach Raw Sex?*, a book that became *the* resource to consult in order to combat SIECUS.[61] The evangelical efforts of Hargis and Drake labeled SIECUS "the pornographic arm of liberal education" and connected it to Communism.[62] Connecting sex education to Communism spoke to the evangelical concern of secular humanism dominating public school education and religion (specifically Protestantism) being removed from education. Furthermore, preventing sex education in public school was a single, values-based issue that many parents easily agreed with, which allowed these small, right-wing organizations to garner needed support.

By 1974, the movement against secular humanism in public schools organized, and white evangelicals considered school literature too sexual. Mass protests occurred in West Virginia, and books like Onalee McGraw's *Secular Humanism and the Schools: The Issue Whose Time Has Come* argued that "humanistic education repudiates values taught in the home and at church," presenting public school education as a direct assault to the family and to Christianity and as a violation of the First Amendment.[63] When evangelical concern reached all subjects and all levels of education, they, en masse, withdrew their children from public schools and began forming private Christian schools. Williams claims that "from 1965 to 1975, enrollment in Christian schools grew by

---

60   Williams, 83.
61   Williams, 41, 83.
62   As quoted in Hartman, *War for the Soul of America*, 75.
63   Williams, *God's Own Party*, 136.

202 percent, and by the mid-1980s, they had more than two and a half million students."[64]

THE (UNITED) METHODIST CHURCH
AND SEX EDUCATION

In 1969, the General Committee on Family Life, the same organization that organized the previous two decades' Methodist Conferences on Family and Life and elected the Methodist Families of the Year, created the Sex Education Task Force, which issued a letter to the "Pastors and Coordinators of Family Ministries" regarding "What church leaders can do to improve family life and sex education in the school, church, and home."[65] It will be quoted at length, for it lays out the newly formed United Methodist Church's view of sex education and the controversy surrounding it:

> A growing number of communities are being involved in an emotional controversy over family life and sex education. Extremist groups are using the issue of sex education to organize a nationwide attack, not only on family life education, but on public education itself. This attack is designed to stir up fear and deliberately falsifies facts.
>
> The United Methodist Church has long had a concern for quality sex education in the home, church, and school. This concern has been expressed in official statements by the General Conference, in manuals and other materials prepared by agencies of the church, as well as in approved curriculum resources of the church.
>
> Pastors and other church leaders have an opportunity to give strong positive leadership, both within the congregation and the community at large. . . .
>
> Sex education is concerned primarily with education for sexuality, the much broader concepts of masculinity and femininity—what it means to be a man or a woman in all aspects of human behavior and not simply with the "sex act" or with reproduction. In a time of rapid transition our boys and girls, young people and adults need help in

---

64 Williams, 85; Self, *All in the Family*, 344.
65 Constituting this task force were: Leon Smith (Board of Education, Division of the Local Church), Leonard Boche (Board of Christian Social Concerns), Norman Klump (Board of Missions), Merlin Outcalt (Board of Health and Welfare Ministries), and Allen J. Moore (School of Theology at Claremont) (Karen Booth, *Forgetting How to Blush: United Methodism's Compromise with the Sexual Revolution* [Fort Valley, GA: Brisol House, Ltd., 2012], 106).

order to mature as men and women and to function in healthy ways as husbands and wives and parents.[66]

The most notable change here from previous chapters is that United Methodists discussed sexuality as "not simply" the sex act. In the 1950s and 1960s, as the divorce rate increased and in light of the sexual revolutions, Methodists began to understand sexuality as a social construct and as a vital part of full personhood. This letter above was signed by representatives of the Board of Christian Social Concerns, the Board of Missions, the Board of Health and Welfare Ministries, the Board of Education, and the School of Theology at Claremont. The letter was accompanied with a packet, which will be referred to as the "Sex Education Folder." It was a massive conglomeration of materials and pamphlets that dealt with everything from marriage counseling to sex education. A few of these materials will also be dealt with below, but many were discussed in previous chapters.

Considering that it was produced by official United Methodist boards and agencies, the "Sex Education Folder" is unashamed of its support of sex education in public schools and of its disapproval of the "well-planned, coordinated, and financed campaign, led by those extremist organizations of the 'Far Right' who specialize in denunciation—vilifying anything that does not fit their peculiarly tainted viewpoints." With statements such as this, it is obvious to say that this packet represents the liberal Methodist point of view. The first article, "The Church Says, 'Our Children have a Right to Know,'" provides a brief background of the official pronouncements in the *Discipline* in regard to sex education. The first was made in 1940, with the penning of "The Christian Home," the same statement that approved the use of artificial contraception within marriage. It read:

> Our children desire and have a right to know before adolescence the facts regarding the origin of life and the nature of their personality as it relates to sex. Parents, if properly instructed, are best fitted to give this assistance; but if they are recreant to this duty, then qualified persons in the church should teach reverently the beautiful truths of life.[67]

---

66 "Sex Education Folder" (Nashville, TN: The General Committee on Family Life, 1969); records of Health and Welfare Ministries, "General Committee on Family Life—Sex Education Task Force," 2080-7-8:4, GCAH.

67 *Doctrines and Discipline of The Methodist Church* (New York: Methodist Publishing House, 1940), 771; as quoted in "The Church Says, 'Our Children Have a Right to Know'" in "Sex Education Folder."

In 1952, with sex education becoming increasingly popular in senior high school and college, and prior to the formation of SIECUS, the General Conference adjusted the statement to read: "We endorse the growing tendency in our public schools to include sex education under competent teachers as a normal part of their curriculum" and produced a pamphlet for parents called, "Teaching Children about Sex in the Home."[68] With the formation of The United Methodist Church in 1968, a completely revised Social Principles reaffirms the support of sex education: "We advocate thorough educational efforts in home, church, and school designed to elevate our whole understanding of the meaning of sexual experience."[69] Historically, the Methodist Church and The United Methodist Church were open to teaching sex education in public schools, in the church, and in the home. These efforts have been documented in previous chapters. For example, young couples were encouraged to talk with their families and their ministers about sex adjustment in marriage and to go to Planned Parenthood clinics to gain scientific information about sex. This book has also shown that many of the courses that the Methodist Church sought to develop for young couples to teach them about sex were controversial due to evangelical concern over what was already being taught in Methodist schools and seminaries. With this in mind, the Methodist Church and The United Methodist Church endorsed sex education in public schools, because it gave them a place to direct their constituents without interfering with the Course of Study at Methodist seminaries or with Sunday school literature.

The "Sex Education Folder" proceeded with a list of "right-wing extremist groups" who "have led the attack on sex education, stirring up other uniformed persons with materials that are frequently falsely documented or obviously distorted to create wrong impressions" and accused these groups of using "their favorite tag of 'Communist plot' and feigned shock and disgust" to garner more followers.[70] This rhetoric directly named and blamed various groups for creating dissension in American society, and many of these groups were part of the rise of the New Christian Right. Included were the John Birch Society's Movement to Restore Decency and the Christian Crusade, both mentioned previously. Gordon

---

68 *Doctrines and Discipline of The Methodist Church* (New York: Methodist Publishing House, 1952), 637; as quoted in "The Church Says"; Roy E. Dickerson, "Teaching Children about Sex in the Home" (Nashville, TN: Department of the Christian Family, 1954) in "Sex Education Folder."
69 *BOD* (1968), 58; as quoted in "The Church Says."
70 "Same Extremists, New Target" in "Sex Education Folder."

Drake's *Is the Schoolhouse the Proper Place to Teach Raw Sex?* is called "the 'bible' for many sex education opponents"; and given the article's warning about "materials that are frequently falsely documented," one can assume that this book was such a document. Other named organizations included Carl McIntire's American Council of Christian Churches, the fundamentalist rival of the National Association of Evangelicals, which accused Protestant Churches and especially the Federal Council of Churches (later the National Council of Churches) of being soft on Communism.[71] The list continued, but these were the few organizations or leaders that had an active role in the rise of the New Christian Right.

Moving on to provide information on what SIECUS was and its intent as an organization, the next article read:

> SIECUS believes that responsible sexuality is many things—the need to understand oneself as a sexual human being, that all children are born and grow up as sexual beings, that men and women need knowledge about sexuality before they can determine their attitudes about what it means to be a man or a woman.[72]

Again, the rhetoric acknowledged sexuality as part of full personhood. Understanding one's sexuality, no matter its form, helped one to understand self and to understand God.

To disprove the misgivings in regard to how sex education usurps the rights of parents, the article continued with a question/answer format. It argued that sex education in public school was meant to complement, not replace, sex education at home, and to improve communication between children and parents. Many parents did not receive proper sex education when they were growing up, and SIECUS sought to correct that for the next generation. SIECUS also provided sex education in a variety of contexts for parents who did not receive proper education and who wished to know more so that they could engage in better conversations with their children. The fear that sex education was demoralizing and was trying to devalue a developing relationship between parent and child was false. Methodists believed the evangelical platform against sex education was a political move to garner support, because sex education was something to which every parent could relate.

---

71 Williams, *God's Own Party*, 38–39.
72 "SIECUS Assists in Understanding Sexuality" in "Sex Education Folder."

The more constructive articles in the "Sex Education Folder" gave practical advice on how to ensure that sex education was taught in home, school, and church. These sections encouraged parents to be fully informed on the various political groups that hoped to sway parents one way or the other in terms of sex education. It encouraged them to hold community meetings and learn what the community wanted taught in their local schools. SIECUS did not present a community with set curricula; it relied on the community to decide what it needed, and SIECUS advised based on those needs. Families were encouraged to be proactive when it came to sex education: "Do not wait until [an] attack comes" but "seek to create a climate of acceptance for family life educations in the schools of your community."[73] Ministers and lay leaders were charged with providing "the community with constructive and positive leadership" by offering "factual information and responsible programs."

Being more direct, both the church and SIECUS deemed it a religious duty of ministers to "counteract" the "religious heresy" of "extremists" who "distort sex with negativism and attempt to separate sex education from the normal pursuits of knowledge" by reassuring their congregations that "Christian theology affirms sex as good and understands sex education in much broader ways than sexual intercourse and human reproduction."[74] To The UMC, learning about sex was "a theological enterprise even if it takes place in the school rather than the church or if the language is scientific rather than religious." Less ideological and more practical advice asked local Councils on Ministry to form a task force on sex education with members who represented a broad range of positions in the local church. The job of such a task force would be to help construct the science-based curriculum of sex education in public schools and complement it with a moral-based curriculum in the local church and open these to the community.[75]

Finally, in the home, parents needed to ensure that they were properly trained to communicate the facts of sex with their children and answer any questions. Churches and communities should have sex education courses for parents who felt that they needed supplemental information. Parents were encouraged to take a look at their own sexual selves and "appreciate their own

---

73   "What Churchmen Can Do" in *Sex Education Folder.*
74   "Improving Sex Education through the Church" in *Sex Education Folder.*
75   "Improving Sex Education through the Church."

sexuality as men and women and . . . find sexual satisfaction in marriage" through manuals, retreats, and counseling. Parents were encouraged to be in constant communication with public school teachers so that both sides were comfortable with what was being taught. Finally, parents should provide ample literature for their children who had questions about sex.[76] The advice given on these two pages addressed how to make parents more comfortable with and more active in their child's sex education. It recognized that sex education in public schools should not be the only place where this education occurs; but it also recognized that parents and churches were not qualified to teach all of sex education. The overall goal of this folder was to parallel the statements of The UMC with those of SIECUS and to provide parents with information on how to help their children develop as sexual beings.

Further cementing the relationship between SIECUS and The United Methodist Church was a SIECUS report written by Leon Smith, a SIECUS board member and director of Educational Ministries in Marriage for The UMC. Entitled "Religion's Response to the New Sexuality," its goal was to establish that "sexuality is a good gift of God" and to "discover and affirm positive healthy ways of functioning as sexual beings."[77] Smith argued for twelve trends on how Protestant denominations in the U.S. and Canada responded to the new sexuality. (1) He witnessed "a great increase in sex education in the churches for persons of all ages" and "for ministers themselves." (2) Churches were supporting "sex education in the public schools." (3) Churches were supporting sex research in general. (4) Churches were moving away from "rigid rules for sexual conduct" and toward "broad ethical principles which individuals might use in specific situations as guidelines in their sexual decisions," also known as the new morality. (5) Churches were beginning to affirm "personal freedom and responsibility in sexual behavior" and were "beginning to support efforts to abolish legal restrictions on private sexual activities." This included overturning anti-sodomy laws, legal access to contraception for all persons, and legal access to safe abortions. (6) Churches were "making efforts to understand" different sexual practices and "provide special ministries" for those persons. (7) Churches were understanding marriage "as a vital, growing relationship that enhances the personal development of both partners with a strong emphasis on sexual enrichment."

---

76 "Improving Sex Education through the Church."
77 Leon Smith, "Religion's Response to the New Sexuality," *SIECUS Report*, 4, no. 2 (November 1975): 1.

(8) Churches were "affirming the equal status of men and women" and attempting to "overcome sex stereotyping and discrimination." (9) Intercourse was being affirmed as a source of pleasure for both men and women and as a primary way to enrich the relationship between the two. (10) Churches were redefining pornography "toward a reverent appreciation of the body and a joyful celebration of the erotic." (11) Churches were beginning to understand masturbation as a healthy form of sexual exploration. (12) Finally, many church leaders were beginning to understand homosexuality not as a "deviant" form of sexuality but as a "variant" of sexuality.

Smith understood that these trends were emerging within the major Protestant denominations, although none had come to full fruition. He also viewed them as rooted in a "deeper understanding of the Bible" and as "an effort to spell out the implications of ethical principles derived from faith." Written in 1975, Smith's article was written alongside the increase in an evangelical voice and perspective on sexuality, which would increasingly take issue with many of his statements. As such, Smith's twelve trends represented an overly optimistic point of view, one that would remain part of the extreme progressive faction of United Methodism.

A larger resource, the *Sex Education Resource Packet*, was created around the same time as the "Sex Education Folder" and contained a variety of pamphlets, articles, papers, and other resources to help parents understand their sexuality and to improve their sex lives, as well as advice on how to talk with their children about sex. One of the more creative resources was an adult comic book, *Escape from Fear: Joan and Ken Harper's Marriage Was on the Rocks— Because They Loved Each Other!*, a book that was included to help parents reaffirm or rediscover their sexual selves. The first page showed that Joan was nervous about having intercourse with Ken after the birth of their first child. After Joan threatened to leave, Ken went to his doctor to get advice, and his doctor recommended that they try contraception: "Tell your wife to see your doctor or to visit the doctor at the Planned Parenthood center in your community." Joan went to the doctor and was told about both "the pill" and "the intrauterine device." The last page of the comic book showed the couple six months later as they rejoiced in their rediscovered bliss. Ken even "told the guys at the plant about the Planned Parenthood Center" when he learned that "they were just as messed up as we were." The comic ended with Joan speaking directly to the reader:

> Planned Parenthood helped us save our marriage. Someday when our
> children are older, we may want another baby. That's why Planned
> Parenthood is so wonderful. It doesn't mean not having children—it
> means spacing them so they come when we can give the kind of love
> and care they deserve!

Produced by Planned Parenthood, this comic book gave the organization
a glowing review, but as the first item in the *Sex Education Resource Packet*, it
reaffirmed the denomination's connection to Planned Parenthood, to a healthy
married sex life, and to the use of contraception. The Methodist Church had
been an advocate on behalf of Planned Parenthood since the mid-1940s, as
chapter 1 of this book showed. The United Methodist Church continued this
tradition, advocating not only family planning, but the use of new birth-control
technology, such as "the pill" and the "intrauterine device."[78]

After pamphlets on marriage counseling (which were discussed in chapter 2),
there was a pamphlet called "Your Child and Christian Attitudes Towards Sex."
Published in 1962 by the Department of the Christian Family and the General
Board of Education, the pamphlet discussed the "unparalleled exposures to sex"
of the early 1960s, calling the "frankness with which sex is brought before us
good and helpful and positive" but also warned that it can lead to "confusion."
The goal of this pamphlet was twofold. First, it showed parents that sex education was not simply providing the facts about intercourse to children. It was
about shaping attitudes of how people interacted daily with each other. It was
also about shaping bodily attitudes. Everything from explaining basic bodily functions to being an example of healthy interpersonal reactions was sex education.

Second, the pamphlet showed that sex education was not something that
was done once a child reached puberty, but was done from infancy. Whether
parents wanted to teach their children about sex or not, "from birth onward"
children "are receiving sex education constantly." Parental reactions to changing a diaper was an early form of sex education. Teaching a child to speak was
an early form of sex education. The Methodist Church was advocating a wholesome approach to sex education, one that defined *sexuality* in the broadest
sense. Sexuality was "maleness and femaleness," "what makes girls girls and

---

78 *Escape from Fear: Joan and Ken Harper's Marriage was on the Rocks—Because They Loved Each Other!*
(New York: Planned Parenthood Federation of America, 1962) in *Sex Education Resource Packet* (Nash-
ville, TN: The General Committee on Family Life, 1969), records of Health and Welfare Ministries, "Sex
Education Resource Packet 1964–66," 2355-6-1:38, GCAH.

boys boys," "the love and tenderness of parents" and how they "express love for each other and a baby," and it was "the factual information about reproduction and birth." The pamphlet's conclusion asked parents to remove emotions from sex education, to not bring their own experiences with sex to the conversation, and to keep answers positive, "brief and factual." It reminded them that "God made us as we are" and that sex is a good, God-given thing.[79]

Sex and the Whole Person

The last article worth mentioning was the most radical. It was an advertisement for the new experimental course, which encouraged teenagers, parents, and clergy to come together for small group discussions about sexuality. The stated goals of an elective youth study entitled *Sex and the Whole Person* were "(1) That you may understand what it means to be male or female; (2) That you may rejoice wholeheartedly in being such a person; and (3) That you may express this joy, in relationship to persons, in appropriate and productive ways."[80] *Sex and the Whole Person* was a course created by the Board of Education in 1962, to live into the General Conference mandate of creating "courses of study for young people regarding Christian attitudes toward sex and personality growth."[81] In a ten-week course, senior high teenagers and parents were to be taught "biblical, psychological, and physiological information" with the goal of developing "Christian standards concerning sex." During the course, "no one is told, nor is the impression given, that a specific action is right or wrong." Instead, "guidelines are set up by giving all the facts concerning all of the facets of sexual relationships, from definitions of terms, all the way through psychological and emotional actions and reactions to all forms of sexual stimuli." The goal was to allow each person to "make his [or her] own decision about his [or her] sex life" using the Christian attitude learned during the course.[82] This course was the first of its kind to teach parents and teens together, to make them more comfortable discussing sex in small groups, and to teach both at the same time the realities of sex in the 1960s. Its willingness to allow for individual

---

79 David B. Treat, "The Child and Christian Attitudes Towards Sex" (Nashville, TN: Department of the Christian Family, 1962) in *Sex Education Resource Packet.*
80 Frank E. Weir, *Sex and the Whole Person* (Nashville, TN: Abingdon Press, 1964), 5.
81 "Guidelines for Using *Sex and the Whole Person.*"
82 Lee Vance, "Sex Education for United Methodist Youth," (Nashville: The General Committee on Family Life, 1969) in *Sex Education Resource Packet.*

moral authority and not mandate rules was radical for the time and, as this book argues, formed the basis for the denomination's new sexual ethic, "the new morality."

These types of courses and books continued to be produced into the early 1970s. In *Youth Views Sexuality*, author Anne C. Blanchard explained that the new morality was "an approach to decision making that consists of trying to discover what is the most loving thing to do in each situation." She connected this idea to the teachings of Jesus, who "placed the value of persons above slavery to the law."[83] She understood the new morality not as an "advocacy of sexual license" but as a reinterpretation of love. In order to better understand love, Blanchard encouraged persons to consult the Bible as well as their own "life plans."[84] Another resource published in 1971 was *God and Human Sexuality*. As a guide for adults, it openly addressed homosexuality and encouraged the readers to reexamine their preconceived notions that heterosexuality was the only morally correct lifestyle to lead.[85]

The administrative branches of Methodism were aware of the disjuncture within Methodism. They recognized that "in the last few years the Methodist Church has made notable strides in helping its teenage members face creatively their capacity for sex and their calling to love"—and yet—"these programs have not always been received gratefully by all segments of the church."[86] Donald Kuhn, editor of *Concern* magazine, which was the periodical of the General Board of Christian Social Concerns, argued that while Methodism was a "pluralistic" denomination, not everyone recognized that it was okay for Methodists to disagree on some aspects of life. The Methodists, he argued, who preferred the "old way of doing things" were "strain[ed]" by diversity, especially when it came to sex. To him, "Methodists do not have to look far to notice marked differences in attitudes toward marriage, use of contraceptives, divorce, abortion, homosexuality, and premarital and extramarital intercourse." While diverse attitudes necessitated reevaluation, Kuhn argued that "universal standards . . . may not be the best way to encourage individual moral responsibility that will

83 Anne C. Blanchard, *Youth Views Sexuality* (Nashville, TN: Graded Press, Methodist Publishing House, 1971), 52.

84 Blanchard, 79.

85 Henry M. Bullock, Horace R. Weaver, and John P. Gilbert, eds., *God and Human Sexuality* (Nashville, TN: Methodist Publishing House, 1971), 98–99.

86 Donald Kuhn, "Goals for Sex Life," *Concern*, January 15, 1964, 12.

withstand the strains of passing time and changing location." He critiqued the church for focusing too much on certain standards in the past without evaluating or explaining the "context of the struggle." Too often, teenagers were told that certain behaviors were morally wrong, but were not given an explanation as to why or recognition that acting a certain way may require struggle.

Kuhn proposed five "goals for sex life." First, laws and statements on human sexuality needed to "strengthen the individual's social responsibility in the midst of diversity." Second, individuals needed to understand "sex-related activities" as a way "to communicate love and/or to make babies." Third, individuals who participated in "sex-related activities" needed "to bring to an end the possibility of unwanted and/or unintended babies." Fourth, society needed to allow "physicians the possibility to perform abortions on the basis of their professional values and judgment without special laws related to abortion." Fifth, society needed to better understand "how to prevent conception." To Kuhn, a contemporary understanding of healthy sexuality needed to account for all five of these goals. He believed that "the key concept is love." Kuhn presented step-by-step goals for the new morality, as "each [goal] provides a perspective for evaluating personal thoughts, interests, ambitions, and outward behavior."[87] His goals necessitated cooperation among individuals who dedicated themselves to acting out of love and in a responsible manner regarding contraception, society that agreed to allow for abortion and education on contraception, and the church (or the lawmakers) who agreed to account for individual responsibility and social diversity. Kuhn's article upheld the new morality, based all actions in love, and accounted for diverse opinions on matters of sex.

These types of pamphlets and books were analyzed in 1976 by James Phillips at Duke University on behalf of the National Council of Churches to "determine the extent and quality of sex education in the mainstream of American Protestantism."[88] In 1966, it was believed that "less than five percent of our churches do anything significant" in regard to sex education. Phillips wanted to see if, since 1966, with the rising popularity of *Playboy*, the churches had changed their approach to sex education. He analyzed eight American Protestant denominations: the Episcopal Church, the Lutheran Church in America,

---

87 Kuhn, "Goals for Sex Life," 12.
88 James H. Phillips, *Sex Education in Major Protestant Denominations* (New York: National Council of Churches in the U.S.A., 1976), 2.

the Lutheran Church–Missouri Synod, The United Methodist Church, the Presbyterian Church (U.S.A.), the Southern Baptist Convention, the United Church
of Christ, and the United Presbyterian Church in the U.S.A. He wrote directly
to the board of education of each denomination and requested their denomi-
nationally produced materials on sex education. His conclusions placed the Lutheran Church–Missouri Synod as the best in terms of sex education, because
in 1964 they produced a four-volume series that explained sexuality for four
different age levels, from kindergarten through high school. Accompanying the
books were four filmstrips, a parent's guide, discussion tools for classes, and a
manual for church leaders to help the church better understand how it can help
parents with sex education. To Phillips, this comprehensive, lifelong approach,
which used multimedia and offered the option for discussion groups, was best.
The [United] Methodist Church ranked fifth on the list, with their *Sex and the
Whole Person* course receiving accolades for its insistence that properly trained
teachers provide the facts of sex education, and parents and churches provide
supplemental information.[89] Phillips applauded the denomination for recognizing that parents, too, need to reevaluate their sexual lives in order to most ef-
fectively teach positive sexuality.[90]

Overall, the Methodist Church and The United Methodist Church sought
to provide sex education to senior high teenagers and their parents. They supported sex education in public schools as early as 1954, and continued to support sex education in public schools throughout the controversy in the 1960s.
They produced dozens of pamphlets across the two decades to guide parents
in discussions with their children, to inform children about their own bodies,
and to recommend other nonreligious resources for both parents and children.
The administrative ranks of the denominations made great strides in trying to
correct the errors of the past when sex was ignored as a vital part of our whole
being. The UMC encouraged proper sex education as a guide to help teenagers decide for themselves how to approach their own sex lives. While this attitude was not an endorsement of premarital sex, it did not demean it. This
rather candid and modern attitude was in direct contrast with the American
evangelical notion of a healthy sex life, which promoted strict celibacy outside
of marriage.

---

89   Phillips, 4.
90   Phillips, 7.

Evangelical-leaning Methodists were (and continue to be) critical of the new morality. They believed the new morality was a "lackadaisical approach to sexual integrity."[91] Karen Booth, director of Transforming Congregations (an organization that advocates sex-conversation therapy and believes that faith in Jesus Christ is consistent only with a heterosexual lifestyle), wrote *Forgetting How to Blush: United Methodism's Compromise with the Sexual Revolution* in 2012. It used many of the same primary sources that this book employs and makes a similar argument that "deliberate curriculum and program choices made in the late 1950s and throughout the 1960s and 1970s laid the foundation for . . . moral revisionism," a move that "began with the then Methodist Church's development of sex education material."[92] However, Booth concludes that these new programs were detrimental and counter to "God's will, purpose and plan for human sexuality."[93]

Booth argues that evangelical Methodists viewed courses like *Sex and the Whole Person* and publications such as *Youth Views Sexuality* and *God and Human Sexuality* as works of "moral ambiguity" where "scripture was tacked on as an afterthought."[94] Instead of prioritizing "God's revealed will for human sexuality and behavior" as revealed in Scripture, these works and their accompanying ethic of the new morality "exalt[ed] human intellectual reasoning as the ultimate guide to making moral decisions."[95] These works, according to evangelical Methodists, were full of "psychological jargon," their "scripture lessons were sketchy and superficial," and their ethical lessons often provided "loopholes to justify [any] behavior."[96] Evangelicals tended to uphold Scripture as the sole authority; thus any inference that human reasoning, without scriptural guidance, was sound enough to make moral and sexual decisions was a direct threat to their understanding of the world. As the evangelical United Methodist voice grew louder in the 1970s, the new morality was increasingly challenged. As a result, The UMC would increasingly restrict its attitude toward sex. It began advocating a sexually gray area that endorsed the new morality and understood sexuality as a God-given good, while, at the same time, tried to restrict what

91   Booth, *Forgetting How to Blush*, 96.
92   Booth, 98.
93   Booth, 99.
94   Booth, 103.
95   Booth, 103.
96   Booth, 104–5.

sexual acts were moral based on Scripture. This dual sexual framework, which sought to appease all Methodists, led only to confusion as to where The UMC stood in terms of sexual ethics.

THE METHODIST FISSURE—THE FORMATION OF THE GOOD NEWS MOVEMENT

Without an organized evangelical voice in the denomination, it is hard to know exactly how evangelical Methodists felt, at the time, about sex education in the public schools during the 1960s. Karen Booth's work examined the new morality from a historical context and provided primary source criticism of the new morality. As previously mentioned, Robert Schuler retired in 1960, leaving the movement without an advocate. However, in 1966, Charles Keysor penned his famous "Methodism's Silent Minority," which reignited the evangelical flame in the new United Methodist Church. The context for his article was the debate on sex education and the new morality (along with a host of other issues, such as civil rights, women's rights, and a newly emerging gay rights movement). Spann argued that "many Methodist leaders in the 1960s accepted the proposition that 'the world sets the agenda for the church.'" He continued, "The social ferment of the 1960s presented the church with a plethora of problems and proposed solutions," which led the "program of Methodism" to more and more become one focused on social activism.[97] Given the amount of resources produced for the promotion of sex education in schools, at home, and at church, it was plausible that one of the problems evangelical Methodists tried to resolve was sex education. Spann followed this comment with a critique of the Board of Evangelism for being more concerned with changing the structures of society instead of redeeming humanity, the General Board of Christian Social Concerns for acknowledging the "increasing 'diversity' of attitudes toward 'marriage, use of contraceptives, divorce, abortion, homosexuality, and premarital and extramarital intercourse,'" and of Methodist leaders for "minimiz[ing] the importance of theological affirmation in the Christian experience."[98] For him and other evangelicals, this theologically lax denomination was being taken over by cultural concerns and being guided by a secular agenda. This was the context that created the first crack in the "Methodist Fissure," the deep divide

---

97 Spann, "Evangelicalism in Modern American Methodism," 339.
98 Spann, 340–41.

between liberal and evangelical Methodists, a divide that began decades prior but that truly took form in the late 1960s due to the increased concern with matters of sexuality.

Charles Keysor, minister of Grace Methodist in Elgin, Illinois, was also trained as a journalist and worked as managing editor of *Together*. He attended Garrett Biblical Institute and was converted during a Billy Graham revival. In 1966, Keysor penned an article for the *Christian Advocate*, "Methodism's Silent Minority," through which he spoke for "those Methodists who are variously called 'evangelicals' or 'conservatives' or 'fundamentalists.'" Keysor preferred the term "orthodox" for these persons, who, like himself, "hold a traditional understanding of the Christian faith." Orthodox Methodists (who for the purposes of consistency will still be referred to as "evangelical Methodists" in this book), Keysor claimed, were "not represented in the higher councils of the church" and their "concepts are often abhorrent to Methodist officialdom at annual conference and national levels."[99]

Orthodoxy, for Keysor, was a belief "that the Christian faith is comprehensively declared in the Holy Scripture and is succinctly summarized in the Apostle's [sic] Creed." It was based in five fundamentals that "constitute a common ground for all who are truly orthodox": the infallibility of the Bible, the virgin birth of Christ, the substitutionary atonement of Christ, Christ's physical resurrection, and Christ's physical return. Keysor separated himself from fundamentalists in that he did not agree with premillennial dispensationalism, believing this idea to be "perverted."[100] Using the rhetoric of Sloan, Schuler, and Robb, Keysor portrayed the evangelical Methodist voice as absent from Methodist administrative ranks, where liberalism was dominant. Keysor lamented that evangelical Methodists were referred to by their counterparts as "narrow-minded, naïve, contentious, and potentially schismatic."[101] Despite this, Keysor believed that he was not a lone evangelical, for "10,000 Methodist churches are using some Christian education materials based on orthodox theology," a reference to Schuler's attack on Methodist Sunday school literature as part of the progressive Methodist agenda, and the desire for more "'good old gospel songs'" in the new Methodist Hymnal. Keysor challenged other evangelicals to "become

---

99 Charles W. Keysor, "Methodism's Silent Minority," *Christian Advocate* (July 14, 1966): 9.
100 Keysor, 9–10.
101 Keysor, 9.

the *un*-silent minority" and "enter forthrightly into the current theological debate." In their speaking, he warned, evangelicals "must not speak as right-wing fanatics, intending to subvert the 'establishment' and remake it in our own orthodox image."[102]

After publication, "more letters poured into *Christian Advocate* as the result of [this] article than from any other single article in the history of the magazine."[103] With such overwhelming support, Keysor decided, in the spirit of his predecessors, to begin his own magazine, one that would "articulate historic Methodism," "exalt Jesus Christ," and "be a forum for the discussion of church issues and a rallying point for people of like-minded convictions."[104] The first issue of *Good News* was printed in 1967 and mailed to six thousand persons. The reaction to the first issue was mixed. Some agreed with Keysor's theology but were timid concerning its divisiveness. Others believed that the magazine represented a needed voice in Methodism but were not fond of Keysor's theology. Others were excited that their voice had finally been heard and spoken in an official forum. Officially, the Methodist Church did not respond to the first issue.[105]

A couple of years later, Keysor decided that he had garnered enough support through his periodical to officially organize a movement. Sponsored by *Good News*, the "Convocation of United Methodists for Evangelical Christianity" gathered in Dallas, Texas, August 26–29, 1970. In attendance were sixteen hundred people during the day and three thousand for the evening worship services. Keysor proclaimed it as a "*kairos* moment for evangelicals and for church renewal." His description of the event provides a history of the evangelical Methodist movement from his perspective:

> In a dramatic way, the four days of meetings mark the end of an Exile which has seen Methodist evangelicals wandering in a wilderness for roughly 40 years. Somewhere back in the 1920s, liberals gained control of the power structure of Methodism. Since then, evangelicals have been squeezed out of influence in denominational affairs. For many years, it has appeared to the world as if evangelicals could not survive in the increasingly humanist, universalistic climate. But a remnant has survived! They have endured spiritual starvation. They

---

102 Keysor, 10, emphasis original.
103 Case, *Evangelical and Methodist*, 29. Again, Case provides no citation for this claim.
104 Case, 29–30.
105 Case, 30–31.

have seen colleges and seminaries bearing the Methodist name to-
tally repudiate what once made that name great. They have been
force-fed church school literature that is repugnant to New Testament faith and experience. They have seen pulpits taken captive by
humanism, secularism, politics, institutionalism, and psychology. Their
money has been used to finance many programs with which they
violently disagree. They have heard themselves slandered, ridiculed,
and castigated by those for whom Biblical faith was "not relevant."
. . . *We are coming out of exile!*[106]

Keysor's overall point is relatively accurate, even if his styling and wording
are exaggerated. This book, thus far, has shown that the administrative ranks
of the various Methodist denominations since the 1920s had been largely controlled by progressives, and the evangelicals had a small voice present throughout the denomination, but rarely in a place of power. And the evangelical voice
had survived this. The movement, which would eventually be given the name
the Good News Movement, provided evangelical Methodists with a sounding
board, a place to discern their faith with others. Speaking at its convocation
were a few Methodist "officials," Bishop Gerald K. Kennedy and Ira Gallaway
from the Board of Evangelism. Also present were non-Methodist evangelicals
E. Stanley Jones, Oral Roberts (who eventually became Methodist), and Howard
Ball of Campus Crusade. Cementing the movement's eventual connection to
Asbury Seminary, Dennis Kinlaw, president of Asbury College, and Frank Stan-
ger, president of Asbury Seminary, also spoke.[107] Its initial board "was truly a
grassroots, populist, bottom-up movement" with "no aspiring episcopal candidates," "no large-church pastors . . . or seminary professors," and "no wealthy
laymen." Instead those who joined were "young evangelicals, fundamentalists
in established churches, revivalists, Sunday school teachers, mavericks, naïve reformers, and populists of several varieties."[108]

After the Dallas convocation, a survey was sent to those who attended to
discover their demographics so that the movement could progress knowing its
audience. Twenty percent were aged twenty-five to thirty-five; 45 percent were
aged thirty-five to fifty; and 25 percent were aged fifty to sixty-five. They represented forty-eight states and four continents. A slight majority were laypersons

---

106 Charles Keysor, "Coming Out of Exile," *Good News* (March 13, 1970), 22, emphasis his.
107 *MEA*, vol. 1, 503.
108 Case, *Evangelical and Methodist*, 32.

(58 percent) and the remaining identified as clergy. Of the clergy, an equal percentage, 18 percent each, attended an official United Methodist seminary or a non-UM school. In regard to denominational literature, 40 percent admitted to using only UM-published materials. In terms of theology, 80 percent believed that there was a discrepancy between what the average layperson believed and how the clergy interpreted faith. Furthermore, in 1970, 99 percent believed that divinely sanctioned miracles occurred daily.[109] These statistics are arguably the greatest contribution Case's work brings to the history of Methodist evangelicalism. Prior to his work, other historians and leaders relied on vague language such as "a large percentage" or a "substantial number" without providing data from actual Methodists to support their claims. While the sampling of 1,600 people is a small fraction of the membership of The UMC (10,671,774 lay members in 1970), the numbers do confirm what evangelical Methodists had stated since the 1920s: laypersons held a different theology than their clergy.[110] What is missing from this data is information on the size of town the attendees came from, their education level, their income, and their ethnicity. If we combine Case's data with conclusions from Spann's book, which argues the evangelical Methodists were largely white, from rural areas, held little college-level education, and made a low to modest income, then a larger picture forms of the persons represented in Dallas.[111]

Methodist historians have characterized the Good News Movement as a highly organized "parachurch organization" that benefits from the "support of an energetic and outspoken board, through connections with the burgeoning political-religious, conservative-evangelical movement, with . . . the larger Asbury networks." This foundation provides them with a multitude of authors ready to offer a "prophetic critique" through the pages of Good News.[112] Riley B. Case argued that as early as January 1970, prior to the Dallas convocation, Good News and Charles Keysor had already been labeled "reactionary and confrontational."[113] This label was due to Keysor's editorial "Cyanide in the Church School," where he labeled all United Methodist publications for church school as "poison." Prior to this, the magazine was not without its controversial

---

109 Case, 38–39.
110 Hempton, Empire of the Spirit, 212.
111 Spann, "Evangelicalism in Modern American Methodism," 261.
112 MEA, vol. 1, 503.
113 Case, Evangelical and Methodist, 46.

or accusatory articles; however, the majority of the issues prior focused on re-claiming orthodoxy,[114] disproving historical criticism,[115] advising laypersons and clergy how to petition General Conference,[116] and pointing followers to ortho-dox resources.[117] In 1970, many articles turned toward church school curricu-lum, beginning with Keysor's "Cyanide in the Church School." Case argued that "frustration over church school curriculum, more than over any other concern, basically launched the Good News movement." However, this editorial also had "friends of Good News r[unning] for cover" and "disassociat[ing] themselves from [its] language."[118]

According to Keysor, each week, church school curriculum "repress[ed] and stifl[ed]" evangelicals with the liberal Protestant theology of official United Methodism. The main problem for Good News' followers was that the only sanctioned materials, including Sunday school literature, audio-visual materials, music, and hymnbooks, that could be used in a United Methodist Church were those produced by the United Methodist Board of Education, as sanctioned by General Conference.[119]

Keysor and his followers argued that the problem with United Methodism was multifold. First, the Board of Education was, like other administrative ranks of the denomination, controlled by "white male liberals": seven clergy, thirteen professors, and the remaining nineteen were bishops. Second, they argued that the "whole educational system was under attack" from both the left and the right, making Sunday school "irrelevant." Third, "the new cultural ferment" brought with it "a new philosophy of Youth Ministry . . . in which youth were to be given not answers, but rather tools so they could find answers for them-selves"—a direct attack on the new morality and *Sex and the Whole Person*.[120] When viewed in light of sex education and the philosophy behind *Sex and the Whole Person*, which sought to provide senior high teenagers with guidelines to help them figure out their own sexual selves, it becomes apparent that one of the things Good News was fighting against was sex education.

---

114 "Listen to the Wesleys," *Good News*, Winter 1967, 42–44.
115 David R. Hunsberger, "Where Does an Alien Go to Register?" *Good News*, October 1968, 18–21.
116 Robert M. Neely, "When Did You Last Use Your Voice?" *Good News*, Fall 1967, 4.
117 "Books to Help You," *Good News*, Winter 1967, 32–35.
118 Case, *Evangelical and Methodist*, 46–47, 59.
119 Case, 47.
120 Case, *Evangelical and Methodist*, 61.

In the January–March 1970 issue, evangelical Methodists directly addressed sex education in the "for Christian Women" section. Mrs. Philip E. Worth wrote the article from the point of view of a pastor's wife. The year 1969 was when sex education in public schools became a "controversy." Mrs. Worth argued that the best place for sex education was in the home, where parents could ground sex education in "the authority of the word of God." Her article portrayed a particular reading of certain passages in Genesis as sufficient for sex education:

> Genesis 1:27 (KJV): "God created man in [H]is own image . . . male and female."
>
> Genesis 2:18 (KJV): "It is not good that the man should be alone; I will make him a help meet."
>
> Genesis 2:24 (KJV): "Therefore shall a man cleave unto his wife; and they shall be one flesh."
>
> Genesis 1:28 (RSV): "God blessed them and [. . .] said to them, 'Be fruitful and multiply, and fill the earth.'"[121]

She argued that "sex is plainly set forth in the Word of God as God's method for continuing society" and "the sanctity of sex and the wholesome relationship of marriage is sufficiently repeated throughout the New Testament." She understood that the climate of 1970 was sexually explicit, but if parents followed the mandate in Proverbs 22:6 to "train up a child in the way he should go" then that child was guaranteed to "not depart from it."[122] Worth placed primary responsibility with parents, but her wording was peculiar: "the primary responsibility in sex education rests with parents who by their own example demonstrate the joy of the marriage relationship." Were parents simply supposed to be an example of a healthy sexual relationship, or were they supposed to talk with their children about sex? It was unclear. She believed that the churches "should supplement the work of the home by presenting to parents the biblical plan of sex and marriage," with the biblical plan using the scripture quoted above. Finally, she acknowledged that some public schools taught sex education and encouraged parents to "concern" themselves "with who does the teaching and what is taught" and ensured that "moral restraint" was taught.[123] On the surface, this

---

121 Mrs. Philip E. Worth, "Sex Education—Whose Responsibility?" *Good News* (January–March 1970): 45.
122 Worth, "Sex Education," 46.
123 Worth, 46.

does not seem an unreasonable request, but given her argument for only the biblical view of sex and marriage to be discussed, it is plausible that any other instruction, including scientific, was unacceptable.

The first place that evangelicals sought an official voice within the ranks of United Methodist administration was on the Board of Education. After a few meetings with the editors of church school curricula, in an effort to include the evangelical voice in its publications, they published a new series for children called "Exploring the Bible." Unhappy with this, Charles Keysor, Riley Case, and Diane Knippers produced *We Believe*, a Good News–sponsored and evangelical curriculum for confirmation. In the early 1980s, the organization began its own publishing house, Bristol House (now called Seedbed), which as of November 2016, does not advertise a curriculum for sex education.[124] As Case argued, "frustration over church school curriculum, more than over any other concern, basically launched the Good News movement."[125]

Up to now, Methodists had dealt with sexuality rather politely. Methodists in the administrative ranks observed the world around them and made theological adjustments accordingly. In many cases, they listened to clergy and annual conferences, such as the 1930s requests for courses on preparation for marriage. Finally, in the 1960s, Methodists heard the cries for an honest and frank new look at sexuality, and they directed the denomination in experimentation with the new morality through *Sex and the Whole Person*. While evangelical Methodists were not fond of these steps, prior to 1967, they acquiesced and continued to silently preach a different message in their local context, because they did not want to create dissent. A few leaders spoke up but were too militant to garner any substantial following or influence. However, desiring to have a balanced administration that honored both liberal and evangelical theology, Good News unknowingly and perhaps unintentionally created a deep division in United Methodism over sexuality.

---

124 Based on search result: accessed 1/23/2017, http://store.seedbed.com/search?type=product&q=sex. Instead, three Seedbed resources that discuss sexuality (and which, in my view, are highly biased) are: Christopher West's *Cultural Shifts in Sexuality* (April 27, 2016), which gives West's view of sexual changes in the mid-twentieth century and seems to argue against contraception; Karen Booth's *Forgetting How to Blush: United Methodism's Compromise with the Sexual Revolution* (2012), which is her particular viewpoint and historically inaccurate, is not shy to cite Wikipedia for definitions of words such as *pornography*; and Mark Ongley's *Into the Light: Healing Sexuality in Today's Church* (2016), which seeks to offer healing for "sexual brokenness" on everything from "homosexuality" to "infidelity, sexual abuse, incest, emotional adultery, and sexual addiction."

125 Case, *Evangelical and Methodist*, 47.

CONCLUSION

This chapter shows that sex education was included in Good News's frustration over church school curricula. The philosophy of the Board of Education, through courses like *Sex and the Whole Person,* was radical for a denomination in the early 1960s. It was radical to teach psychology and physiology alongside Christian morality, and it was radical to hope that by using these guidelines "each individual" would "weigh all of the facts involved and make his [or her] own decision about his [or her] sex."[126] With parents involved in the courses, parents rediscovered their sexual selves, some of whom may have come to accept their own latent homosexuality. The administrative levels of the denomination witnessed cultural change, and the church was impotent to stop it. The best Methodist clergy could do was to be a guide and provide a small, positive influence in the way sexuality was approached. The dichotomy between the new morality, as advocated by some Methodists, and the sexual ethic of Good News, which argued that the Bible was the only true guide, could not be starker.

With the debate over sex education and the new morality, a disjuncture between Methodists was established. Was it okay for Christians to be autonomous over their own sexuality, or was the Bible the only source for answers about one's sexual self? The answer to this question is grounded in theology. Progressive Methodists tend to use the Bible as a guide, one of many sources of authority that can provide adequate answers, but one that is always considered as part of a specific historical context. They believe that the best way to know God is to know one's self, and this includes one's sexual self; and the best way to better society is by breaking down barriers that prevent others from truly knowing and expressing themselves. Evangelical-leaning Methodists tend to use the Bible as *the* answer, an infallible resource that provides an answer to any question. They believe that the best way to know God is to turn to the Scriptures, and the best way to better society is to the spread the Word of God to others. The different answers to this question created the United Methodist fissure that led to the formation of the Good News Movement and its increasing popularity across the last third of the twentieth century. As this book turns toward abortion and homosexuality, other political caucus groups join the Good News Movement in either collaboration or confrontation; and the way that The United Methodist Church approaches sexuality would never be the same again.

---

126 Vance, "Sex Education for United Methodist Youth."

4

AMERICAN METHODISM AND THE POLITICS OF ABORTION

I n May 1967, twenty-one Protestant ministers and Reformed Jewish rabbis serving New York City organized the Clergymen's Consultation Service on Abortion (CCSA) in order to counsel women and refer those wanting an abortion to reputable physicians willing to perform the operation. At this time in New York, and most other states, abortion was legal only if pregnancy threatened the physical life of the mother. The CCSA recognized that women whose lives were not threatened by their pregnancy might also need an abortion, and they sought to provide these women with safe alternatives to "back alley" or self-abortions. Their mission statement claimed that "although there may be embryo life in the fetus, there is no living child upon whom the crime of murder can be committed." It continued: "Confronted with a difficult decision and means of implementing it, women today are forced by ignorance, misinformation, and desperation into courses of action that require humane concern on the part of religious leaders." Of the twenty-one ministers and rabbis offering their referral and counseling services, six were Methodist.[1] The United Methodist support of abortion continues; however, it has become increasingly less permissive and more restrictive, adding to the growing dissention on matters of sexuality.

This chapter will begin with a history of the abortion debate in American politics and society, and then turn toward a discussion of abortion within the Methodist Church and within the newly formed United Methodist Church (UMC). Chronologically, the chapter will focus on 1964–1980 for abortion in American society, and through 1992 for abortion within The UMC.

---

1   Rev. Lee H. Ball of Methodist Federation for Social Action, Inc; Rev. Robert W. Howard, Christ United Methodist Church; Rev. Charles W. Lee, Bushwick Avenue Methodist Church; Rev. Finley Schaef, Washington Square Methodist Church; Rev. Max A. Schwindt, Middle Village Methodist Church; and Rev. Anthony Shipley, Union Methodist Church.

The chapter will argue that the debate within The UMC is parallel to that of American politics due to the increasing influence of both the New Christian Right in American politics and evangelical Methodists in the denomination. It will also argue that within the denomination, the formation of political caucus groups further distanced evangelical Methodists from the administrative efforts of the denomination, specifically, the General Board of Church and Society. This dissention created political extremes and left a large portion of the denomination, largely those who do not overtly advocate for political, social, or theological causes, without a voice.

Unlike the rights and status of LGBTQ persons (which will be discussed in the next chapter), abortion was not advocated solely by political caucus groups. Instead, political caucus groups—such as Good News and Lifewatch, which viewed abortion as a theological issue; and the United Methodist General Board of Church and Society (GBCS), an official general agency of the denomination, which viewed abortion as a social justice issue—advocated for or against abortion rights. In accordance with the new morality, all sexual (and other) decisions, including whether or not to have an abortion, were to be decided according to personal reflection and experience, without constraint or rules. The denomination originally took a progressive, even radical, stance on abortion, one that received pushback from evangelical Methodists, and abortion continued to be a subject of discussion through the most recent General Conference of 2016.

HISTORY OF ABORTION IN AMERICA, 1964–1980

Daniel K. Williams's *Defenders of the Unborn: The Pro-Life Movement before Roe v. Wade* provides an intellectual and political history of the pro-life movement. He argues that the pro-life movement began earlier than American historians typically argue. He places its origins in the rights-based rhetoric of New Deal liberalism and its expansion of the welfare state. Williams successfully argues that early pro-life advocates were not necessarily conservative or Republican but were in fact liberal Democrats. He concludes with a discussion of how pro-life rhetoric, when combined with the Religious Right, aligned with the Republican Party and promoted evangelicalism at the federal level. The problem with Williams's line of reasoning is, however, that the timeline goes back further, to the 1870s and anti-vice efforts that were actually an early form of pro-life rhetoric.

In *All in the Family*, Robert O. Self focuses on abortion in chapter 5, "Bodies on Trial: The Politics of Reproduction." In this chapter, he contends that the feminist reconstruction of abortion rights cast women's bodies into "the place where the intimate and personal became the legal and public, where the personal became the political" which, in order to have mass appeal, was changed in the mid-1970s to "pro-choice."[2] The problem with Self's book is that it lacks an analysis of the pro-life movement. This, in turn, would support his argument that pro-choice appealed to masses and pro-life did not.

Mary Ziegler, in *After* Roe: *The Lost History of the Abortion Debate*, argues that *Roe v. Wade* did not create the vast divide in the abortion debate that many contemporaries believe. While *Roe* changed the location of the abortion debate, moving it from the public sphere to the courts, the abortion debate was divisive prior to *Roe*. However, there is some problem with not crediting *Roe* for causing deeper divides in the abortion debate, as it forced states that were not ready to liberalize abortion laws to do so. This arguably interrupted the progress that was made state by state and created a new politicization of Supreme Court appointments that arguably would not have happened without *Roe*.

Donald T. Critchlow, in *Intended Consequences: Birth Control, Abortion, and the Federal Government in Modern America*, argues that overpopulation was the original basis for the legalization of both birth control and abortion as part of a federal program to expand the welfare state. Focusing on family planning, Critchlow provides a non-rights explanation of how abortion gained support.

Finally, Tom Davis's *Sacred Work: Planned Parenthood and Its Clergy Alliances* provides a wealth of information about how liberal Protestant clergy advanced not only the birth-control movement but also the abortion rights movement. He provides helpful insights into the Clergy Consultation on Abortion to better understand how clergy helped women gain abortions prior to *Roe*.

With the help of these books, this chapter will sketch the history of the abortion debate in America, beginning with a discussion of the social and political movements and then proceeding to a religious discussion of abortion.

ABORTION AT THE TURN OF THE TWENTIETH CENTURY

The American medical profession was the first to disagree with the legal status of abortion in the 1850s. In early American society, abortions were sought by

2   Self, *All in the Family*, 134.

mostly unmarried women who had no intention to marry the father. After the 1840s, abortions increased slightly due to a new awareness of the medical procedure and the availability of herbal abortifacients and their advertisements in mass periodicals. In this era, abortion was, according to one doctor, "democraticizing." It was a viable option for "the married and the unmarried; the rich and the poor; the learned and the unlearned."[3] These abortions were conducted prior to quickening, the time when a mother first feels fetal movement, typically between sixteen and twenty-four weeks.

Abortion, as a controversial procedure, was rarely discussed publicly prior to 1859, and Protestant ministers made no public proclamations against the procedure. Denominational periodicals discussed abortion twice prior to 1859, with those two instances citing criminal cases for botched abortion procedures. American historians agree that "no scholars have yet uncovered a single instance of a Protestant clergyman denouncing abortion or advocating tighter laws between 1776 and 1857."[4] Even the Catholic Church rarely discussed the issue in American society prior to 1859, for a few different reasons. First, the Catholic Church, at the time, believed that abortion prior to quickening was less of a sin than abortion performed after quickening. Second, by the 1850s, Catholics were only 5.3 percent of the United States population, and thus were able to teach about the sin of abortion in less public ways. Third, the Catholic Church most likely made their stance on abortion known through private means: sermons, confessionals, penance, and other instructional tools.[5]

Abortion entered the public stage in the late 1850s for two reasons, both stemming from the professionalization of medicine. Until the mid-nineteenth century, midwives were the primary authority on all matters regarding pregnancy. With an increase in scientific and medical knowledge about women's reproductive systems and embryonic development, medical doctors made new conclusions regarding the stages of pregnancy, which undermined the authority the midwives. One of these conclusions stated that "life" existed prior to quickening. Furthermore, in 1859, professional medical doctors, via the American Medical Association (AMA), claimed that abortion was the "unwarrantable destruction of

---

3   Mark A. Smith, *Secular Faith: How Culture Has Trumped Religion in American Politics* (Chicago, IL: University of Chicago Press, 2015). 143–44.
4   Smith, 144.
5   Smith, 145–46.

human life" and unsafe for women.[6] When combined with an increase in urbanization, "vice," immigration, and the anti-obscenity movement led by Anthony Comstock, it is understandable that abortion was outlawed relatively easily. As a result of the AMA's efforts, after 1860, abortion was outlawed throughout the United States except for *therapeutic abortion* or if there was a physical threat to the mother's life.[7] Women and practitioners who sought or performed an abortion for any other reason were subject to criminal punishment. With the passage of the Comstock Act in 1873, abortifacients and the surgical procedure itself could no longer be discussed or advertised in print. Abortion, therefore, went from mostly legal to mostly illegal within the short span of fourteen years.

Those who sought to ban abortion, like Comstock and the AMA, turned to clergy for support. Catholic clergy were ready and willing to make public their private statements against abortion; and in 1869, Pope Pius IX declared that all abortion was equally sinful, prior to quickening or not.[8] Protestants were less willing to respond publicly because Scripture was unclear on abortion. Based in *sola Scriptura*, the Protestant faith did not have a clear answer or position on abortion.[9] The only Protestant denomination to take a stance against abortion was the Presbyterian Church in the United States of America (Old School Presbyterians), which in 1869 declared that "the destruction by parents of their own offspring, before birth, [is] a crime against God and against nature."[10]

ABORTION IN MID-TWENTIETH-CENTURY AMERICA

Legal prohibitions did not mean that women no longer sought abortions. Similar to the ban on contraception, it simply made the procedure accessible to mostly white women of privileged economic means. Private clinics and liberal physicians stretched the meaning of "threat to a woman's physical health" and performed the operation in a safe environment (if the woman could afford it) through the 1940s. Historian Tom Davis argues, "Abortion in the fifties was invisible, unspeakable, and ubiquitous."[11] As of the 1950s, medical procedures were performed more often in hospitals and no longer in small private clinics,

---

6   Smith, 149.
7   Davis, *Sacred Work*, 123.
8   Smith, *Secular Faith*, 151.
9   Smith, 157–67.
10 Smith, 150.
11 Davis, *Sacred Work*, 122.

meaning that the decision was no longer that of the doctor. Seeking to limit the number of abortions performed in order to avoid the label "abortion mill," hospital boards created therapeutic abortion committees who decided whether or not the life of the mother was truly at risk. Along with the emotional distress and social embarrassment of seeking an abortion, in the 1950s, women were subjected to an interrogation as to why they needed an abortion. For example, one committee member remarked, "Now that she has had her fun, she wants us to launder her dirty underwear. From my standpoint, she can sweat this one out."[12] Remarks such as this discouraged women from seeking the legal, safe option and led to an increase in self-abortions or "back alley" abortions, often performed in a non-hospital, non-clinical, unsanitary environment. Many of those who sat on abortion committees viewed women who sought abortions as lesser, as women who were trying to avoid motherhood without taking responsibility for their prior actions. Under the auspices of hospitals committees, the number of safe, legal abortions performed in the 1950s was less than one-third the number performed in previous years. Postwar America also saw an increase in the number of persons prosecuted for performing illegal abortions, or those performed for any reason other than the physical threat to the mother. The number of women treated for complications from illegal abortions in 1939 was around one thousand; by 1959, it had increased to three thousand, and by 1962 to five thousand.[13] As a result, women sought less safe means; they either traveled abroad to seek the operation or attempted abortion themselves.[14] Self argues that "alongside the Lavender Scare and other wartime and Cold War efforts to guard domestic normalcy, the mid-century resurgence of a hallowed, and anxious, vision of motherhood drove abortion underground" by the 1950s.[15]

In the context of postwar America, with veterans coming home and women leaving their wartime employment, societal pressure forced many women back into the domestic sphere. Americans wanted prewar and pre-Depression life to return, and the fastest way to guarantee "normalcy" was to send women

---

12 As quoted in Davis, 74–75.
13 Davis, 123.
14 Davis, 72–75.
15 Self, *All in the Family*, 139; Smith, *Secular Faith*, 149–52; Mary Ziegler, *After Roe: The Lost History of the Abortion Debate* (Cambridge, MA: Harvard University Press, 2015), 4–5. Note: The "Lavender Scare" was a period of purging suspected homosexual persons from federal employment, resulting in thousands of layoffs in the 1950s.

home to be mothers.[16] In order to provide women with safe alternatives to multiple pregnancies, the American Law Institute (ALI) called for the legalization of abortion in the case of rape, incest, fetal deformity, or threats to the physical or mental health of the mother in 1959. With the threat of overpopulation, the increased popularity of birth control, the women's rights movement, and the sexual revolution, ALI began the fight to expand legal the definition of therapeutic abortion at the state level.[17]

The threat of overpopulation set the stage for the abortion debate by helping birth control become a norm in American society and marriage by the 1950s. Mary Ziegler argues that it was solely the threat of overpopulation that allowed religious leaders to favor birth control, an argument that is too narrow and leaves out the vast changes in marital life and sexuality that also contributed to its acceptance.[18] However, the threat of overpopulation allowed ministers to frame the use of birth control as a philanthropic measure. Overpopulation was viewed as hurting the impoverished developing countries the most by limiting access to food, housing, and health care. American politicians framed overpopulation as a threat to national security for these same reasons and feared that it would spread Communism. Therefore, any means to prevent overpopulation, including the use of artificial contraception, was moral and patriotic.[19]

World War II exposed the consequences—political, social, and economic instability—of what could happen if the population increased in certain areas. In order for American democracy to spread around the world, the population must be controlled. Since it was originally an international concern, John D. Rockefeller III worked with social scientists, demographers, and contraceptive researchers to find the best technology to limit population growth worldwide through education and access. In the 1960s, the population movement turned to domestic concerns. Combating overpopulation through family planning was an official federal domestic program from the Kennedy administration through the Nixon administration; in fact, it received bipartisan support as a means to

---

16   Davis, *Sacred Work*, 73.
17   Ziegler, *After Roe*, 6; Self, *All in the Family*, 139–40; Williams, *Defenders of the Unborn*, 64; Smith, *Secular Faith*, 152.
18   See chapters 1 and 2 of this book for this argument.
19   Ziegler, *After* Roe, 5.

control welfare costs.[20] The height of "family planning," the euphemistic phrase to discuss contraception and abortion at the federal government level, was 1964–1974, according to Donald T. Critchlow, historian and author of *Intended Consequences.* Critchlow uses these ten years to argue that those who sought to control the population at home and abroad did so through the limited means of family planning, an indirect solution, as he argues, that did not address larger social concerns of "social inequality, wealth and income redistribution, racism, and imperialism."[21] He argues that the intended efforts to curtail world population through family planning and the use of contraception were successful because most societies were ready to accept the use of contraception, but the efforts ultimately failed because reducing the population did not also reduce welfare, poverty, or out-of-wedlock births.[22]

American federal efforts for family planning failed as soon as moral arguments surrounding abortion and women's rights entered the debate. Under Nixon, a Committee on Population Growth and the American Future (CPGAF) was established to research and determine the best means to reduce domestic population. Led by John D. Rockefeller III, this committee was divided internally over two issues: (1) Some members preferred coerced sterilization as a means of reducing population, putting the status of the whole nation over the reproductive rights of individuals; others preferred voluntary sterilization, offering it only to those who requested it as a means of permanent contraception. (2) Should abortion be included as an effective means of population control? The first issue lost popularity quickly in light of the civil rights movement and the fact that African American and lower-income women were forcefully sterilized more than white middle-class women, and often without their knowledge and against their request.[23] The second issue, abortion, imploded the bipartisan support of family planning. The CPGAF released its findings in a divided report in 1971. The majority believed that abortion should be considered a means for population control in the instance that prior contraception had failed. It called for the liberalization of American abortion laws to allow women to have an abortion at any point during their pregnancy and granted minors

---

20 Critchlow, *Intended Consequences*, 13–14, 88.
21 Critchlow, 16.
22 Critchlow, 11.
23 Critchlow, 157–64.

access to contraception (a right that only married persons enjoyed in 1971). The minority opinion held that legalized abortion would create a society that was sexually permissive, an argument that evangelicals would later use to combat abortion rights. In light of forced sterilizations, they feared that legalized abortion would further target African Americans and lower-income persons. Finally, legalizing abortion, in their eyes, would not address the larger concerns of unemployment, housing, poverty, and hunger. Nixon, hoping to be reelected in 1972 by earning the Catholic vote, rejected the findings of the majority report due to its endorsement of abortion legalization. In contrast, the National Council of Churches endorsed the majority report in 1972; this decision will be discussed in a later section.[24]

To put Nixon's decision in context, abortion legalization occurred at the state level, beginning in 1964, and against the wishes of a majority of Catholic leaders. State legalization was due not to population concerns to the fact that women had abortions despite their legal status. As has been mentioned, women had sought illegal abortions since the 1870s through any means necessary. By the 1960s, the estimated number of illegal abortions performed each year was just under one million.

One woman's story gained intense media coverage and convinced some Americans that abortion was necessary in cases other than a threat to the mother. Sherri Finkbine, a mother of four, took headache pills that contained thalidomide. While banned in America, the drug caused horrific birth defects in Europe. Panicked, Finkbine sought an abortion and informed the media about the drug's complications in order to inform other women who might have also taken the headache pill. Due to the popularity of the story and worry about legal implications, Finkbine's abortion was denied by the hospital committee. As a last resort, Finkbine flew to Switzerland to have an abortion, and the media followed her there. Most historians agree that Sherri Finkbine's story brought abortion out of the legalistic and medical fields and into the suburban home. Davis states, "Until this saga, the media represented a woman seeking an abortion as furtive, unmarried, possibly a prostitute, or of otherwise dubious character. But Sherri Finkbine was the perfect suburban mother with four small children." Media coverage of her story made abortion the topic of the dinner

---

24 Critchlow, 165–70.

table, and many believed that the ordeal the Finkbines had to endure was not only "outdated" but "cruel."[25]

THE FIGHT FOR AND AGAINST ABORTION RIGHTS

In order to care for these women and ensure that they received safe abortions, and to ensure that children were born into welcoming and loving homes, organizations such as the American Law Institute (1959) and the American Medical Association (1965) began to fight for abortion liberalization. State discussions of liberalization originated in California in 1966, but Colorado was the first state to expand therapeutic abortion in 1967. Following suit, California and North Carolina (1967), Georgia and Maryland (1968), Arkansas (1969), South Carolina and Virginia (1970), and Delaware, Oregon, New Mexico, and Kansas (1971) expanded the legal definition of therapeutic abortion, either including or excluding fetal deformity.[26] At the time, those against abortion, who called themselves "pro-lifers," holding to the idea that life begins at conception, were neither exclusively Republican nor Democrat. Most pro-life supporters were Catholics who still voted Democrat in the late 1960s due to the party's support of an expanded welfare state and civil rights. In fact, a November 1969 Gallup poll revealed more Republicans than Democrats (46 percent to 35 percent) favored elective abortion during the first trimester of pregnancy.[27]

Most abortions (approximately 91 percent) were performed for mental health reasons, proving that doctors expanded the definition of physical health to allow for abortion. However, therapeutic abortions still placed the final decision in the hands of hospital boards, which meant that the same case could have different results depending on the hospital and its board. However, legal therapeutic abortion did not decrease the number of illegal abortions performed each year, and thus it was not a solution to a still-present problem, the danger of self-abortions and back-alley abortions.[28] In 1969, a California Supreme Court case, *People v. Belous*, found that the California abortion law was unconstitutional due to the vagueness of the phrase "necessary to preserve a woman's life." Did this legalize abortion for *present* physical harm or *potential*

25 Davis, *Sacred Work*, 124–25.
26 Williams, *Defenders of the Unborn*, 82–84, 100.
27 Williams, 100–101.
28 Self, *All in the Family*, 143.

physical harm (a threat that all pregnancies carry)? The court defined poten-tial physical harm as enough to warrant an abortion, and thus women had an overall right to abortion. Prior to *Belous,* hospitals in California approved 3,775 abortion cases in 1967, for reasons of mental or physical health; in 1971, after *Belous*, 117,000 abortions were performed; and, in 1972, 160,000 abortions were performed for reasons of mental or physical health.[29]

As more and more therapeutic abortion laws were determined to not solve the problem of dangerous illegal abortions, states argued for the repeal of all laws and the removal of abortion from the criminal code. In 1969, the National Association for Repeal of Abortion Laws (NARAL) organized and joined the calls of the Society for Humane Abortion and the National Women's Organization to repeal all abortion laws, allowing the decision to be solely between a woman and her doctor, without interference, regulations, or criminal punishment.[30] New York was the first state to remove all abortion laws, allowing for elective abortion until the twenty-fourth week of pregnancy (1970). With no residency requirement, 60 percent of the two hundred thousand abortions performed in the first fifteen months of the law were for out-of-state women. Washington, Maryland, and Colorado followed suit.[31] According to a Harris poll, in 1970, 40 percent of Americans wanted to repeal all abortion laws, and 41 percent be-lieved that abortion killed a human being. Thus, by 1970, prior to *Roe v. Wade*, Americans were highly divided on abortion.[32]

In *After* Roe*: The Lost History of the Abortion Debate*, historian Mary Ziegler examines the decades surrounding *Roe v. Wade* and argues that a divide on the morality and legality of abortion was already in existence prior to *Roe*, as the statistics support, and would have continued to become more divisive without *Roe*. She argues that *Roe* is ascribed more meaning than it truly holds in Amer-ican history, for the debate would have become politicized and polarized with-out the Supreme Court's ruling.[33] Prior to *Roe*, pro-life advocates were mainly Catholic Democrats who focused on expanding the welfare state in order to

---

29 Williams, *Defenders of the Unborn*, 116–18.
30 Williams, 105–8.
31 Williams, 124–30.
32 Williams, 131–32. The religious breakdown of these numbers will be discussed in a different section but are worth mentioning here: 49 percent of Protestants, 71 percent of Jews, and 36 percent of Catholics supported full repeal of abortion laws.
33 Ziegler, *After Roe*, xv.

better society by uplifting the impoverished and securing civil rights for all. They used this rhetoric to make a pro-life argument: the state had a responsibility to protect "the rights of a defenseless minority (in this case, the unborn)."[34] Early pro-life advocates, especially women, believed that instead of focusing on how to eliminate a pregnancy, society needed to focus on more informed sex education, increasing the availability of contraception, and making pregnancy less of a burden for all women through equal pay, better day-care options, parental leave, and adoption services.[35]

By the 1970s, this liberal pro-life rhetoric gave way to a pro-life argument that was more conservative and that called abortion "murder." In 1965, *Life* magazine published Lennart Nilsson's color photos of embryonic and fetal development from conception through birth, images that shocked and amazed Americans. "The pictures created a sensation; eight million copies of the magazine were sold within four days of its release." Pro-lifers believed they now had proof that a fetus was "human," as it had eyes, fingers, and toes as early as eight weeks. Abortion rights activists, they argued, sought to kill a human baby not a "cellular growth." After these images, pro-life advocates based their arguments on saving human life instead of making pregnancy less of a burden.[36] Five years later, after the images in *Life* magazine failed to change the minds of all Americans, pro-life advocates used their own, more graphic images of aborted fetuses and abortion procedures to convince Americans of what they believed to be the brutality of abortion and the destruction of human life. Pro-life organizations, like the National Right to Life Committee, mailed postcards of aborted fetuses to elected politicians, asking them to vote against liberalized abortion laws.[37] The pro-life movement now focused on convincing Americans that abortion was murder, a move that silenced pro-life liberal women who wanted to advocate for equal pay, women's rights in the workplace, day care, contraception, and adoption as alternatives to abortion.[38] By 1973, the new pro-life movement unsuccessfully brought a Human Life Amendment (HLA), which sought to add the "unborn" to the list of those protected by the Fourteenth Amendment,

34 Williams, *Defenders of the Unborn*, 4.
35 Williams, 7, 113.
36 Williams, 69.
37 Williams, 133.
38 Williams, 151–52.

to the floor of Congress and would continue its efforts to pass the HLA through the early 2000s.[39]

On the other side of the debate, the abortion rights movement was gaining ground in many states. As mentioned previously, four states (New York, Washington, Maryland, and Colorado) repealed all abortion laws up to twenty-four weeks in 1970, and fourteen other states relaxed their abortion laws.[40] Robert O. Self argues that 1969 was a turning point for abortion rhetoric. Prior to 1969, abortion rights rhetoric focused on abortion as a public health measure. As a medical procedure, the state, they believed, should not interfere with this medical decision; it should remain between the patient and her doctor. As the 1960s progressed, abortion became part of the civil rights movement: no woman should be required by law to have a child if she does not desire one. It was also alarmingly clear to activists that abortion was a racial justice issue; white women of the middle and upper classes could afford access to safe abortions, whether legal or not, whereas other women were left with more dangerous options.[41]

Women entered the male-dominated debate over the course of the 1960s and began to argue that women would never be fully equal to men without full control of their reproductive lives. According to Self, this idea shocked many Americans, as it "posited women as prior to, even outside, the family" and was "an unacceptable breach of how they understood womanhood."[42] Abortion, for more socially conservative persons, contradicted the American notion of family by giving women a constitutional right to have an identity outside of motherhood and by casting motherhood as a burden. In order to increase support for abortion rights, women needed a platform that was more palatable for the American public at large.

In 1965, the Supreme Court's ruling in *Griswold v. Connecticut* legalized all contraception for married couples; in 1972, *Eisenstadt v. Baird* legalized all contraception for unmarried persons.[43] These two decisions were based on a person's right to privacy. Married couples and unmarried persons should have access to contraception to uphold their right to a private sexual life. Women also had the medical right to private discussions with a doctor who prescribed

---

39 Williams, 212–16.
40 Smith, *Secular Faith*, 154.
41 Williams, *Defenders of the Unborn*, 52, 62–63.
42 Self, *All in the Family*, 137.
43 Self, 141; Ziegler, *After* Roe, 10; Williams, *Defenders of the Unborn*, 200.

contraception. Was abortion included as part of this medical right? Harriet Pipel, member of President John F. Kennedy's Commission on the Status of Women, argued that *Griswold* extended the right of privacy to include abortion. In 1973, the right to privacy between a woman and her physician was expanded to include abortion in the Supreme Court ruling *Roe v. Wade*. Jane Roe (whose real name was Norma McCorvey) had no legal access to abortion in Texas and sought one in Mexico. In 1970, she sued Henry Wade, the Dall County district attorney, for violation of her "right to privacy or liberty in matters relating to marriage, family, and sex," the right guaranteed her by *Griswold*. Her suit was taken to the Supreme Court in 1972, and decided in her favor in January 1973, by a 7–2 vote. The Supreme Court granted her, and other women, a constitutional right to have an abortion based on the right to privacy. *Roe* did have restrictions. During the first trimester, the decision to have an abortion was solely between a woman and her physician. The state was allowed to safeguard a woman's health and allow for abortions under certain conditions during the second trimester. During the third trimester, the state was allowed to interfere to protect fetal life.[44]

In the social context of *Roe*, the sexual revolution was at its peak. *Deep Throat* was playing in theaters across America. *Penthouse* had replaced the less racy *Playboy* as the preferred "gentleman's magazine." The gay liberation movement and women's movement were at their peak. Eighty-five percent of college seniors believed that there was nothing wrong with premarital sex. Abortions sought by unmarried women accounted for a healthy majority (two-thirds) of all abortion procedures. A 1972 Gallup poll showed that 54 percent of Americans believed abortion was a decision to be made by a woman and her physician alone (40 percent believed this three years prior). And by 1972, contraception was legally accessible to married and unmarried persons. As Williams suggests, "the sexual revolution, environmentalism, and feminism were all chipping away at support for the pro-life cause."[45] *Roe*, many believed, was the final blow to the pro-life movement.

Immediately after the decision, abortion clinics opened across the country. In 1973, 750,000 legal abortions were performed; these numbers increased to over one million in 1975, and one and a half million by 1980. Two states, North

---

44 Ziegler, *After* Roe, 11.
45 Williams, *Defenders of the Unborn*, 180–82.

Dakota and Louisiana, managed to block abortions from occurring within their borders during 1973. Mississippi, Utah, and West Virginia prevented abortions, except in life-threatening cases for the mother, in 1973. After 1973, these states were forced to allow abortion to occur. Pro-lifers—who originally believed that state resistance to *Roe* would keep access to abortion from increasing—failed to prevent abortions from occurring. By March 1973, abortion was increasingly becoming more affordable, as it was covered under maternity care by insurance companies and was considered a tax-deductible expense.[46] The lax attitude many Americans had toward abortion pushed some Americans, mainly evangelicals and liberal pro-life advocates, fully into the conservative pro-life movement, and reinvigorated the movement toward political action.

After *Roe*, the pro-life movement fought at both the federal and state levels. At the federal level, advocates focused on passing amendments to restrict or undo *Roe*, and increasingly on the appointment of pro-life Supreme Court Justices. One week after *Roe*, Rep. Lawrence Hogan of Maryland and Rep. Jesse Helms of North Carolina introduced the Human Life Amendment (HLA) to both the House and Senate, respectively. The HLA was a constitutional amendment to protect the unborn under the Fourteenth Amendment. They both failed but were repeatedly used as a barometer to judge where politicians and potential Supreme Court Justices stood on abortion.[47] By the end of 1976, more than fifty constitutional amendments to ban abortion were introduced into Congress. One, the Hyde Amendment, was passed and restricted federal funding of abortion through Medicaid or Title X programs.[48]

Since 1983, the Supreme Court has become a partisan branch of government. Starting with Reagan's appointment of Sandra Day O'Connor, based on her critique of *Roe* and its trimester system, justice nominees have had their abortion records scrutinized to uncover whether or not they support *Roe*. Between 1973 and 1993, the Supreme Court issued twenty major decisions concerning abortion, casting the Supreme Court as a newly partisan branch of government. In these rulings, they have preserved the basis of a woman's constitutional right to choose an abortion, but they have also let states restrict abortion access.[49]

---

46 Williams, 211–12.
47 Williams, 213–15.
48 Critchlow, *Intended Consequences*, 201–2. Of the 1.1 million abortions performed, 260,000 were paid for through Medicaid or Title X.
49 Critchlow, 201; Ziegler, *After* Roe, 224.

And it was here, at the state level, that pro-life advocates focused on restricting abortion access. By 1975, approximately 449 abortion-related bills were introduced into state legislatures, and 58 of those passed. In 1977, 80 percent of public and 70 percent of private hospitals still refused to perform abortions despite *Roe*. By 1990, thirty-eight states had strict enough laws to prevent women from practicing their constitutional right to an abortion.[50]

Since Nixon's 1972 rejection of the CPGAF's report, due to its endorsement of abortion, presidential candidates have taken stances for or against abortion in order to court specific voting blocs. In 1972, Nixon, trying to cater to the Democratic Catholics who felt abandoned by the party's concern with women's rights (and not fetal rights), claimed he was pro-life. The 1976 election politicized abortion even more, as both Republican and Democratic official presidential platforms included stances on *Roe,* and a third-party candidate ran on the Right to Life ticket. In 1976, 48 percent of Democrats favored the HLA, with 44 percent opposed to it. The Democratic platform officially supported *Roe* and opposed the HLA. Even though it recognized that both pro-life and pro-choice voices should continue to be heard in the public realm, this stance alienated the 48 percent of its Catholic and conservative constituents, which favored the HLA. The Republican platform did not support the Supreme Court's decision but refused to take an official stance on the HLA.[51]

To combat the rejuvenated pro-life movement, abortion rights advocates again tried to find a platform that all Americans could agree with in support of a woman's right to abortion. They settled on "pro-choice." A choice-based platform argued that *all* women had the right to choose whether or not to reproduce despite class, race, age, or social status. This platform did not put abortion in the context of women's equality to men or discuss women's sexuality directly. Instead it relied on personal autonomy and privacy, ideals with which many Americans agreed. At the end of the 1970s, when the pro-life movement connected abortion to the Equal Rights Amendment, a constitutional amendment that guaranteed equal rights to women, the pro-choice movement avoided any connection between abortion rights and women's equality. Put simply, abortion should be an individual, moral choice for a woman and should not have

---

50 Critchlow, 200–201.
51 Critchlow, 202–3; Williams, *Defenders of the Unborn*, 228–32.

government interference, they claimed.[52] The problem with this argument was that not everyone was guaranteed equal access to abortion without government interference. Some women, mainly those of lower income levels, needed the help of the government to exercise their constitutional right through programs like Medicaid and government-funded access. Thus, by 1981, the pro-choice platform included providing contraception, health care, and child care to all, a platform that should have been familiar to earlier pro-life liberals.[53]

LIBERAL PROTESTANTS, EVANGELICALS, AND ABORTION

Protestants, both evangelical and not, were mostly silent on abortion until the mid-1960s. Young liberal Protestant ministers were the first to break the silence. Influenced by the civil rights movement, these ministers sought to challenge any law that prevented persons from being able to live their full lives as they pleased. They witnessed young women in crisis and believed it "unconscionable that women who had gotten pregnant out of wedlock faced the choice between having their lives ruined by an 'illegitimate' child and risking the dangers of an illegal abortion."[54] In terms of civil rights, they were astonished to learn that more African American and low-income women died from illegal abortions than white middle-class women, who could afford safer alternatives. These ministers concluded that the only course of action that was both socially just and truly Christian was to liberalize abortion laws. The Episcopal Church called for legal therapeutic abortion in 1965, a full two years before abortion was discussed at the state level. The American Baptist Church and United Presbyterian Church followed suit in 1968 and 1970, respectively, calling for the repeal of all abortion laws until the twelfth week of pregnancy. The newly formed United Methodist Church called for abortion "upon request" in 1970, taking a progressive stand with the Universalist Unitarian Church by advocating the repeal of all abortion laws at any point during pregnancy.[55]

Since 1961, women had spoken publicly about their abortions and shared the horrendous scenarios they endured in order to gain an abortion. Pat Maginnis

---

52   Ziegler, *After* Roe, 129–39.
53   Ziegler, 153.
54   Williams, *Defenders of the Unborn*, 65.
55   Williams, 108.

began the Society for Human Abortion in 1961, which, unlike the ALI and AMA, sought the repeal of all abortion laws. She argued that the reform of abortion laws would not give women a full say in what happens to their bodies. Calling abortion a woman's right, Maginnis and her colleagues shared personal stories with the public for the first time. They handed out pamphlets about where to get an abortion, what to say when speaking to doctors, and how to perform self-abortions if necessary. They demanded to be heard at the legislative level and gave an often graphic but moral voice for those who had been punished or turned away. Similar to the way Margaret Sanger's stories proved that women suffered without reproductive rights, Maginnis's efforts helped convince clergy that abortion reform was a moral necessity.[56]

The Clergy Consultation Service on Abortion

Howard Moody was an American Baptist minister in New York City. As a social activist, he tried to help a few women of his congregation gain an abortion, but he did not know where to begin. Wanting to help, he gathered a few other New York City ministers and rabbis at the United Methodist Church on Washington Square and asked women to come and share their stories. Women shared horrific tales of abortions performed without anesthesia while they were wearing a blindfold. Without hesitation, the clergy set to work. They met with a lawyer to determine their legal risks; they met with doctors to learn exactly what happened during an abortion; they hired Arlene Carmen to pose as a pregnant woman in order to find doctors who were respectful of women seeking abortions. On May 22, 1967, the Clergy Consultation Service on Abortion (CCSA) announced their services in a *New York Times* article and proclaimed publicly their willingness to help women find safe abortions as a moral imperative of the Christian faith. All consultations between clergy and women were confidential due to legal protections; therefore, women's identities, desires, and actions remained private, which allowed them to seek counsel without informing their husbands or legal authorities.

The CCSA's statement of purpose argued that current abortion laws caused "severe mental anguish, physical suffering, and unnecessary death of women." As the birth of a child should be "an occasion for genuine celebration" and not "the imposition of a penalty of punishment upon the mother," they believed

---

56   Davis, *Sacred Work*, 125–26.

that current abortions laws were immoral for both mothers and society. Their goal was to reform laws at the state level, to "educate and inform the public to the end that a more liberal abortion law . . . should be enacted," and to "give aid and assistance to all women with problem pregnancies." The statement continued and declared current abortion laws classist and racist; it determined that the fetus was not a living child; and it unashamedly proclaimed that those physicians who performed abortions were "living by the highest standards of religion and of the Hippocratic oath."[57] The CCSA became a popular, albeit unexpected, refuge for women who needed help and guidance. In their first six months of operation, they counseled and helped more than eight hundred women gain access to a safe abortion. The next year they assisted three thousand women, and by 1969, they counseled five thousand women.[58] The CCSA spread across America, eventually becoming a network of almost two thousand clergy and rabbis.[59]

Eventually, the CCSA went beyond assisting women to find safe abortions and began to advocate for the full repeal of abortion laws. Recognizing that liberalized therapeutic abortion laws, like those of California, did not reduce the number of illegal and unsafe abortions performed every year, they believed that the only way to really help women was to repeal all laws. They worked for full repeal in New York, and they won in 1970, when New York was the first state to repeal all abortion laws. After full legalization, they worked with other organizations to establish clinics to meet the high demand for abortion services. The CCSA eventually opened their own clinic, the Center for Reproductive and Sexual Health, and while they did not own the building, it was their sole clinic for referral. It proved that abortions could be safely performed outside of a hospital setting and at a lower cost, $200 as compared to $600. The clinic was open seven days a week, 7:00 a.m.–11:00 p.m., and performed around one hundred abortions each day. In its first thirteen months, there were no maternal fatalities out of the twenty-six thousand abortions performed.[60]

---

57   As quoted in Davis, 129–30.
58   Davis, 131.
59   Davis, 121.
60   Davis, 133–35.

The Religious Coalition for Abortion Rights

After *Roe*, with abortion now legal, the CCSA ceased all efforts to protect the legal right to an abortion. The pro-life movement increased their campaign efforts through legislative means with the help of evangelicals (as discussed below), and thus, in order to maintain the liberal Protestant voice in support of abortion rights, there had to be a new organization. In 1973, under the guidance of The United Methodist Church's General Board of Church and Society and the Women's Division, sixteen Jewish and Christian religious groups gathered together and formed the Religious Coalition for Abortion Rights (RCAR). It was funded by John D. Rockefeller III, who believed that RCAR had a unique voice and helped educate the public on the moral correctness of abortion. RCAR's goal was to ensure that a religious voice was present in the pro-choice movement, and that the pro-life movement would not dominate the moral viewpoint of the abortion debate.[61]

The coalition wrote pamphlets addressing abortion from a religious point of view; they worked to protect abortion clinics from antiabortion rhetoric and blockades; and they were a moral voice in support of abortion for congressional sessions, including statements against the Hyde Amendment.[62] For example, in March 1976, RCAR sent Theresa Hoover—associate general secretary of the Women's Division of the Board of Global Ministries of The United Methodist Church, chairperson of the Racial Justice Commission of the Young Women's Christian Association, and National Sponsor of RCAR—to speak against the Human Life Amendment before the Subcommittee on Civil and Constitutional Rights of the Committee on the Judiciary of the U.S. House of Representatives. She stated that RCAR was founded after it was evident that "there would be continuing efforts by a vocal and determined minority to overturn the Supreme Court decisions," and believed that the various religious views represented within RCAR "gives the Coalition a unique character, the very nature of which explains our presence here today in opposition to any constitutional amendments which would limit abortion rights."[63] She explained to the

---

61 Critchlow, *Intended Consequences*, 197; Rockefeller gave $115,000 to support the work of RCAR between 1973 and 1978.

62 Davis, *Sacred Work*, 145–46.

63 "Statement of the Religious Coalition for Abortion Rights before the Subcommittee on Civil and Constitutional Rights of the Committee of the Judiciary U.S. House of Representatives" (March 24, 1976), Folder: "Religious Coalition for Abortion Rights 1979, Women's Division, 2593-7-6:1, GCAH.

committee that religious groups who held vastly different opinions on when life began and the morality of abortion agreed "that every woman should have the legal choice with respect to abortion, consistent with sound medical practice and in accordance with her conscience and religious beliefs."[64] Using the First Amendment, she asked the committee not to impose upon women the teachings of one religion. She continued:

> It must be emphasized that our opposition to the proposed constitutional amendments stems from the recognition that the question most basic to the abortion debate is the question of when life begins. We believe this to be above all a theological question on which each denomination or faith group must be permitted to establish and follow its own teachings, but *must not* be allowed to impose them through law on society at large.[65]

Emphasizing the fact that a constitutional amendment would prohibit certain denominations from practicing what they believed, she quoted the American Baptist statement, which recognized the freedom of personal conscience in matters of family life, marriage, and sexuality. A constitutional restriction on abortion limited persons' ability to make their own decisions about their sexual life according to their creedal faith. Finally, Hoover appealed to the health of women who needed access to safe, legal abortions in order to have the right to determine their own destiny, and argued that banning abortion would not stop it from occurring, as history had shown.[66] She concluded with a clarification that

> none of our members advocate abortion or consider it an easy solution to a problem pregnancy. Certainly, none consider it a desirable means of birth control. But each is aware that there are circumstances under which abortion may well be the most acceptable among a series of difficult alternatives, and each believes that women should have the full range of choices available to them—including safe, legal abortion.[67]

After each of these statements (and in additional instances not referenced here), Hoover quoted from various denominations' social stances on abortion, family

---

64 "Statement of the Religious Coalition," 2.
65 "Statement of the Religious Coalition," 3, emphasis hers.
66 "Statement of the Religious Coalition," 7.
67 "Statement of the Religious Coalition," 8.

life, and sexuality to support her argument that, while members of RCAR varied according to the morality of abortion, all agreed that it was an important right to maintain. This was, and is, the work of RCAR (now called the Religious Coalition for Reproductive Choice or RCRC). They lobbied to protect abortion rights, educated the public on the religious view of abortion, and spoke the stances of all its member denominations. They recognized that each denomination had a different view of abortion, but they all agreed that the right to a legal, safe abortion was a right worth protecting.

The National Council of Churches

As an umbrella group for mainline Protestants, the National Council of Churches (NCC) endorsed John D. Rockefeller III's CPGAF's report, which recommended abortion as a means for population control. In 1973, shortly after *Roe*, the NCC released "A Study Paper on Abortion," which was written by an NCC task force to establish a Protestant stance on abortion. It recognized that, due to creedal differences, different denominations would hold different opinions on abortion and on *Roe*, but it asked that all of its member denominations take the report seriously and consider the societal situation in which abortion was morally necessary.

The goal of the NCC in terms of abortion was to affirm the sanctity of human life, provide women the opportunity to "live with dignity and equality," increase the chances of women having happy and healthy pregnancies, and construct a supportive climate in which all children are raised. With these goals, the NCC recognized that to meet these objectives certain obstacles had to be overcome. First and foremost, the rights and desires of women had to become center of the conversation. The NCC recognized that throughout history, legal and religious authorities, who historically were only men, dominated the abortion conversation; if the conversation was to change, it needed to hear the voices of women. Other obstacles included improving the quality of medical care for women including pre- and postnatal care, reproductive care in general, and pediatric care; making this quality care affordable for all; providing adequate child-care services for working mothers; granting women equal pay for equal work; improving the standard of care for disabled children and making this care affordable; expanding adoption services; bettering welfare services for low-income families; distributing contraception to all who need it, free of charge if necessary; improving sex education for young boys and girls and continuing this education through high school; and providing women with support to express their sexual selves without being labeled a "temptress."[68]

The NCC called upon Protestant denominations to work together to help society overcome these obstacles through Christian education, dialogue, and advocacy. It concluded that while denominations held varying views of abortion, the NCC believed that "it is imperative to end the *need* for abortion." It called denominations to work together to overcome obstacles so that abortion truly was a last resort when all else has failed:

> Alternatives to abortion must be real if freedom of conscience and responsibility are to be more than rhetoric. This means that society must offer good health care, both pre- and post-natal; day care facilities; homemaker services where needed; maternity and paternity leave; family service centers; and expert counseling services.[69]

It was a Christian's responsibility to maintain the right to abortion as a last resort and to work to remove obstacles that prevented it from being a last resort.

Evangelicals and Abortion

For evangelicals, historian Mark Smith argues, "abortion became and remains a proxy for a range of questions involving sexuality, the family, traditional values, and women's role in the workplace and society."[70] Abortion was connected to women's fight for equal rights, women's fight for reproductive rights, the fight for civil rights, and the sexual revolution, all of which many conservative evangelicals viewed as threats to the traditional American family, as epitomized in the 1950s and discussed previously in this book. However, evangelicals remained silent on abortion until the late 1960s for two reasons: (1) they were suspicious of any stance that was in agreement with Catholicism; and (2) they were unsure of how to view abortion, as Scripture did not address it directly. Most agreed in the 1960s that abortion on demand or the repeal of all abortions laws would encourage promiscuity and extramarital relationships. However, in cases of rape, incest, or risk to the mother, evangelicals believed that abortion should be permissible.

---

68 "A Study Paper on Abortion," National Council of Churches, 1973, 2–4; folder "NCC Task Force on Abortion 1972–1973", administrative records of the Division of General Welfare of the General Board of Church and Society, 1443–4–3:11, GCAH.

69 "A Study Paper on Abortion," 8, emphasis theirs.

70 Smith, *Secular Faith*, 156.

In August 1969, twenty-five evangelical scholars gathered to participate in "A Protestant Symposium on the Control of Human Reproduction." After their gathering, a consensus was released to the public in a document holding the same title as the symposium. The document was divided into three parts: "Theological Basis," "Principles of the Christian Physician," and "Guidelines to Professional Practice." It stated that a sexual relationship was best expressed between two married persons, and while procreation was a major piece of this act, it was not the only purpose for a married sexual relationship.[71] Scripture did not condemn contraception, but it did uphold the sanctity of human life and the command to multiply. Appropriate reasons for the use of contraception included "disease, psychological debility, the number of children already in the family, and financial capability." A physician should determine how one prevented pregnancy. In regard to abortion, those gathered agreed that abortion was necessary and permissible in certain circumstances. It asked the Christian physician to consider two factors when deciding whether or not to perform an abortion:

> 1) The human fetus is not merely a mass of cells or an organic growth. At the most, it is an actual human life or at the least, a potential and developing human life. For this reason the physician with regard for the value and sacredness of human life will exercise great caution in advising an abortion.

> 2) The Christian physician will advise induced abortion only to safeguard greater values sanctioned by Scripture. These values should include individual health, family welfare, and social responsibility. From the moment of birth, the infant is a human being with all the rights which Scripture accords to all human beings; therefore, infanticide under any circumstances must be condemned.[72]

These two statements suggest that the symposium was divided on whether or not the fetus was a human life or only held potential for human life, a conundrum that many evangelicals wrestled with, because they did not have a coherent theology of when human life began. They also allowed for abortion in the case of "family welfare" and "social responsibility," suggesting that the

---

71 "A Protestant Affirmation on the Control of Human Reproduction," *Journal of American Scientific Affiliation: Science in Christian Perspective* (June 1970): 46–47.

72 "A Protestant Affirmation," 46–47.

statements from this 1969 symposium cannot be easily categorized as pro-life. Without a definition of family welfare, one could assume that having too many children, which was a viable reason to use contraception, could also be a viable reason to have an abortion. One could also assume that social responsibility could include a person's need to serve the community in a way that pregnancy might prohibit.[73]

These inferences were confirmed further along in the document when it affirmed therapeutic abortion. It stated that it was the duty of the Christian physician to preserve human life at all costs. The world was a threatening place: "We live in a world pervaded by evil. Human relationships become distorted; unwanted children are born into the world; genetic defects are not uncommon and harmful social conditions abound." It then separated fetal life from human life as a potential threat to family life and stated that, in some circumstances, "when principles conflict, the preservation of fetal life . . . may have to be abandoned in order to maintain full and secure family life." This document placed living family life as a separate and superior entity to fetal life. Recognizing that "unwanted children" can harm the security of these families, this document also supported abortion as a form of contraception when other methods failed. The only negative statement against abortion was that it should not be used for "convenience only or on demand." Based on the prior statements on the sanctity of family life, it is logical to conclude that evangelicals believed that only unmarried women used abortion for convenience or on demand.[74]

Evangelicals in the 1960s were relatively progressive when it came to abortion, agreeing with most of the state legislatures and efforts of some abortion rights organizations that therapeutic abortion was justified and necessary for the preservation of family life. Some evangelicals who did not agree with this or with the official proclamations of their Protestant denominations joined Catholic pro-life organizations like the National Right to Life Committee. *Christianity Today* first discussed abortion in 1966. In a 1968 article, "The Relation of the Soul to the Fetus," it is clear that evangelicals still did not have a consensus on when life began. The author, Paul K. Jewett, examined Scripture, philosophy, and history, trying to find an argument that confirmed when life began. Concluding that human life was dependent on the soul, he tried to decipher

73   "A Protestant Affirmation," 46–47.
74   "A Protestant Affirmation," 46–47.

when the soul entered. He concluded, "It seems that the Christian answer to the control of human reproduction must be found principally in the prevention of conception, rather than in the prevention of birth." He desired that "abortion" remain a "last recourse" because it was "burdened with uncertainty."[75] Evangelicals' liberal stance in the 1960s shifted drastically after 1970, when four states legalized elective abortion.

As mentioned above, in 1970, New York was the first to repeal all abortion laws. It was quickly followed by three other states, and the number of abortions performed increased drastically. In 1970, two-thirds of abortions performed were for unmarried women.[76] As a result, evangelicals put aside their uncertainty and joined the (mostly Catholic) pro-life cause for the purposes of preventing sexual promiscuity. In 1971, Carl F. H. Henry proclaimed, "The connection between easy abortion and sexual promiscuity is obvious." Going a step further, Henry called abortion "murder." Evangelicals began to work with Catholics, and by the end of 1972, 63 percent of Protestant evangelicals opposed abortion legalization. The number jumped to 75 percent if the pool was limited to only those evangelicals who attended church weekly.[77]

Historian Daniel K. Williams argues that Francis Schaeffer, an American evangelical theologian who spent his days in Switzerland, "may have done more than any other person to mobilize evangelicals on behalf of the pro-life cause, [by framing] the abortion issue as part of a broader narrative of national moral decline."[78] Schaeffer created documentaries and movies about *Roe* and morality that depicted legalized abortion as the apex of moral decline, for, to him, it provided evidence that women were sexually promiscuous and wanted to continue to be so without punishment. In 1979, Jerry Falwell joined Schaeffer and announced a campaign against abortion as top priority for the Moral Majority. Williams argued that "by the end of the 1970s, after the gay rights movement, the rising divorce rate, and the explosion of pornography," abortion should be seen as part of "a larger context of moral decline." This led evangelicals to believe that "*Roe* [was] far more disturbing" than they originally imagined.[79] Believing it their Christian duty to bring Christian morality back to the federal

75   Paul K. Jewett, "The Relation of the Soul to the Fetus," *Christianity Today*, 13 (November 1968): 9.
76   Williams, *Defenders of the Unborn*, 182.
77   Williams, 146.
78   Williams, , 237.
79   Williams, , 238.

government, evangelicals looked for political allies, and they found them in the Republican Party.

The Republican Party in 1980 was looking for a victory after their defeat in 1976 to Jimmy Carter. Paul Weyrich, a Catholic and chief architect of the New Right, used the evangelical rhetoric of abortion as a threat to the American family to gain the Democratic Catholic vote and the evangelical vote. According to Ziegler, "The New Right made *Roe* into a symbol of sexual license, women's exit from the home, and the decline of religion."[80] Key to securing the evangelical vote was convincing evangelicals that the Republican Party was the only party that sought to protect traditional family values.

To do this, Weyrich partnered with Phyllis Schlafly and connected abortion to the Equal Rights Amendment (ERA). Schlafly viewed the ERA as demeaning to women by lowering their privileged status, "Why should we lower ourselves to 'equal rights' when we already have the status of special privilege?"[81] Schlafly convinced evangelicals that abortion was directly tied to women's rights and the ERA, and convinced pro-life advocates that women's rights and the ERA would strengthen the abortion rights movement. Schlafly secured the relationship between evangelicals, the New Right, and the pro-life movement, thus cementing the New Christian Right to the Republican platform. The New Right and the New Christian Right joined forces to restore traditional Christian moral values at the federal level. They agreed that abortion and sexual immorality could be eliminated only through a massive pro-family campaign. Falwell declared in a 1980 sermon:

> If we had not gone to sleep for the last thirty years, there could never have been a climate that would have allowed the existence of a Supreme Court that could legalize murder on demand, [and] there could not have been legislation to allow pornography as it exists today. . . . There would not be all of this homosexual explosion today. The problem is that we have been silent too long.[82]

The New Christian Right took over the pro-life movement and rebranded it as a fight to restore Christian morality. Ronald Reagan, the Republican presidential

---

80 Ziegler, *After* Roe, 15.
81 Phyllis Schlafly, "What's Wrong with Equal Rights for Women?" *The Phyllis Schlafly Report* 5, no. 7 (February 1972): sec. 2.
82 As quoted in Williams, *Defenders of the Unborn*, 255.

candidate in 1980, secured the political power of the New Christian Right when he denounced abortion and promised, if elected, to protect fetal rights through the Human Life Amendment.[83]

UNITED METHODISTS AND ABORTION

This section will argue that The United Methodist Church's stance on abortion, in accordance with the new morality, called for the repeal of abortion laws through the 1960s and supported *Roe* after 1973. Evangelical-leaning Methodists insisted that according to Scripture, life began at conception. Thus, as part of the evangelical desire to return to a rules-based morality, which looked to Scripture alone to know morality from immorality, they began an antiabortion campaign. Methodists in the administrative ranks of the denomination, specifically the General Board of Church and Society and the Women's Division, resisted the evangelical stance as much as they could. However, at almost every General Conference since 1972, The UMC's stance on abortion has become more and more restrictive.

The Methodist Church (MC) and the Evangelical United Brethren (EUB), in 1968, made the following statements in their respective *Disciplines* regarding family planning:

> We believe that planned parenthood, practiced with respect for human life, fulfills rather than violates the will of God. It is the duty of each married couple prayerfully and responsibly to seek parenthood, avert it, or defer it, in accordance with the best expression of their Christian love. Families in all parts of the world should have available to them necessary information and medical assistance for birth control through public and private programs. This issue must be seen in reference to the pressing population problem now before the whole world. [84]
>
> The result of a rising birthrate, the decrease of infant mortality, the increase in longevity and improved general health created the increase in world population. To meet this situation, the Church affirms: (1) that the members uphold the highest standards of love and marriage and urgently teach young people to sanctify marital relationships. (2) that the parents assume the responsibility of planning at long range the family they hope to establish and plan wisely the

---

83   Ziegler, *After* Roe, 14–15.
84   "The Family," "Our Declaration of Social Concern," *BOD* (1968), 54.

spacing of children and provide moral guidance and spiritual nurture for all members of the family; and (3) that the married persons regard as ethically and morally right the proper use of methods and techniques, especially approved, for the purpose of achieving planned and responsible parenthood.[85]

The EUB declaration called for essentially the same things as that of the MC. Abortion was not fully addressed in either, but it was clear from these statements that abortion would be a topic of conversation during the 1968 General Conference. Both denominations upheld family planning, defined as the overt attempt to space children using all available medical and scientific techniques. Understanding the climate of the late 1960s, it is not a far stretch to assume that one of these techniques sought by members of both denominations was abortion. Methodist involvement with the CCSA confirms two things: one, some Methodist ministers believed that abortion was a moral necessity, and two, Methodists were trying to live into the new morality, creating space for persons to make their own sexual decisions. With the claims that "planned" and "responsible parenthood" were moral necessities, one can conclude that abortion was included, at least as a last resort.

In 1970, this inference was confirmed when an addendum to the *Discipline* endorsed abortion. In a section entitled "Population Crisis," The UMC claimed that "the population explosion brought on by medical and technological advances in the prolonging of life poses for man an unprecedented threat." Overpopulation brought with it "mass starvation" and "depletion of natural resources," and threatened "rich and poor nations alike." It called the denomination to action and asked that "the church recognize population growth to be a matter of great religious and moral concern." Two of its final requests of the church involved family planning. First, it asked the church to adopt "the small family norm" in order to improve family life for all. Second, all UM hospitals should "take the lead in eliminating those hospital administrative restrictions on voluntary sterilization and abortion which exceed the legal requirements in their respective political jurisdictions."[86] As this chapter has shown, hospital boards often prevented women from obtaining a safe, legal abortion. This

---

85 "Family Life," "Basic Beliefs Regarding Social Issues and Morals Standards of The Evangelical United Brethren Church," *BOD* (1968), 63–64.

86 "Population Crisis," *BOR, 1970 Addendum*, ed. the Program Council (Methodist Publishing House, 1970), 17–18.

pronouncement requested that UM hospitals grant an abortion to all women who wanted one so that families who did not desire more children were not forced to have them. The resolution also called on the federal government to "remove the regulation on abortion from the criminal code, placing it instead under regulations relating to other procedures of standard medical practice. Abortion would be available only upon request of the person most directly concerned."[87] With this additional statement, it is clear that in 1970, The UMC called for the repeal of all abortion laws, leaving the decision to have an abortion between a woman and her doctor alone, a stand that "was approved by an overwhelming majority of the delegates to the General Conference."[88] The statement concluded with an acknowledgment that its requested action was of "a grand scale," but it was such so that "children may not be born to suffer and to experience despair." The UMC believed its requests, including the repeal of all abortion laws, were necessary.[89]

By 1972, the radical endorsement of "abortion . . . upon request" was already amended, signaling that abortion was and would remain a heated discussion for the new denomination, reflecting the social and political climate of the early 1970s. In the 1972 *Discipline*, a section entitled "Birth and Death" states:

> Our belief in the sanctity of unborn human life makes us reluctant to approve abortion. But we are equally bound to respect the sacredness of the life and well-being of the mother, for whom devastating damage may result from an unacceptable pregnancy. In continuity with Christian teaching, we recognize tragic conflicts of life with life that may justify abortion. We call all Christians to a searching and prayerful inquiry into the sorts of conditions that may warrant abortion. We support the removal of abortion from the criminal code, placing it instead under laws relating to other procedures of standard medical practice. A decision concerning abortion should be made only after thorough and thoughtful consideration by the parties involved, with medical and pastoral consent.[90]

---

87 "Population Crisis," 19.
88 *Abortion: A Human Choice*, Division of General Welfare, Department of Population Problems. Board of Christian Social Concerns of The United Methodist Church, May 1971. 5; folder: "Abortion Packet 1972," administrative records of the Division of General Welfare of the General Board of Church and Society, 1443–4–2:6, GCAH.
89 "Population Crisis," 20.
90 "Birth and Death," "Social Principles," *BOD* (1972), 86.

From the differences among the 1968, 1970, and 1972 statements involving family planning and abortion, one can see that this topic was debated tirelessly. The statement above does not mention the population crisis, and instead situates abortion as a complex moral decision made by husband and wife under the guidance of pastoral counseling. It states that the denomination is "reluctant" in its approval of abortion, a sense that was not present in the 1970 statement, which recognized that it was asking for action on a "grand scale." It is easy to see that this is a compromise statement. It recognizes the "sanctity of unborn life," a common pro-life sentiment, while acknowledging that unwanted pregnancies can be "devastating" for women, a common abortion rights sentiment. It does not call for "abortion upon request" but for abortion after "thorough and thoughtful consideration . . . with medical and pastoral consent." However, it does still request that abortion be removed from the criminal code and treated as other medical decisions; therefore, The UMC was still in support of the full repeal of all abortion laws.

Abortion: A Human Choice

As with evangelicals outside of United Methodism, evangelical Methodists were originally silent on abortion between General Conferences. From the periodicals, agency publications, and caucus group statements, progressive and evangelical Methodists were relatively content with the 1972 paragraph on abortion. In order to compete with and correct information that was disseminated by the pro-life movement, the General Board of Church and Society and the Women's Division of the General Board of Missions published books that sought to educate Methodists on the moral and medical aspects of abortion. One booklet, *Abortion: A Human Choice*, was published in 1971 and included in a sixty-four-page "Abortion Study Packet," prepared by the Department of Population Problems, the Board of Christian Social Concerns, and the Women's Division. It was meant to educate United Methodists on the denomination's stance on abortion, and to help calm the anxiety of the minority of General Conference delegates who did not endorse the 1970 resolution on abortion.[91]

Abortion: A Human Choice was offered as an ethical, theological, and legal guide to United Methodists who were conflicted on abortion. It is divided into three articles written by Tilda Norberg, an ordained minister and feminist

---

91 Grover C. Bagby and Rodney Shaw, "Foreword," *Abortion: A Human Choice*, v.

activist who worked on the New York Task Force on Status of Women in The UMC and a member of the CCSA; John M. Swomley Jr., an ordained minister in the Kansas East Conference, professor of Christian ethics at Saint Paul School of Theology, and member of the General Board of Christian Social Concerns of The UMC; and Allen J. Moore, an ordained minister, professor of religion and personality and Christian education at Claremont, and the national director of Methodist Young Adult Work.[92]

Norberg begins with an article entitled "Female Anguish and Abortion," which, in the abortions rights sentiment, shares stories from women who sought abortions: a fifteen-year-old girl whose parents believed that the only "humane way out of an already emotionally damaging situation" was to have an abortion; an African American woman who finally found the courage to divorce her abusive husband only to learn that she was pregnant by him; a forty-five-year-old woman whose last of four children had just gone to college and was looking forward to the opportunity to self-improve only to find that she was again pregnant; and a woman with four children, all under age seven, whose husband's income could barely cover the expenses for their current family. She describes the options available to these women, from trying to afford an illegal abortion, "begging" a hospital board for a legal therapeutic abortion, or self-abortion. She argues that most unwanted pregnancies are the result of a failure of contraception and occur within the marital relationship. Providing evidence that unwanted children have more mental health issues and problems adjusting to society than children who are welcomed into homes, Norberg concludes by stating that "women are angry" about their victimization, the high cost and limited access to a medical procedure, and the double standard that does not hold men accountable for unwanted pregnancies. In order to "affirm the wholeness" of a woman's "personhood," which The UMC claims it upholds, women must have access to abortion.[93]

John Swomley Jr. provides a legal argument for abortion and its removal from the criminal code in his "Abortion and Civil Liberty." His argument is easily summed up by his first two sentences, which reference the First Amendment:

> In a secular state, such as the United States, laws relating to abortion must have a validity apart from church doctrine or religious dogma. This means that if a local, state or national government adopts

---

92 Bagby and Shaw, vii.
93 Tilda Norberg, "Female Anguish and Abortion," *Abortion: A Human Choice*, 1–7.

legislation about abortion, it may do so constitutionally only because abortion affects the public health or welfare, and not because a church or denomination is convinced that abortion is an appropriate or inappropriate course of action.[94]

This statement foreshadows later arguments regarding the Human Life Amendment and unknowingly endorses the soon-to-be-heard *Roe v. Wade*.

Swomley places the abortion debate in the context of public health, arguing that it is better for society at large to have legal access to abortion, especially in light of the world population crisis. He analyzes current legal statutes to demonstrate that the law and constitution do not currently consider a fetus a living person based on the minimal severity of punishments for those who seek illegal abortions and the lack of constitutional protection afforded to the unborn. Adding to the denigration of public health is the fact that women who do seek legal abortions are often denied them and subjected to harsh criticism and embarrassment by hostile hospital boards. Swomley argues that legal abortions are overwhelmingly granted to white, middle-class women and not to African American, lower-income women, proving that the present laws are not only a hindrance to public health but racialize public health standards. Finally, he argues that current laws inhibit the rights of physicians who are not allowed to make medical decisions for their suffering patients, forcing them to break the Hippocratic oath to do no harm. Swomley concludes by stating that the only way to "protect the civil liberties of women, physicians, clergymen, and others who are directly or indirectly involved in the process of seeking, advising, or performing abortions" is to abolish all laws concerning abortion.[95]

Finally, Allen J. Moore, whose name is recognizable from chapter 3's discussion of *Playboy* and chapter 4's discussion of sex education, places abortion in the context of the new morality, as a moral choice that, while difficult to make, is a necessary right to have. He argues that "there are few questions in our time that call forth as fully our theological understanding of who we are as persons and our ethical responsibility for all of life as does the abortion issue."[96] After tracing the history of abortion as a continuous human and theological problem for all of humankind, Moore states that one of the main arguments against

---

94 John Swomley Jr., "Abortion and Civil Liberty," *Abortion: A Human Choice*, 9.
95 Swomley Jr., 9–20.
96 Allen J. Moore, "Abortion: A Human Choice," *Abortion: A Human Choice*, 23.

abortion legalization is that it would increase promiscuity. He quickly denounces this argument by arguing that persons should never be "punished for sexual enjoyment" and arguing for their punishment is "not based in either on sociological fact or theological insight."[97] Moore flips this argument around and states that the "real evidence that a sexual act has resulted in human failure" is not evident in an unwanted pregnancy but is more often found in the "maiming of dignity and personhood, as well as body, that thousands of women undergo each year at the hands of the criminal abortionists." To this list he adds

> the rejection that thousands of young girls suffer by peers, parents, and adult society . . . [due to] an illegitimate pregnancy, . . . the number of deformed children born each year whose possibility for a meaningful life is greatly reduced by the growing inability of society to provide adequate institutions for their care, . . . the unwanted additions to the growing population problem which threatens . . . the natural environment, . . . [and] the fact that pregnancy has come to represent for thousands of women a negation [of] their personhood.[98]

Moore argues that these reasons are more punishment than a sexual interaction could ever be. Addressing the second major argument against abortion, that the fetus is human, Moore argues that the fetus is "unique tissue that is in the process of becoming a human life," but is not yet human.[99] He agrees that life is present at conception, but it is not yet human life. God imbued humanity with a special kind of life when God breathed life into humanity, and "under no condition, has the fetus obtained the full worth of a human being."[100] Moore concludes with a brief statement on the value that The UMC and other denominations give to parenthood, a value that implies that parenthood should be a welcome and enjoyable experience and not a burden.

The purpose of this booklet was to get United Methodists to view abortion not as "murder," but as a complex theological, legal, and moral issue, which was being wrongly portrayed in the media during the early 1970s. The article showcased the plight of women fighting for an abortion and for equal rights, highlighted how abortion legalization would benefit the public welfare,

---

97 Moore, 28.
98 Moore, 28.
99 Moore, 30.
100 Moore, 30.

and wrestled with the theological arguments that morally allowed for abortion. The evidence supporting the impact of this booklet could be seen in the 1972 resolution on abortion, which was stated above. The revised statement asked for thoughtful and careful examination of the reasons an abortion was being sought while still calling for the full repeal of all abortion laws. It recognized the moral predicament that abortion presented to women and to families and encouraged pastoral counseling—all themes stated in *Abortion: A Human Choice*.

Other Methodist Publications on Abortion

Other items included in the "Abortion Packet" dealt directly with making the decision to have or not have an abortion. R. Bruce Poynter wrote "The Abortion Dilemma," and argued that those "who participate in the decision to abort a pregnancy must consciously, deliberately, and actively choose to end a human life." He believed that fetal life was life, albeit not self-aware, self-conscious life, and thus not fully human life. Making this decision was impossibly difficult because many "oversimplified the moral situation." In making this ethical decision, other ethical decisions needed to be made, including the "quality of life available to the unborn fetus," "the quality of life available to the mother," and "the quality of life available to a family." His solution to the abortion dilemma was to legalize abortion as a last resort through the first twenty-six weeks; to make all prenatal, postnatal, contraception, and abortion services available to the poor free of charge; and to increase sex education in society including contraceptive education, pregnancy education and counseling, and sterilization education.[101]

The next article, "Problem Pregnancy Counseling," was written by Judith Whiddicombe, a registered nurse and executive director of the Clergy Counseling Service of Missouri. She began the article by stating that she was "not unequivocally *for* abortion and certainly not against abortion." Instead, she supported "the individual's legal right to make the decision to terminate or not terminate a pregnancy, without the guilt-producing presence of . . . law."[102] In Missouri, she stated that, statistically, 42 percent of women who sought an abortion were married, 38 percent were Roman Catholic, and 18 percent were African American. In the sixteen months that the CCS Missouri was operational,

---

101 R. Bruce Poynter, "The Abortion Dilemma"; folder: "Abortion Packet 1972."
102 Judith Widdicombe, "Problem Pregnancy Counseling," GCAH UMC; folder: "Abortion Packet 1972," emphasis hers.

it alone counseled 4,700 women. For many, "quality of life and not quantity of reproduction is becoming more important," which included "terminating an undesired pregnancy" but also "becoming responsible about . . . sexual activities both in and out of marriage by means of adequate contraceptive measures." As a nurse, she called on other nurses, clergy, and doctors to help women with family planning. As a counselor, she called on parents to not be "moralistic, judgmental, and punitive" with their children who have unwanted pregnancies. Children in this situation needed love, support, and sex education. She concluded with a recommendation to read the Women's Division statement on "Responsible Parenthood" and believed that as a United Methodist "it can indeed be an act of Christian love and responsibility to terminate a pregnancy."[103]

The rest of the "Abortion Packet" follows a similar pattern to the above three items. Included were "Letters from Three Women," which gave women's voices to the question of fetal or human life, asked readers to consider all aspects involved in a woman's decision to have an abortion, and asked readers to recognize that more factors were involved in the decision than simply a desire to not have a child; resolutions on abortion from other religious groups; the current status of abortion laws in each state; information on the Clergy Consultation Service; questions and situations to prompt discussion in small groups; a question-and-answer section; and a list of books, articles, and films for further reference.

All of these materials have common themes. First, they recognize that fetal life is life, but not yet fully developed, self-aware human life. Second, they recognize that a woman has the right to make the decision to have a child or not have a child based on her own moral conscience and religious beliefs, that the government has no say in this decision, and that clergy should provide counsel if desired. Third, in line with the new morality, the decision to have an abortion is not simply one of convenience but involves a whole host of ethical issues that must be put into context for each individual. This is why only the individual can make the final decision. Fourth, the right to an abortion is a moral necessity for all women—rich and poor, educated and uneducated, young and old—and all women should have equal access to abortion services. Fifth, sex education

103 Widdicombe.

needs to be more common and include more information on all aspects of reproductive care. Sixth, health care needs to be improved for all women, including the availability of contraception, prenatal and postnatal care, and general health care. Seventh, pregnancy can occur even if contraception is used, and thus abortion needs to be available as a last resort. Those seven items formed the basis of the United Methodist position on abortion in 1971. This position would be maintained in 1972, but after *Roe*, it would receive increasing opposition from many evangelicals within the denomination, particularly due to the United Methodist involvement in the founding and advocacy efforts of the Religious Coalition for Abortion Rights in 1973 and the resolution on Responsible Parenthood, which was approved by General Conference in 1976.

The Religious Coalition for Abortion Rights (Reproductive Choice)

In 1973, *Roe v. Wade* legalized abortion according to a trimester system as a constitutional right for all women, and polarized the religious discussion of abortion in the years to come. The UMC, in 1975, witnessed an increase in abortion rhetoric as a result of the impending 1976 General Conference and in accordance with the increase of abortion rhetoric in the public at large just prior to the 1976 presidential election. Believing that such discussions and protests against *Roe* would increase and would continue to use a religious argument to overturn *Roe*, The UMC's Women's Division and the General Board of Church and Society gathered clergy and rabbis within the United States to form a religious coalition to protect a woman's right to choose, the Religious Coalition for Abortion Rights (RCAR).

RCAR, as mentioned previously in this chapter, was an advocacy group and educational organization that brought together various faiths to educate the public on the moral aspects of the right to obtain an abortion. In 1994, RCAR changed its name to the Religious Coalition for Reproductive Choice (RCRC) and expanded its program to include comprehensive sexual education, reproductive health care, and advocacy. As of 2004, RCRC was composed of thirty-eight faith groups and had coalitions in twenty-five states.

There is virtually no historical research on RCAR/RCRC as a women's rights or abortion rights organization. It is mentioned in some historical accounts but given only a few sentences or paragraphs. This silence is odd, as the organization is public with its information and has been quite active over the last forty-three years. The only academic work dedicated solely to the work of RCAR is a master's thesis written by Melissa Winham in 2004, *Voices of Reason: The Story of the Religious Coalition for Reproductive Choice.*[104]

RCAR was founded just after *Roe*. Its stated goals were to combat legislation aimed against *Roe* in Congress, to educate the public on how abortion was viewed by a variety of faiths, and to organize faith groups to protect abortion rights. It never advocated abortion as the only answer to pregnancy and, instead, continuously sought to educate society on why abortion was a moral necessity when other methods failed.[105] After *Roe*, other faith-based abortion groups, such as the CCSA, believed that their work was done when abortion was legalized. RCAR believed the contrary to be true; their work was just beginning. RCAR picked up the work of the CCSA, providing counsel, education, referrals, and advocacy on behalf of women's moral right to have an abortion. It was a religiously oriented pro-choice voice in the movement to counteract the religiously oriented pro-life voice that was dominant at the time (and would become only more dominant throughout the rest of the century).[106]

Through 1976, RCAR was largely on the defensive, counteracting any statements made by pro-life religious organizations, especially those of the third-party presidential candidate, Ellen McCormack, who ran on the Right to Life party in 1976. Its objectives during the 1976 election were exemplary of the type of work RCAR engaged in:

1. Working with other abortion rights groups [to] distribute abortion rights materials to candidates, the media, and to interested persons within religious groups.

2. Promoting church and synagogue right-to-choice days in areas respective to such a program and where anti-choice religious groups are highly vocal, providing ideas for sermons, bulletin articles, seminars, study groups, etc.

3. Providing national religious publications with articles on abortion as an election issue.

4. With respect to the 1976 Congressional candidates, compiling positions on the abortion rights issue for circulation in states with Coalitions; and with

---

104 Melissa Winham, "A Voice of Reason: The Story of the Religious Coalition for Reproductive Choice" (master's thesis, University of Southern California, 2004).

105 For more on the RCAR (now Religious Coalition for Reproductive Choice), see their website, http://rcrc.org.

106 Winham, *A Voice of Reason*, 5–7.

the assistance of the Policy Council members, devising ways of circulating this data among religious constituents in states without Coalitions.[107]

RCAR functioned the same way that prior organizations, like the CCSA, did. It was an advocacy group, an educational organization, and a place for referral and counseling for all reproductive needs. The UMC founded the organization in order to bring faith groups who had varying views of abortion together to work for a common good.

The main rhetorical tool of RCAR was pamphlets. One pamphlet sought to differentiate RCAR from pro-life groups like the National Right to Life Committee, which distributed pamphlets full of graphic images of aborted fetuses. It said:

> Pro-choice people often ask, "Why don't we have a brochure with pictures?" We could. We could print pictures of women who have bled to death from illegal abortions. We could print pictures of rape victims. We could print pictures of babies with fatal birth defects; babies that lived only a few minutes after birth. But we don't. Those pictures would shock and upset you. We'd rather you take the time to think seriously about the real issue. THE ISSUE IS FREEDOM. YOU CAN'T TAKE A PICTURE OF FREEDOM.[108]

The interior of the brochure focused on the individual's right to make the final decision on abortion based on her own "conscience and personal religious principles." In all of RCAR's materials, it mentioned how "each denomination and faith group represented among us approaches the issue of abortion from the unique perspective of its own theology." This ideology formed the basis of the organization and defined why the organization fought for the final choice to be solely with the woman, not with the government. Staying on the defensive, this brochure sought to correct misinformation that was made public by anti-choice organizations: "[Roe] did NOT 'mandate abortion on demand to the moment of birth.'. . . Rather, it placed clear restrictions on the woman and on the state giving neither an absolute right to 'demand' or to prohibit abortions."[109]

---

107 "RCAR's Program 1976–1977"; folder: "Religious Coalition for Abortion Rights 1979," Women's Division, 2589-6-4:1, GCAH.

108 "The Issue Is Freedom," RCAR Brochure; folder: "Abortion and RCAR Grant folder 1 1979," Women's Division, 2593-7-6:1, GCAH; emphasis theirs.

109 "The Issue Is Freedom," emphasis theirs.

Throughout the 1970s and 1980s, RCAR remained on the defensive, especially related to statements made against the organization by Good News and the Institute on Religion and Democracy (IRD).

The UMC general agencies, specifically the General Board of Church and Society and the Women's Division, maintained the denomination's progressive stance on abortion from 1968 through 1984. Their main achievements were the founding of RCAR and General Conference's approval of "Responsible Parenthood," a resolution passed by the General Conference of 1976. The resolution reiterated many of the themes found in the earlier statements on responsible parenthood supported by the Methodist Church, such as the use of artificial birth control, premarital counseling, and family planning. It read:

> When through contraceptive or human failure, an unacceptable pregnancy occurs, we believe that a profound regard for fully developed personhood, particularly when the physical, mental, and emotional health of the pregnant woman and her family show reason to be seriously threatened by the new life just forming. We reject the simplistic answers to the problem of abortion, which on the one hand regard all abortions as murders, or on the other hand, regard abortions as medical procedures without moral significance. When an unacceptable pregnancy occurs, a family, and most of all the pregnant woman is confronted with the need to make a difficult decision. We believe that continuance of a pregnancy which endangers the life or health of the mother, or poses other serious problems concerning the life, health, or mental capability of the child to be, is not a moral necessity. In such case, we believe the path of mature Christian judgment may indicate the advisability of abortion, we support the legal right to abortion as established by the 1972 Supreme Court Decisions. We encourage women in counsel with husbands, doctors, and pastors to make their own responsible decisions concerning the personal and moral questions surrounding the issue of abortion.[110]

The 1976 resolution had more in common with the 1970 resolution regarding abortion than it did with the 1976 Social Principles paragraph on abortion. The Social Principles' statement is "reluctant" to approve abortion because of the "sanctity of unborn life." In the General Conference resolution, however,

---

110 "Responsible Parenthood, 1976," in "Quotes on Abortion Rights from United Methodist Conference Resolutions," RCAR, Abortion Pamphlets, Records of the Division of General Welfare, General Board of Church and Society, 1439–1–3:11, GCAH.

an abortion is a "difficult" decision without "simplistic answers," but a decision that if made in "mature Christian judgment" can support an abortion. While the family should be consulted, the final decision should remain solely in the hands of the pregnant woman. Instead of reluctance and calling the fetus "unborn life," this resolution deems abortion a moral choice that should be made solely in accordance with the new morality.

Later Evangelical Methodist Responses

Until the late 1970s, evangelical Methodists were primarily concerned with three things. The first and second, bringing a more orthodox Wesleyan voice to the denomination and to church school curriculum, as discussed in previous chapters. The third, homosexuality, will be discussed in the next chapter.[111] Abortion was seldom mentioned in *Good News* during the early 1970s. It first appeared as a topic of concern in a special edition of *Good News* in 1977. Entitled "What about Abortion?," a special issue of the periodical included six articles dedicated to "a fuller understanding" of abortion. On the front cover of the issue was a small fetus curled up with its eyes, ears, nose, fingers, and toes in full view. It began by stating that in 1972, The UMC "went on record . . . approving abortion." However, while The UMC approved abortion prior to 1972, as this chapter has shown, Good News claimed that since 1972, "a growing uneasiness has crept across the church about this issue." The purpose of this special edition issue of *Good News* was to help United Methodists find "a truly biblical solution" to the question of abortion's morality, a stance in direct opposition to the ethical framework of the new morality. It did so in four parts: part 1 "present[ed] the opinion of a mature Christian gynecologist"; parts 2 and 3 examined biblical sources—the Old Testament and New Testament, respectively; part 4 examined historic views of the church, the United Methodist position, and the denomination's activities regarding abortion.[112]

In part 1, Dr. Hammell P. Shipps argued emphatically that life begins at conception, although he never called abortion "murder." His article, unfortunately,

---

111 See "The Church in Crisis," *Good News*, October/December 1970, "In the Aftermath of Atlanta," *Good News*, Summer 1972, 34–53; "Ten Petitions for General Conference," *Good News*, January/March 1972, 50–65; "You Ought to Know," *Good News*, September/October 1979, 63–65; and "The 1980 Indianapolis General Conference" *Good News*, May/June 1980, special insert.

112 "What about Abortion?" *What about Abortion? A series of articles published in the interest of fuller understanding by Good News* (Wilmore, KY: Good News, 1977), 2.

began with a factual error, stating that *Roe v. Wade* was decided in 1972. In a few clinical paragraphs, Dr. Shipps defined abortion and the methods of abortion without going into graphic detail.[113] Halfway through, Dr. Shipps lost the clinical tone and began preaching morality. He claimed that "one cannot be aware of the medical evidence without acknowledging the fact that abortion is clearly destructive of a living being."[114] At first, his logic followed that of earlier discussions of fetal life. He argued that when sperm and egg meet, a new life was formed; this idea was upheld in *Abortion: A Human Choice.* However, Dr. Shipps then argued that this life was not part of the mother; it did not belong to her. Using an analogy of a kidney transplant in which the kidney was the mother's to choose to give away, he argued that, because the fetus had its own DNA, it was "another person;" and therefore, it was not the mother's to freely give away.[115] Moving on, he described the "astounding" rate of fetal development that made it "recognizably human" within four weeks, when "this tiny being has a head with eyes and ears." Shipps combined anatomical development with gestures that birthed babies performed in order to support his argument that the fetus was a child: "This little one will even turn his head away if the nose is tickled" and "The unborn child also moves, squints, swallows, and sucks a thumb!"

This rhetoric was meant to conjure images of a fully developed infant sucking its thumb in the womb. For those who believed that life truly did begin at conception, images and statements such as this proved their worst fear: millions of babies were being legally murdered, and the church condoned it. Shipps then returned to the methods of abortion, but this time he did so without being clinical: "Anyone who has seen a fetus pulled apart in early abortion, or poisoned with a strong salt solution in second-trimester abortion, or struggling for life after hysterectomy must be impressed with the inhumanity of the whole proceeding."[116]

While Shipps did not use graphic imaging to make his point, his contrast of a child sucking its thumb with that same "child" being pulled apart, poisoned, or struggling was a stark juxtaposition. For Shipps, abortion was not an individual moral choice based on a complex set of ethical circumstances; to him,

113 Hammell P. Shipps, "A Christian Gynecologist Speaks," *What about Abortion?*, 3–4.
114 Shipps, 4.
115 Shipps, 5.
116 Shipps, 5–6.

"abortion is the logical consequence of human sin, and the sin-accepting direction of our society."[117] This statement suggests that Shipps (and evangelical United Methodists who agreed with him) believed that abortion was sought only by those who had "illegitimate" sex, and thus ignored all of the statistics that showed married women requesting abortions for the sake and health of their families. His claim that abortion signaled a new direction toward sin in the 1970s blatantly ignored American (and world) history, which supported the fact that women sought abortion whether or not it was legal.

Trying to remain balanced, *Good News* asked Theresa Hoover to speak on behalf of those who supported abortion rights. She responded to Dr. Shipps's article and argued that Dr. Shipps placed "an absolute value on the life of the fetus" and ignored the full life of the mother.[118] To support her claim that the life of the mother must be taken into account and had more value as a fully living person, she quoted from the National Council of Churches study on abortion (1973) and from *Abortion: A Human Choice* (1971). Her second argument stemmed from Dr. Shipps's statement that abortion was an answer for young persons "living sexually promiscuously." Hoover countered, stating that Dr. Shipps was defining *sin* in a very limited way, and he believed that pregnancy was an apt punishment for certain lifestyles. Furthermore, she stated, he ignored the other issues for which women sought abortion—fetal deformity, rape, and incest—and she took issue with his lumping all of these together as mere "social issues."[119]

Hoover then criticized Shipps's authority as a medical doctor by correcting some of his medical facts. First, Shipps incorrectly stated that abortion can prevent women from having safe, healthy pregnancies later in life. "This is factually incorrect," Hoover stated and continued, "Abortion in the first trimester is tenfold safer when compared with deaths from full-term pregnancy and delivery."[120] Second, when discussing the safety of abortion, Shipps ignored the fact that complications from illegal abortion were no longer an issue after *Roe.* Third, Shipps did not mention that 80 percent of abortions were performed in the first trimester when it was safest to do so.[121] Hoover continued, dismissing various arguments that Shipp made about the Supreme Court's decision. She

---

117 Shipps, 6.
118 Theresa Hoover, "The Other Side," *What about Abortion?,* 9.
119 Hoover, 10–11.
120 Hoover, 11.
121 Hoover, 11.

concluded with a request to Good News to find a pastor who had done pastoral counseling for women who were deciding whether or not to have an abortion, in order to get a more well-rounded Christian viewpoint of all the ethical issues involved.

Part 4 explored the United Methodist stance on abortion from the evangelical standpoint. Written by James V. Heidinger II, a United Methodist pastor in Ohio and later president of Good News, it was a glaring critique of the United Methodist stance on abortion. He began with a survey conducted by the United Methodist Reporter in 1976, which showed that 45.3 percent of United Methodists disagreed with the *Roe* decision, and 45.5 percent agreed with it, proving that, early on, Methodists were split on the morality of the issue.[122] Heidinger argued that the open call for "abortion on demand" by The UMC and its participation in RCAR went against "the thinking of many"; yet he refused to recognize that not endorsing the two would also go against the thinking of many.[123]

The basis for his critique was that, as a pastor, he counseled many women who had unwanted pregnancies that turned into wanted children: "I have seen the initial anguish, shock, and depression of pregnancy-discovered become the acceptance, joy, and responsibility of pregnancy-completed." This statement assumed that women who had unwanted pregnancies would eventually come to love the child born from that pregnancy, a fact that is especially unlikely to be true when the child was born of rape. Heidinger then broke down the article into three sections which, to him, needed "serious consideration and discussion."

First, he believed that the Supreme Court decision to legalize abortion "represents a sharp turn from the Western ethical tradition and early church history." He argued that *Roe* granted women "abortion on demand during the first two trimesters of pregnancy," and "an almost unqualified right to abortion in the final three months."[124] Second, Heidinger examined when life begins. Admitting

---

122 James V. Heidinger II, "Perspectives in the Church," *What about Abortion?*, 24. Only 1,514 people were surveyed.

123 Heidinger II, 25.

124 Heidinger II, 26. *Roe* is based on a trimester system, as described previously but reiterated here. During the first trimester, the decision is between a woman and her doctor. This is as close as *Roe* gets to abortion on demand. However, as shown by hospitals and individual doctors who refused to provide abortions after *Roe*, it is evident that one could not simply demand an abortion and receive one. During the second trimester, therapeutic abortion is allowed, prioritizing the life of the mother. During the third trimester, the life of the fetus is believed to be equal to that of the mother, as the fetus is viable during the third trimester. While many early church fathers were against abortion, the Catholic Church, the prime

that it was hard to determine when life begins by medical, scientific, theological, or philosophical means, Heidinger was confident that it begins at conception. He referenced the two articles in parts 2 and 3 and two Methodist theologians. One, Albert C. Outler argued that human life exists on a continuum and is "sacred at every point along that continuum." This leads to the conclusion that abortion is "an attack upon the sacredness of human life," an attack that he believed, if left unchecked, would lead to "euthanasia and Nazi-like attempts to wipe out individuals and groups judged no longer socially useful or wanted by the society in which they live."[125] The second, Paul Ramsey, a United Methodist and professor of religion at Princeton, argued that the idea that the unborn are not recognizably human by law is "demonstrably erroneous."

Finally, Heidinger analyzed the "weakness of the major proabortion arguments," delineating six: (1) Heidinger argued that women do not have a legal right to do with their bodies as they please. (2) He argued that unborn children have biblical rights, but provided no specific analysis or references for this statement. (3) Unwanted children and fetal deformity were, for him, not valid arguments for abortion. (4) He believed that all children were wanted and quoted uncited studies that stated that 84 percent of women were glad they had their children.[126] (5) He argued that abortion legalization would not reduce the number of illegal abortions. (6) Heidinger argued that morality cannot be legislated. In his conclusion, Heidinger undermined his own argument when he simplified his statements to proclaim, "Our protest is with abortion on demand" and "that therapeutic abortions are acceptable."[127]

The end of "What about Abortion?" is an editorial by Charles Keysor, who argued that abortion was both a theological and political topic. Theologically, United Methodists did not agree on whether to emphasize evangelism or social action, and thus it was not surprising that these different theological foundations tended toward different theological views of abortion. Politically, the General Conference, the Board of Church and Society, and the Women's Division had the power to sway the church toward their pro-choice—or as Keysor

---

authority of these early church fathers, allowed abortion until the point of quickening, which is between the fourth and fifth month. While the Catholic Church did consider abortion a sin at any point, it was a lesser sin if done prior to quickening. Major Protestant theologians did not take issue with abortion until the twentieth century when the procedure was already politicized.

125 Heidinger II, 28.
126 Heidinger II, 31.
127 Heidinger II, 32.

stated, "pro-abortion"—stance.[128] At the end of his editorial, he called for "pro-life United Methodists to form an effective coalition . . . who would express the view of Scripture" on abortion. This coalition could "deluge pastors, bishops, superintendents, leading laypeople, and the 1980 General Conference with evidence that many United Methodists are pro-life."[129]

Throughout the 1970s and 1980s, Good News became less of a "forum for scriptural Christianity" within The UMC and more of a political caucus group, lobbying on behalf of the evangelical United Methodist position on abortion, on human sexuality, and on theology. Prior to each General Conference, *Good News* published petitions that they submitted to amend the *Discipline*, and encouraged their readers to submit the exact same petition. They highlighted issues to monitor during and leading up to General Conference, creating a "Good News agenda." Especially of interest were

> those [issues] which would offer a positive program emphasis for the church (i.e. the family life emphasis); prevent serious erosion of our church's moral witness (i.e. the efforts to weaken UM disapproval of homosexual practice); and augment the voice and perspective of grassroots United Methodists in contrast with the often-more-powerful agency bureaucracies.[130]

In 1979, they officially formed a Good News Political Strategy Task Force to organize prior to General Conference and to advocate during General Conference.[131] They held training seminars in U.S. annual conferences to teach evangelicals how to elect delegates that would represent their message and to advocate on behalf of Good News. At these training seminars, attendees were given a "petitioning packet," complete with sample petitions to send to General Conference. More than fourteen thousand packets were distributed in 1979. They successfully "generate[d] a flood of petitions reflecting particular Good News concerns." The Political Strategy Task Force also sent "a series of informational mailings to delegates outlining positions on family life, homosexuality, and accountability of general boards and agencies."[132] They participated for the

---

128 Charles Keysor, "The Double Roots of Abortion," *What about Abortion?*, 35.

129 Keysor, 37.

130 "The 1980 Indianapolis General Conference," *Good News*, May/June 1980, 10.

131 "The 1980 Indianapolis General Conference," 10.

132 "The 1980 Indianapolis General Conference," 10.

first time in a pre–General Conference press briefing, where they provided an "alternative to much of the radical social action agenda promoted by general church agencies and other caucuses."[133]

During the 1980 General Conference, sixty-five men and women worked on behalf of Good News and distributed materials advocating their stances on the issues. They hosted meals, provided transportation for delegates, and had a special "hospitality room" for delegates to gather with members of Good News. During the first week of General Conference, they divided up and monitored legislative committees to see if their petitions were discussed and in what way. In the evenings, they wrote minority reports and amendments and developed strategies for the next day. They took note of delegates who were sympathetic to their cause in order to "[have] data on previous delegates' track records" to "increase confidence in the elective process."[134]

In September/October 1979, the section "You Ought to Know" of *Good News*, which often highlighted General Conference issues, named "special women's concerns" and discussed the denomination's support of the ERA, an incoming petition to remove "sexist" language from all denominational publications and abortion. It stated that

> at least six annual conferences endorsed the official UM free-choice position . . . [and] three conferences want to add a statement to the Social Principles warning that abortion-on-demand in certain circumstances is morally wrong.[135]

Thus the General Conference of 1980 had petitions to General Conference from not only individuals but also entire annual conferences, meaning that abortion was discussed at all levels of the general church. By 1980, Good News was a highly organized and effective political caucus group.

While many of their petitions failed or did not make it out of legislative committee, they were "heard and even respected" in 1980.[136] Their efforts concerning abortion were less successful early on. The 1980 General Conference did not change the church's position on abortion. But *Good News* editor Charles Keysor was hopeful after the 1980 General Conference:

---

133 "The 1980 Indianapolis General Conference," 10–11.
134 "The 1980 Indianapolis General Conference," 12–14.
135 "You Ought to Know," *Good News*, September/October 1979, 65.
136 "The 1980 Indianapolis General Conference," 9.

There was more noticeable sensitivity to the "grass roots" than I can remember at the five previous General Conferences. . . . These attitudinal changes are just the tip of the iceberg; its base is widespread dissatisfaction with the denominational status quo.[137]

He believed he witnessed "a narrowing of the unfortunate gap that . . . separates the expectations of many 'grass roots' United Methodists from what is said and done by the hierarchy."[138]

Keysor's language is telling. He believed that evangelical Methodists were the grassroots of the church: the laypersons, those not in pulpits, bishop seats, or at the administrative level. He was in agreement with Glen Spann's argument that many laypersons in the denomination held more conservative beliefs than persons at the general church level.[139] However, as General Conferences progressed, the Good News Movement did increase its voice and made substantial efforts to limit the rights of persons who identify as LGBTQ (the subject of chapter 5) and to limit the church's position on abortion.

The first victory for the Good News Movement was in 1984, when two sentences were merged into one. The 1980 Social Principles statement read, "In continuity with past Christian teaching, we recognize tragic conflicts of life with life that may justify abortion. . . . We support the legal option of abortion under proper medical procedures."[140] In 1984, it was amended to read, "In continuity with past Christian teaching, we recognize tragic conflicts of life with life that may justify abortion, and in such cases support the legal option of abortion under proper medical procedures."[141] This small change amends the statement to state that only when the mother's life is in danger, when "life" conflicts with "life," is abortion supported. It was a subtle change, but it had drastic consequences for years to come. In 1988, the sentence "We cannot affirm abortion as an acceptable means of birth control, and we unconditionally reject it as a means of gender selection," was added.[142] Evangelical-leaning United Methodists believed that the United Methodist stance was still an endorsement of "abortion on demand" or abortion as a means of birth control. Since 1972, it

---

137 "The 1980 Indianapolis General Conference," 42–43.
138 "The 1980 Indianapolis General Conference," 42–43.
139 Spann, "Evangelicalism in Modern American Methodism," 265–67.
140 "Abortion" in "Social Principles" *BOD* (1980), 91.
141 "Abortion" in "Social Principles" *BOD* (1984), 91.
142 "Abortion" in "Social Principles" *BOD* (1988), 96.

had not endorsed abortion "upon request," but instead endorsed abortion's re-moval from the criminal code. This 1988 change was a victory for evangelicals and a sign that the denomination was listening to the evangelical voice.

The Durham Declaration

In 1991, evangelical Methodists expressed their opinion against abortion in an overt statement, "The Durham Declaration." The statement was the product of a new political caucus group, the Taskforce of United Methodists on Abortion and Sexuality, also known as Lifewatch. Formed in 1987 by nine pastors and lay-persons to "promote a biblical and Wesleyan moral responsibility in the church and society," as opposed to the new morality, which they believed to be nei-ther biblical nor Wesleyan. They focused solely on abortion and sought to "en-gage in abortion prevention through theological, pastoral, and social emphases that support human life."[143] To date, about four thousand persons receive their quarterly newsletter. In 1993, Abingdon Press published an extended version of "The Durham Declaration," *The Church and Abortion*.

"The Durham Declaration" focuses on "the church's morality and minis-try with regard to abortion" and "calls the church to a 'scriptural, theological, and pastoral approach to abortion.'"[144] It begins with a rather bold statement: "Abortion is testing our church today as deeply as slavery tested our church in the nineteenth century." For evangelical Methodists, this was a legitimate argu-ment; any denominational support of abortion, no matter how "middle of the line" it seemed, still condoned murder. They believed that The UMC had ap-proached abortion from solely a political standpoint and not a theological stand-point, and they sought to correct this. Lifewatch believed that United Methodist theology upheld the notion that "we are not our own . . . God owns us." There-fore, we do not have a full say in what happens to our bodies; only God does, a theological foundation that is in direct opposition to personalism, the preferred theological foundation of liberal Methodists. Evangelical-leaning United Meth-odists stated that all children, born and unborn, are gifts from God. The dec-laration calls for the following confessions: "We have often compromised the Gospel by submitting to the seductions of society. . . . We have treated matters

---

143 "Origin and History of Lifewatch," *Lifewatch*, accessed 1/23/2017, https://www.lifewatch.org/origin_and_history_of_lifewatch.html.
144 "The New Durham Declaration," *Good News*, May/June 1992.

related to marriage, sex, and children as if they were merely lifestyle questions." It continues by acknowledging that The UMC, according to Lifewatch, has not confronted abortion in an honest manner, but has reduced it to "private choice" and "partisan politics." It calls for "fidelity in marriage and celibacy in singleness" as a new sexual ethic, one that would be reiterated in the debate regarding the rights and status of LGBTQ persons. Regarding abortion, it calls for the church

> to teach . . . that the unborn child is created in the image of God and is one for whom the Son of God died. This child is God's child. This child is part of God's world. So that life of this child is not ours to take. Therefore, it is a sin to take this child's life for reasons whether of birth control, gender selection, convenience, or avoidance of embarrassment.[145]

It further calls for increased counseling for women who have had children and who have had abortions and the end of UM involvement in RCAR.

Lifewatch is not a large group. Much of their current rhetoric is proclaimed through joint efforts with Good News and IRD. "The Durham Declaration" is their only major publication, and it was signed by a few hundred United Methodists. However, it was picked up and endorsed by Good News and IRD. The statement arose out of the belief that the General Board of Church and Society and the Women's Division were not adhering to the 1988 General Conference mandate to denounce abortion as a means of birth control. Lifewatch, Good News, and IRD viewed involvement with RCAR as supporting abortion as birth control.[146] It also viewed the "Responsible Parenthood" resolution in the 1976 *Book of Resolutions* as supporting abortion as a means of birth control.

"The Durham Declaration" did not change 1992 General Conference in a drastic way. Good News, angered by the General Board of Church and Society co-sponsoring a National March for Women's Lives in April 1992, rallied their voting bloc to try and reverse the United Methodist support of abortion and of RCAR at the 1992 General Conference.[147] United Methodists voted to maintain their membership in RCAR; however, it was a close vote, with support retained by only 37 votes (485 to 448). Good News referred to the floor debate on abortion as "one of the most heated, yet clearly articulated debates of the 1992

---

145 "The Durham Declaration," *Lifewatch*, accessed 12/20/2016, https://www.lifewatch.org/durham.html.
146 "A Sanctuary from Abortion," *Good News*, May/June 1992, 31.
147 "Abortion-Rights March Lacks Diversity," *Good News*, May/June 1992, 36.

General Conference."[148] The United Methodist Church still supported *Roe* and refused to amend the resolution on Responsible Parenthood in order to make it more restrictive or "more consistent" with the *Discipline*.[149] The only concession made in the Social Principles text was the insertion of two small sentences requesting that the church provide "nurturing ministries" for those who both terminate a pregnancy and those who give birth.[150] These sentences do not change the overall meaning of the statement, as it had already and continued to call for pastoral counseling.

ABORTION IN THE TWENTY-FIRST CENTURY

There were no other major changes to the statement on abortion until 2000.[151] In 2000, Good News declared, "Abortion has ushered in a culture of death instead of life, created division instead of unity, and promoted injustice for the most vulnerable members of the human family."[152] From 2000 until 2016, all five General Conferences amended the stance on abortion, making it more conservative and supporting the increasingly present evangelical voice. By 2012, qualifications were added to the Social Principles' statement on abortion that: disavow and call for an end to partial-birth abortion;[153] request ministries and counseling services to reduce unintended pregnancies;[154] support parental or guardian consent for any minors who seek an abortion;[155] and commit the denomination to reducing the number of abortions performed each year.[156] It further calls for the denomination to improve sex education, to advocate for contraception use, and to a renewed commitment to improving the lives of women and girls around the globe. The statements regarding the quality of life for women and girls reflect those arguments made by liberal pro-life advocates in the 1960s, and calls for better reproductive care for women. They read:

---

148 "RCAR Reaffirmed by 37 Votes" *Good News*, May/June 1992, 15.
149 "RCAR Reaffirmed by 37 Votes."
150 "Abortion" in "Social Principles" *BOD* (1992), 92.
151 In 1996, delegates voted down an attempt by United Methodist Evangelicals to affirm the rights of the unborn in the paragraph on abortion ("Delegates reject 'rights of the unborn,'" *Good News*, May/June 1996, 22).
152 "A Sanctuary from Abortion," *Good News*, May/June 2000, 31.
153 *BOD* (2004), 102.
154 *BOD* (2008), 105.
155 *BOD* (2008), 105.
156 *BOD* (2012), 113.

We support initiatives that enhance the quality of life for all women and girls around the globe. Young adult women disproportionately face situations in which they feel that they have no choice due to financial, educational, relational, or other circumstances beyond their control. The Church and its local congregations and campus ministries should be in the forefront of supporting existing ministries and developing new ministries that help such women in their communities. They should also support those crisis pregnancy centers and pregnancy resource centers that compassionately help women explore all options related to unplanned pregnancy We particularly encourage the Church, the government, and social service agencies to support and facilitate the option of adopted. We affirm and encourage the Church to assist the ministry of crisis pregnancy centers and pregnancy resource centers that compassionately help women find feasible alternatives to abortion.[157]

While the entire statement on abortion became more restrictive, the above wording indirectly supports efforts of both Planned Parenthood and the RCRC, organizations that provide women with reproductive care and non-abortion services. United Methodist support of RCRC was emphasized in a new resolution, "Support for the Religious Coalition for Reproductive Choice," in 2004. It named The UMC as a "founding member," recognized the "wide variety of views" present at the table, listed the services available through RCRC, including "sexuality education, family planning services, contraception, abortion services, and affordable and quality health and child care," and it recognized RCRC as a "non-government organization within the United Nations." The resolution directly mentions the evangelical United Methodist position against RCRC:

Whereas, factions within The United Methodist Church whose stated goal is to have the General Conference go on reccrd in opposition to all abortions regardless of the reason are working towards the goal of severing all United Methodist ties with the Religious Coalition for Reproductive Choice. Therefore, be it resolved, that the United Methodist 2004 General Conference go on record in support of the work of the Religious Coalition for Reproductive Choice, and Be it further resolved, that the 2004 General Conference affirm the continued membership of the General Board of Church and Society and the

---

157 *BOD* (2012), 113.

Women's Divisions of the General Board of Global Ministries in the Religious Coalition for Reproductive Choice.[158]

The relationship between The UMC and RCRC was a continuous debate in the 2000s. In 2008, the vote to withdraw was denied (416 to 384). Progressive Methodists continued their efforts to maintain what they believed to be a vital relationship with RCRC. However, in 2016, by a vote of 425 to 268, United Methodist delegates voted to withdraw all membership from RCRC, thus affirming the evangelical voice in the denomination.[159]

The resolution on "Responsible Parenthood," which was originally adopted in 1976 was amended in 1996 and 2008. In 2012, it stated:

> We reject the simplistic answers to the problem of abortion that, on the one hand, regard all abortions as murders, or, on the other hand, regard abortions as medical procedures without moral significance.[160]

Pregnancies that "endanger the life or health of the mother, or pose other serious problems concerning the life, health, or mental capability of the child to be" were not a "moral necessity." In these cases, the woman had the right to "mature Christian judgment," which might lead her to decide to have an abortion. The resolution had not changed much since its 1976 penning, except for a deletion in 2008 of the provision that allowed for abortion in the case of "contraceptive or human failure."[161] It still supported *Roe* and a woman's right to control her reproductive life. It asked the church to provide comprehensive sex education, counseling, comprehensive health care to women and children, materials on contraception options, to "safeguard the legal option of abortion under standards of sound medical practice," to "make abortion available to women without regard to economic status," among other things.

The resolution was less nuanced than the Social Principles statement regarding abortion. It called for abortion, education, and reproductive care for all and did not stipulate which procedures were allowed or who was allowed to

---

158 *BOR* (2004), 321–22.

159 Kathy L. Gilbert, "Church Ends Membership in Reproductive Health Coalition," United Methodist News Service, May 19, 2016, http://www.umc.org/news-and-media/church-leaves-membership-in -reproductive-health-coalition.

160 "WhatWeBelieve," UMC website, accessed 1/15/2017, http://www.umc.org/what-we-believe/responsible -parenthood.

161 "Initiatives for the Unborn," *Good News*, May/June 2008, 35.

receive care, as the *Discipline* did. For these reasons, the resolutions on Responsible Parenthood and on United Methodist support for RCRC were targets of evangelical United Methodists during General Conference 2016; they successfully blocked re-adoption by votes of 310 to 445 and 561 to 167, respectively.[162] The vote to withdraw from RCRC and to not reaffirm the resolution on Responsible Parenthood showcased the evangelical presence and dominance within the denomination.

Conclusion

What began as radical support of abortion's removal from the criminal code and of abortion "upon request" in order to allow women to exercise their right to control their reproductive lives and bodily selves, was, by 2016, a highly restrictive statement, which still supports a woman's right to an abortion but only under certain conditions and if performed in a certain way. Since the early 1980s, and especially after "The Durham Declaration," evangelical United Methodists united to combat The UMC's stance on abortion using the rhetoric of the pro-life movement and of the New Christian Right. The General Board of Church and Society and the Commission on the Status and Role of Women fought to undo these restrictions and maintain the relationship with RCRC; but as of 2016, their efforts were thwarted by the evangelical voice. In 2016, the General Conference voted to withdraw United Methodist membership from RCRC, ending the relationship with the organization it founded more than forty years earlier, and the General Conference did not support "Responsible Parenthood," a resolution that endorses women's health care and a woman's right to an abortion. Due to these actions, five annual conferences—Oregon-Idaho, California-Nevada, New England, New York, and Pacific Northwest—voted to independently support RCRC at the national and state level.[163]

Evangelicals believed that these two General Conference decisions were a "necessary and good step towards affirming that the unborn are persons of sacred worth," and proved that The UMC was "moving away from other liberal, declining, 'mainline' denominations to embrace a new faithful, global

---

162 "General Conference Legislative Summary," Good News website, June 21, 2016, http://goodnewsmag
.org/2016/06/general-conference-legislative-summary/.

163 Kathy L. Gilbert, "5 Conferences Join Faith Coalition on Reproductive Rights, Abortion," United
Methodist News Service, June 22, 2016, http://www.umc.org/news-and-media/oregon-idaho-takes
-up-support-for-rcrc-denied-at-gc2016.

identity."[164] Others saw the move as a denial of United Methodist support of women's health and women's rights. Harriet Jane Olsen, top executive of United Methodist Women, believes that "abortion is just one procedure available for one part of a woman's life cycle," and that RCRC was more concerned with women's whole health and not just an advocate for abortion.[165] She continues, "The need for women to have the care they need in order for them to thrive so that their families can thrive is very compelling." To some United Methodists, withdrawal from RCRC and the removal of Responsible Parenthood was a sign that The UMC was no longer willing to openly support women's healthcare.[166] The official withdrawal from RCRC and the removal of "Responsible Parenthood" proves that evangelical United Methodists dominate the abortion debate at the General Conference level. However, the choice of individual annual conferences to support RCRC and to create their own resolutions on parenthood showcases how the denomination is continually divided over issues of sexuality. The tension of the sexuality debate increases exponentially when the rights and status of LGBTQ persons in the life and ministry of the denomination are considered.

---

164 Gilbert.
165 Gilbert.
166 Gilbert.

5

AMERICAN METHODISM
AND HOMOSEXUALITY

A BREAKING POINT

Joanne Carlson Brown was a self-identified lesbian attending Garrett-Evangelical Theological Seminary in the late 1970s, when two of her classmates were expelled from the school for being "self-avowed homosexuals." After graduation, she sought ordination in the Rocky Mountain Annual Conference, under the authority of Bishop Melvin Wheatley, a progressive bishop who refused to sign the Episcopal Address of the 1980 General Conference due to its endorsement of the "incompatibility clause." Bishop Wheatley, aware that Brown was a lesbian, ordained her in 1982, as the *Discipline* did not yet prevent him from doing so. Reverend Brown was the first self-proclaimed, practicing lesbian to be ordained in The United Methodist Church, and never stood trial for being so. Her ordination was upheld by the Judicial Council, which stated that there was nothing in the *Discipline* that prevented her ordination, a fact that would soon change.[1]

The rights and status of persons who identify as gay or lesbian have been discussed at every General Conference since 1972; however, Methodists discussed the theological foundations of homosexuality and were actively involved in the homophile movement prior to that. This chapter will trace the history of the (United) Methodist stance regarding the rights and status of gay and lesbian persons. It will argue that 1972 was a pivotal turning point for The UMC, creating a breaking point between Methodists, invigorating the formation and politicization of caucus groups within the denomination, and moving the denomination from a progressive stance on homosexuality toward a conservative

---

1   R. W. Holmen, *Queer Clergy: A History of Gay and Lesbian Ministry in American Protestantism* (Cleveland, OH: Pilgrim Press, 2013), 474; "Rev. Dr. Joanne Carlson Brown," The Lesbian, Gay, Bisexual, and Transgender Religious Archives Network, accessed January 7, 2017, https://www.lgbtran.org/Profile.aspx?ID=22.

position. Homosexuality, unlike any other aspect of sexuality discussed previously, solidified the authority of General Conference as the only official voice of the denomination, specifically through decisions regarding chargeable offenses. This invigorated annual conferences, bishops, local clergy, and laypersons to take stances against the power and proclamations of General Conference. This chapter will proceed in the same method as previous chapters. It will begin with a brief examination of the social and political history of the U.S., focusing on the homophile and gay liberation movements of the 1950s through 1970s, followed by an examination of Protestant reactions to these movements (prioritizing Methodist sources when available), and finally, it will end with a thorough examination of how United Methodism reacted to those movements. The United Methodist section will follow consecutive General Conferences, looking at the events that happened between them and the legislation passed during each.

THE HOMOPHILE MOVEMENT AND GAY LIBERATION

In chapter 2, this book argued that the cult of togetherness was promoted by American Protestantism and the American government as a way to ensure healthy, heterosexual family life as a patriotic duty and Christian responsibility. Heterosexuality was the recognized norm during the 1950s, and the sexual intimacy of married heterosexual couples was promoted as proper Christian morality by Protestant ministers. This new ideology of healthy sexuality created an "other," the unhealthy or deviant sexual person, the homosexual. In the 1950s, a growing subculture brewed and then fully emerged into society in the 1960s as the homophile movement, a movement advocating homosexual self-affirmation and acculturation into heterosexual society. Gay, white men sought to prove that they were not a threat to the heterosexual social-sexual order, while fighting for the right to be sexual citizens in American society. However, according to historian Robert O. Self, "Gay men in the homophile movement questioned both heterosexuality and conventional manhood, upending the most indomitable taboo of modern American life." In a similar manner, Self continues, "lesbians challenged similar, but distinct, sexual and gender ideologies."[2]

Homosexuality was rarely a topic of public discussion until after World War II. During the war, homosexual persons were barred from service, and any

---

2   Self, *All in the Family*, 75.

persons suspected of homosexual activity were dishonorably discharged and subsequently labeled sexual deviants. In the context of Cold War America, government officials were convinced that homosexual persons were vulnerable to blackmail from Communist organizations, and the federal government began the Lavender Scare, a period of purging any and all suspected homosexual persons from federal employment, resulting in thousands of layoffs in the 1950s. Federal agencies were not the only organizations suspicious of homosexuality. Local police viewed homosexuality as a cause of urban vice, and homosexual persons were arrested and charged with everything from lewdness and solicitation to vagrancy and sodomy, the latter of which could carry a twenty-year sentence.[3]

As of 1952, the American Psychiatric Association in their *Diagnostic and Statistical Manual* labeled *homosexuality* as a type of "sexual deviation," and subsequently classified it as a "sociopathic personality disorder." Believing homosexuality could be cured, and that all persons were naturally heterosexual, doctors sent homosexual persons to psychiatrists for help, where they were often subjected to aversion therapy and electric-shock treatment. Gay men, more than lesbians, were thought to be a threat to American society, because they directly threatened the foundation of American society: American manhood. Gay men were believed to be either hyper-feminine—"weak, womanish, and laughably unmanly; they were convenient foils for heterosexual manhood and its breadwinner and soldiering prototypes" or hyper-masculine—"gay men were just the opposite, exhibiting too much of the wrong kind of manliness—sexual voraciousness."[4] Either way, gay men, in the Cold War imagination, were not viewed as fully men. In a similar vein, women who identified as lesbian challenged the social order in two ways: their economic independence of the male breadwinner and their challenge to conventional notions of womanhood, specifically motherhood. As a result, Self argues, lesbians represented a rejection of "two of America's most powerful mythologies and a subversion of how the country defined itself, the family, and its priorities."[5]

In response to this negativity, in 1950 and 1955, respectively, two organizations, the Mattachine Society and the Daughters of Bilitis, formed and sought

3   Self, 76–79; Smith, *Secular Faith*, 98–99.
4   Self, 79.
5   Self, 172.

to prove to the American public that homosexuality was not a disease, not a crime, and not a sin. These organizations struggled throughout the 1950s without proper organization and under the scrutiny of Cold War America.[6] However, in the early 1960s, their efforts began to challenge existing laws that inhibited their civil rights.

In 1961, Frank Kameny, a Harvard-trained astronomer who was fired from his job with the Army Maps Service in 1957 for being gay, helped form the Washington, DC, branch of the Mattachine Society in hopes of overturning regulations that discriminated against employment of homosexual persons. He believed respectable protest—the donning of suits and ties, heels and skirts—was the best form of protest. His idea was to prove to America through example that homosexual persons were respectable citizens. These types of protests caught media attention and "by the end of the 1960s, this pioneering band had succeeded in disseminating widely a point of view that diverged sharply from the dominant consensus about homosexuality."[7]

The homophile movement changed the conversation about citizenship to include sexuality. No longer was "minority status" based solely on "race, sex, ethnicity, nationality, or religion," but also on "sexual or erotic identity." By the end of the 1960s, the homophile movement forced Americans to recognize a different type of life that did not exist within a heterosexual perimeter and to acknowledge that "citizens don't just have a sex; they *have* sex."[8]

Around the same time, another version of homosexual rights made social strides. Whereas the homophile movement sought to fight for gay rights by proving that homosexuals were no different than heterosexuals, others celebrated the fact that homosexuals *were* different than heterosexuals. In March 1968, the first "gay in" occurred in Griffith Park, Los Angeles, California. Hundreds of homosexual persons gathered in a local park dressed in a variety of non-conforming attire. Led by a drag-queen, the celebration called homosexual persons to "come out of the dark shadows of fear and paranoia and to establish themselves as free American citizens."[9] Deemed "swishes" or "exhibitionists," Self argues that these persons wanted the "freedom for sexual expressiveness

6   John D. Emilio and Estelle B. Freedman, *Intimate Matters: A History of Sexuality in America*, 3rd ed. (Chicago: University of Chicago Press, 2012), 320; Smith, *Secular Faith*, 100–101.
7   Emilio and Freedman, 320.
8   Self, *All in the Family*, 84–85, emphasis original.
9   As quoted in Self, 88.

and gender transgression" and "personal freedom through sexual authenticity."[10] Thus two versions of the gay rights movement existed by the end of the 1960s: one sought equal rights in the eyes of the law; the other sought to assert a separate gay identity in American society.

The two, arguably, merged their efforts after the events of Stonewall Inn. On June 27, 1969, New York City police raided the Stonewall Inn, a gay bar in Greenwich Village. Tired of continual police harassment, this time, the patrons of the bar fought back. The hubbub attracted a crowd, which joined in resisting and protesting the police. Riots continued throughout that night and the subsequent night, and "graffiti proclaiming 'Gay power' were scribbled on walls and pavements in the area." With these riots, a new movement emerged, one focused on gay liberation.[11] Within weeks, hundreds of new gay organizations, including the Gay Liberation Front and the Gay Activist Alliance in New York City, sprang up across the country, signaling the beginning of the gay liberation movement. The next summer, on the one-year anniversary of Stonewall, the "largest mass demonstration by homosexuals . . . to date" gathered in New York City and around the U.S., proudly marching in defense of their sexuality.[12]

The 1970 march was covered by national media, with gays and lesbians using their own voices to participate in the national debate. A Harris poll conducted in both 1965 and 1970 asked the same question to measure what Americans thought of homosexuality: "America has many different types of people in it. But we would like to know whether you think each of these different types of people is more helpful or more harmful to American life." The list included "homosexuals," "prostitutes," "beatniks," "young men with beards and long hair," and "women who wear bikini bathing suits." In 1965, 70 percent believed that homosexuals were harmful to American society. By 1970, 53 percent believed homosexuals were harmful. Historian Mark Smith argues that "in public opinion polls, changes this large in only five years are rare, occurring only in special situations when people encounter new information."[13] The homophile movement and public affirmation of homosexuality, along with the events of Stonewall, changed the minds of many Americans. By 1973, the American Psychiatric

---

10   Self, 88.
11   Emilio and Freedman, *Intimate Matters*, 319.
12   White, *Reforming Sodom*, 138–39. Marches were also held in Chicago and Los Angeles in 1970. Today the Gay Pride parade is celebrated in most major cities in the U.S. and is a commemoration of Stonewall.
13   Smith, *Secular Faith*, 101–3.

Association removed homosexuality from its list of personality disorders, an act largely due to the research and efforts of persons like Evelyn Hooker, a clinical psychologist who argued that gay and straight men had the same psychological function; and to gay rights activists who picketed annual events of the APA.[14]

PROTESTANT RESPONSES TO THE HOMOPHILE MOVEMENT AND GAY LIBERATION

Historian Heather R. White's *Reforming Sodom: Protestants and the Rise of Gay Rights* is an exceptional work that brings together American religious history and the history of LGBTQ persons. She makes three basic arguments to prove that Protestants were not silent regarding homosexuality in the early-to-mid-twentieth century. First, she argues that the biblical antihomosexual stance is a modern-day invention that was not, as some might assume, inserted into biblical translations by evangelical Christians; but instead, was inserted into Scripture through the work of liberal Protestants who, in their desire to use scientific methods and terminology to better understand the Bible, replaced certain scriptural terms and phrases with "homosexuality." Second, White argues that the liberal Protestant determination to create a new, healthy, non-procreative heterosexual ethic (the topic of chapters 1 and 2 of this book) created a heterosexual/homosexual binary, which favored the former as natural, healthy, and moral. Third, she argues that Protestants played a major role in forming and supporting the homophile movement in the 1960s as part of their efforts of *therapeutic orthodoxy*, at first hoping to cure homosexuals and later hoping to reform the Christian sexual ethic to be accepting of homosexuality.

In chapters 1 and 2, this book argued that Protestant clergy in the 1940s and 1950s preached a new sexual ethic, one that encouraged marital sexual intercourse for pleasure's sake as part of a new construction of Christian marriage. This type of healthy sexuality was now considered a part of one's natural, divinely created self. Young adults were encouraged to take sex education courses during high school and premarital courses during college; and married couples were encouraged to seek marital or pastoral counseling, where they learned about healthy sexuality and sexual adjustment in marriage. White argues that this "priz[ing] of sexual health and normalcy" through pastoral

---

14   Smith, 101–3.

counseling was "an expression of actualized spirituality," or what she calls *therapeutic orthodoxy*.

Protestants in the 1940s argued that non-procreative heterosexual sex should not be categorized as sodomy; instead, they argued, this form of marital sex increased marital intimacy, which, in turn, glorified God. In other words, liberal Protestants "reformed religion in order to emancipate healthy sexuality." In doing so, however, they unintentionally created an unhealthy sexuality.[15]

Something had to be substituted for non-procreative heterosexual sex now that sodomy was redefined, and that something was homosexuality. In the 1946 translation of the Bible, the Revised Standard Version, the term *homosexual* is first used in place of *sodomy*.[16] The problem with this substitution was twofold. First, it limited the original definition of sodomy when, in actuality, sodomy referred to a whole host of acts and not only same-sex acts. Sodomy originally included masturbation, oral and anal sex, and non-procreative heterosexual sex; and it was also a term for "perceived enemies of the faith" including "Muslim infidels, American Indian pagans, perverse Papists, and sodomitical Reformers." Essentially, sodomy referred, negatively, to any sexual act that was not heterosexual, reproductive sex. White argues that to simply replace one act, non-procreative sex, with another act, homosexual sex, ignores an entire history of "religious, racial, and colonial alterity."[17] The second problem was that the substitution assigned to Scripture and to homosexuality a history of condemnation that was not previously there, and it did not qualify the difference between individual same-sex acts and the homosexual orientation or identity, which developed in the late nineteenth century and came to the forefront of American society in the 1950s and 1960s. Thus, when people interpret Scripture as condemning certain same-sex acts, they are in fact interpreting their own twentieth-century concept of homosexuality—something foreign to biblical intent—into the text.

American society has limited itself to a binary of two categories: homosexual and heterosexual. Some members of society consider only one of those to

---

15   White, *Reforming Sodom*, 8.
16   White, 2. For a full, exegetical explanation of the translation of homosexuality into scripture see Smith, *Secular Faith*, 122–28.
17   White, 11.

be moral, and have applied this limited binary to Scripture, placing it in a historical context in which it did not originally exist. Queer theorist Kathy Rudy argues:

> Thus it is only because we live in a culture that divides gay and straight (and uses one category to define the other) that we see certain historical practices as "gay" even though the people who participated in those practices would not have recognized them in such terms, . . . To use the categories of homosexuality and heterosexuality to understand the construction of sexuality in any past era is to ignore the reality that sexualities and their meanings are produced within specific cultural contexts.[18]

When liberal Protestants translated *sodomy* as *homosexuality*, they created future controversy over the morality of homosexuality in Scripture. Their translation deemed homosexuality a sin, assigning it a scriptural context, a Christian history, and an immoral connotation that it did not originally have. Some may refute this claim and argue that homosexuality was always understood as sinful. But this is where queer theory is vital to this project. It is vital to remember that the morality of sexual action is dependent on historical context, and sexual morality is not consistent across history. The translation of *sodomy* as *homosexuality* is subject to its historic context of the early twentieth century; in a similar manner, sodomy meant something very different when it was originally written into the scriptures.

In order for liberal Protestants to create a new Christian sexual ethic that was not limited to procreative sex, they had to disassociate non-procreative sex and sodomy. "By the 1950s," White states, "a new map of sexuality was firmly in place: it prized the wholesome goodness of heterorelationality, the affectionate bond between husband and wife, and the necessity of sexual pleasure within marriage."[19]

PASTORAL COUNSELING: THE HENRY FOUNDATION

During the first half of the twentieth century, as chapters 1 and 2 have shown, pastoral counseling increased in popularity. However, homosexual persons also sought pastoral counseling. Pastors focused not only on providing sex education and preventing premarital sex but also on preventing sexual devi-

---

18 White, 94.
19 White, 11.

ancy, which included same-sex desires, and preventing sexual maladjustment, which many believed led to same-sex desires. In the context of Cold War America, thousands of gay men who were dishonorably discharged from the military or recently fired from their jobs flocked to (or were referred to) the clergy for help; and due to new medical research, liberal Protestant clergy sought to cure homosexual persons and not condemn them. In the 1950s, new medical and psychological research suggested that homosexuality was a "thwarted maturation," and homosexual persons, if guided through their "emotional conflicts" could return to the "natural progression of their heterosexual desire."[20] By the mid-1950s, many liberal Protestant clergy viewed homosexuality less as a sin (evangelical Protestants would continue to view homosexuality as a sin) and more as a "developmental condition" that could be cured with therapy.[21]

This construction of sexuality was originally evident in liberal clergy's participation in the George W. Henry Foundation. Founded in 1948, the Henry Foundation was a counseling center begun by George Henry and Alfred Gross to help coach gay men into living the double life, heterosexual in public and homosexual in private. It provided legal counsel, job placement, medical advice, and pastoral counseling. Gross believed that pastoral counseling could help gay men see that there "are no untouchables" in the eyes of God, and he viewed the clergy as a necessary ally in preventing "homosexuals' self-defeating slide into almost certain disaster."[22] Clergy were moral guides and assisted homosexual persons with self-acceptance by encouraging them to acknowledge their sexual desires, a type of Protestant confessional. The end goal of the Henry Foundation was not change, but assimilation. Many of the clergy involved with the Henry Foundation, after many conversations with gay men, began to understand their innermost struggles. As a result, they began to change their minds about homosexuality, seeing it as a natural form of sexuality, one not in need of a cure but in need of full acceptance.[23]

---

20 White, 25.
21 White, 41.
22 White, 51–52.
23 White, 48–55.

The Council on Religion and the Homosexual

The earliest Protestant group to accept homosexual persons as a minority sexual identity was the Council on Religion and the Homosexual (CRH), the brainchild of Methodist minister Ted McIlvenna and based out of Glide Memorial Methodist Church in San Francisco. The CRH was the result of a four-day consultation (May 31–June 2, 1964) between fifteen liberal Protestant clergy and fifteen representatives and members of homophile organizations.[24] For the first time, clergy found themselves listening to and learning from the gay community about the community's needs and how the church could assist them in bettering their lives.[25] Don Lucas, a gay man and representative of the San Francisco Mattachine Society, reported to the consultation:

> The homosexual is a human being. He has a soul and Christ Consciousness just as do all other human beings. He loves, lives, and has feelings and emotions which are really no different from those of his so-called heterosexual counterpart. All human beings are looking for understanding, love, and approval. The homosexual is no exception.

---

24 In attendance were: William Black (Lutheran Church of America), Roger Burgess (Methodist Board of Christian Social Concerns), Hal Call (Mattachine Society, San Francisco), Robert W. Cromey (Protestant Episcopal Church), Lewis Durham (Glide Urban Center), Robert J. Durksen, Cleo Glenn (Daughters of Bilitis), Bill Billings, Darryl Glied (Jumpin' Frog), Bob Koch, Donald Kuhn (Glide Urban Center), Don Lucas (Mattachine Society, San Francisco), Orville Luster (Youth for Service), Phyllis Lyon (Daughters of Bilitis, San Francisco), Jan Marinessen, Del Martin, Ted McIlvenna (Young Adult Project, Glide Memorial Methodist), John Moore (The Methodist Church), Charles E. Mowry (Methodist Board of Education), C. Kilmer Myers (Chicago Urban Training Center), Dennis F. Nyberg (The Methodist Church), Bill Plath (D'Oak Room), Walter Press (United Church of Christ), Keith Right (National Council of Churches), B.J. Stiles (*motive* magazine), Guy Strait (League for Civil Education), Billie Talmijj, Pat Walker, Dale White (Methodist Board of Christian Social Concerns). Those listed without an organization by their name were members of the San Francisco gay community. Glide Memorial was known as a progressive Methodist church. Glide's progressiveness is described by a 1967 news article in the *Wall Street Journal*: "The church holds 'soul jigs'—rock 'n' roll concerts—in its sanctuary. It sponsors a retreat for clergymen and homosexuals; a dance for male prostitutes. It hands out $1,000 to hire Negro gang leaders as 'peace monitors' to help quell a race riot." *Wall Street Journal*, March 13, 1967, http://www.lgbtran.org/Exhibits/CRH/ImageSet.aspx?AID=3&P=10.

25 White, *Reforming Sodom*, 84–86. The more informative document to emerge from this retreat is the "Consultation Report," written by Glide minister Rev. Donald Kuhn. At thirty-nine pages, it chronicles the responses from both the clergymen and the gay activists who attended the retreat and provides background to the founding of the Council on Religion and the Homosexual in 1964, shortly after the retreat. The "Consultation Report" begins with a word from the male homosexual community, with Don Lucas speaking on their behalf. Prior to the retreat, Lucas asked 150 people who identified as male homosexuals, questions on how they perceived the church's outreach or lack thereof to the homosexual community. Only forty agreed to answer his questions, and from these forty interviews he presented the consultation with many conclusions, of which only a few will be analyzed and read: "The church does not understand [homosexuality] because it is afraid to delve into the subject. . . . The church should stop limiting its moral concerns to safe subjects such as alcoholism, etc. . . . The church should study the subject of homosexuality, do research in this field, and make known its findings. . . . The clergy must be educated about homosexuality before they, in turn, can educate their congregations."

It is felt that the church is best suited to demonstrate to all human beings these attributes, because they are primarily of a spiritual nature.[26]

Lucas challenged the church to serve the community by recognizing
and welcoming homosexual persons and by updating its doctrine to reflect
modern notions of sexuality. He stated that the church "is not perceived as
anti-homosexual. Rather it is anti-sexual."[27]

Using language familiar to the clergy, Lucas asked them to be an example
of acceptance and openness. C. Kilmer Myers spoke on behalf of clergy representatives and admitted that there was no consensus on how various denominations view homosexuality, and in fact, there was mostly "mass silence on
the subject" on behalf of clergy and often "hostility and even fear" from Protestantism at large. Myers affirmed White's argument that the church tends to
view "the same sexual patterns" throughout all of history and argues that "the
church is beginning to recognize a new pluralism in this area." He hoped that
the four-day consultation would help "project new paths which are appropriate
for a new age."[28] Both clergy and homosexual persons challenged each other
to drop their preconceived notions of the other and engage in honest dialogue.
This type of dialogue opened up the minds of clergy to better understand that
homosexuality was not a disease, but a natural, God-given form of sexuality. After four days of dialogue, the group agreed to continue their relationship with
each other in a more official capacity.

The goals of the CRH as an organization were to educate the clergy on non-
heterosexual aspects of sexuality; to create opportunities for the gay community
to educate congregations on sexuality; to continue dialogue between the gay
community and pastors; to influence the nation at large on how homosexual
persons were targeted by law enforcement and discriminated against by existing laws; to encourage other denominations, clergy, and homophile organizations to engage in dialogue; and to help the clergy understand more fully their
role as pastoral counselors in a changing sexual climate.[29] The CRH was created

---

26 Donald Kuhn, *The Church and the Homosexual: A Report on the Consultation* (San Francisco: Council on
    Religion and the Homosexual, 1966), 7–8; LGBT Religious Archives Network, accessed 1//2017, http://
    www.lgbtran.org/Exhibits/CRH/ImageSet.aspx?AID=16&P=1; the item can also be found in the records
    for the General Board of Church and Society at the United Methodist Archives, Drew University.

27 White, *Reforming Sodom*, 8.

28 White, 4.

29 White, 32. According to the LGBT Religious Archives, "This was the first group in the U.S. to use the
    word 'homosexual' in its name," http://www.lgbtran.org/Exhibits/CRH/Room.aspx?RID=2&CID=7.

out of "the growing awareness on the part of clergymen of the extent to which homosexuals had been shut out of the church and society." The CRH brought together clergy, local congregations, homosexuals, heterosexuals, and members of local homophile organizations "to embark on an urgently needed action program aimed at disseminating accurate information about human sexuality."[30] Their main goal was education of one another and of the public. The CRH was never an official national organization, although local branches were established in other major cities (Denver, Chicago, Dallas, Kansas City, Boston, Honolulu, and Ottawa, Ontario).[31] The CRH created what White calls "enablers," clergy and congregations who provided "funding, meeting and office spaces, access to communication and publishing services, and support for direct action advocacy" for local homophile organizations.[32] White argues, "For many of these [homophile organizations], the critical connection to start them came through urban ministry programs. At the center of the fledgling organizing efforts were urban ministers working on outreach in 'homosexual ghettos.'"[33] Thus, liberal Protestant clergy, like those who began the CRH, were vital to the formation, organization, and success of various local homophile organizations. Through the community formed of combined civil reform efforts and education, clergy began to see homosexuality, not as a curable disease, but as a natural sexual variation.

This shift was best summarized by the words of the Reverend Cecil Williams, senior pastor of Glide Memorial Methodist, who stated in 1968, "We will be silent no longer. We know that homosexuals are not sick, criminal, or sinful. . . . We must give the word to the professional community—the church must take the lead in showing a way to understanding the homophile world."[34]

This new theological understanding of homosexuality as a God-given form of sexuality made its way into the Christian press and sermons. Robert Cromey, an Episcopal priest who was active in the CRH, wrote in 1967, in his denomination's main journal, that it was a Christian's duty to "lead the way in insisting that homosexuals be given their rights as citizens and be treated as human

---

30   "CRH brochure" LGBT Religious Archives Network, accessed 1/8/2017, http://www.lgbtran.org/Exhibits/CRH/Room.aspx?RID=2&CID=7&AID=18.
31   White, *Reforming Sodom*, 93.
32   White, 88.
33   White, 93.
34   As quoted in White, 105.

beings."[35] Similarly, *Social Action*, a periodical of the United Church of Christ, focused on civil rights. The director of the UCC Council for Christian Social Action, Lewis Maddocks, argued that the Christian church was "the institution most vehement in its opposition to the homosexual," and it was thus up to the Christian church to take responsibility in helping homosexual persons gain civil rights. He asked his congregations to stop "exhorting homosexuals to 'give up their sinful ways'" and to stop their own internal discrimination against homosexuals through denial of seminary admission, ordination, and employment in local churches. Maddocks believed that the new Christian sexual ethic must apply "the same criteria" to all sexual relationships, "whether a relationship is heterosexual or homosexual."[36] *New World Outlook*, periodical of the United Methodist Board of Global Mission, printed a collection of small articles in 1970 that sought to show "a renewed awareness that homosexuals are first of all persons and must be dealt with in a Christian context of respect for persons."[37]

THE SERMONS OF THE REVEREND JOHN V. MOORE

The Reverend John V. Moore was senior minister at Glide Memorial Methodist when the CRH was developed as part of its urban outreach ministry. In response to its development and his congregation's new involvement with the local gay community, he developed a three-week sermon series on sexuality beginning January 10, 1965, which sought to provide his congregation with a new sexual ethic that was based in the "new morality" and that would help all members of the congregation "integrate [their] sexuality into [their] personhood."[38] Like any well-thought-out sermon series, the sermons built on each other. The first sermon, "Man, Sex, and the Gospel," sought to undo the separation between persons and sex that was common in the 1960s. He stated, "The greatest sexual problem of our day is the alienation of sex from persons." He continued, "Men talk about 'having sex'" and yet "they say nothing of the context in which men 'have sex.'"[39] In order to correct this alienation, Moore believed that people

---

35   As quoted in White, 99.

36   White, 99.

37   "The Church and Homosexuality: A Changing Picture," *New World Outlook* (September 1970): 25–29.

38   John V. Moore, "Man, Sex and the Gospel," 1; folder: "Sermons 1965," Moore Papers, 2144-4-3:3, Drew University.

39   Moore, 2.

needed to view each other as persons and not as objects; they needed to learn to see the humanity and the God that exists in each other. One has the ability to "grow in the capacity to see every fact of life in relation to the whole of life"; and by learning to relate oneself to others, "human beings who were things will be transformed into persons."[40] If one no longer sees persons as objects but as fully human, then one will begin to see "sex in relation to persons" and can begin to "integrate our sexuality into our own personhood."[41]

Moore went even further and claimed that "the crisis of sex in our day is not in premarital but is in postmarital relationships."[42] Here, Moore critiqued ministers who placed sexual morality solely in terms of premarital relationships, and ignored the often complicated sexual experiences of married couples. More often, he believed, persons became objects after marriage; they became breadwinners, housekeepers, mothers, fathers, roommates, but they failed to be fully human, appreciated for all aspects of their humanity. And thus, postmarital sex, according to Moore, was where sexuality tended to be most alienated from personhood. Whether within marriage or outside of marriage, persons had to learn to maintain a higher standard for sexuality, and the only appropriate standard was one that respects the full humanity of all actors. He concluded this first sermon with a powerful statement that recognized the need for full expression and acceptance of all forms of sexuality:

> Every human emotion, positive or negative, can be expressed sexually within the bonds of marriage as well as outside of marriage. Jesus said that he came that we might live rich, full lives. Denial of our sexuality, alienation of our sexuality, repression of our sexuality all stand in the way of the full life. We will experience the kind of life which Jesus helped man find only when our sexuality, as every other dimension of our lives, is fused with love, the kinds of love we see in his life.[43]

Moore's second sermon, "Church, Community, and Homosexuality," was most likely the first Methodist sermon on homosexuality that accepted it as a vital form of sexual expression. The sermon was exegetical and focused on Paul, whom Moore considered "the most misunderstood man in the history

40 Moore, 3.
41 Moore, 3.
42 Moore, 4.
43 Moore, 4–5.

of Christian thought."[44] Immediately, Moore argued that it was unfair to Paul to understand his words outside of their historical context. Moore stated that Paul's condemnation of homosexuality was often taken on its own, out of context of the other condemnations which stated that *all* men have fallen short of the glory of God. . . . We're all in the same boat."[45] This sermon, according to Moore, did not focus on homosexuality; it focused on "persons who because of their sexual identification are estranged from both the church and the community." His sermon, in fact, did focus on homosexuality, but he made this claim to critique the homosexual/heterosexual binary and to show that there were persons who claimed one, the other, or neither identity who were still discriminated against due to their implied sexuality. Moore continued:

> There are reportedly 70,000 to 80,000 persons who are homosexual in San Francisco. The difference among these persons, intellectually, socially, in appearance, and in every other way are as great as the difference in the community at large. Most of these citizens work, pay taxes, and contribute to the welfare of the community. Insofar as I know, they are law-abiding, save in reference to certain laws pertaining to sex. There are exhibitionists among them as there are in the heterosexual community. They are rejected by the churches and the community. They live with the fear of exposure. They know anxiety and loneliness. They love and hate. They aspire and create. We are human beings together, different as groups only in sexual identification.[46]

When compared to statements made a few years prior—by Protestant clergy who worked with the Henry Foundation and sought to cure homosexual persons by bringing them back to God, that is, to a heterosexual orientation—Moore's words were incredibly radical.

This statement on its own was evidence that attitudes were shifting in the relationships built between the clergy and the homophile community through the CRH. The CRH exposed the humanity of persons who identified as homosexual and exposed the ignorance of clergy. Fostering dialogue, creating community, and recognizing one another's humanity was the most effective way

---

44   John V. Moore, "Church, Community, and Homosexuality," 1; folder: "Sermons 1965," Moore Papers, 2144–4–3–:3, Drew University.

45   Moore, 3, emphasis his.

46   Moore, 3.

to change how homosexuality was perceived. Moore continued his sermon, touching on the legal discrimination of homosexual persons, how they were perceived as threats to children, and the medical community's misunderstanding of sexual identification. He concluded with a challenge to his congregation, his community, and the church at large, to help every person—young, old, male, female, heterosexual, and homosexual—to "discover and shape their identity." This was solely the job of the church, for "we can't really know who we are, nor create our identity until we see ourselves in relation to God." Once a person had a sense of who he or she was, the church had the responsibility to accept that person for who he or she was for "no good can come from rejecting persons."[47] This second sermon builds off the first. The first was intended for self-reflection, to help congregants understand their own sexuality in relation to God and to recognize the God-given sexuality in others. The second sermon recognized the multitudes of sexuality that existed because everyone had a unique relationship with God and therefore a unique expression of their full selves. If church was a community of God, then it should welcome all persons without qualification.

The third sermon, "Chastity and the Pill," really did not focus on chastity or the pill. Instead, Moore focused on undoing the "old morality" of legalism, which sought to impose restrictions, or "codes of conduct," on individuals. A better morality, which was called the "new morality," was based in ethics, which "aris[e] from within individuals rather than imposed upon them by some external authority." Moore argued that "morality tells you in advance what is right and wrong"; but to "act ethically means to take the insights of others, [and] to make our own decision in the situation in which you find yourself."[48] Living an ethical, as opposed to moral, life was the best avenue for sexual self-expression, which honored the themes of the first two sermons. If persons made their own decisions based on the situation at hand, then they could fully live into how they understood themselves, their sexuality, and their relation to God and others.

Moore's sermons made headlines across San Francisco and as far as New Zealand and Australia.[49] His willingness to preach that all persons were equal

---

47   Moore, 6.

48   John V. Moore, "Chastity and the Pill," 3; folder: "Sermons 1965," Moore Papers, 2144-4-3:3, Drew University.

49   John V. Moore, "Article for *Manna for the Journey*, Feb 1986; Addresses and Papers, 1966–1986, Moore Papers, GCAH, 1.

in God's eyes, regardless of their sexuality, and that all persons should, there-fore, be equal in the church's eyes, brought ministers from all over the U.S. to Glide Memorial to learn how to relate to their communities and how to edu-cate their congregations on matters of sexuality.[50] Moore was not alone in his willingness to make such proclamations, but he was the first Methodist to do so from a pulpit.

OTHER METHODISTS SUPPORT GAY RIGHTS

Other publications called for "homosexual marriage." Paul Jones was a Meth-odist minister in Kansas City, who, along with his associate Van Anderson, be-gan a night ministry where the two donned their clerical collars and ventured into gay bars to be available for counsel if desired; they began the Phoenix So-ciety for Individual Rights, which sought to educate local clergy, faculty, and students at the local Methodist seminary (St. Paul's Theological Seminary). He wrote "Homosexuality and Marriage: Exploring on the Theological Edge," pub-lished in *Pastoral Psychology* in 1970. He began the article describing what was to be the first same-sex wedding to occur in a United Methodist Church. In the

---

50 The work of Glide Memorial Methodist was emulated throughout Methodist congregations in the U.S. The reverends Alex Smith and Ken Wahrenbrock, Methodists from Southern California, came to Glide and later created their own local CRH. Clarence Colwell, a UCC minister, did the same. Other CRHs formed in Denver, Dallas, Kansas City, Boston, Honolulu, and Ottawa, Ontario. Other ministers came to Glide and then created their own organizations modeled after the CRH. Methodist ministers Paul Jones and Vann Anderson created the Young Adult Project and the Phoenix Society for Individual Rights. The former was a night ministry that ventured into local communities and bars and offered pastoral counsel-ing on-site to anyone who wanted it. The latter was an educational endeavor to teach local Methodist congregations, pastors, and students and faculty at St. Paul's Theological Seminary about homosexual-ity. In Dallas, Doug McLean, a Methodist minister, created the Circle of Friends, which brought together local homophile organizations and clergy and gave them space to work and coordinate. Methodist min-ister Harper Richardson of Portland, Oregon, began a coffeehouse ministry, which provided a safe space for community action organizing of gay and lesbian organizations (White, *Reforming Sodom*, 92–95). Twenty years later, Moore reflected on his sermon series in an article for *Manna for the Journey*, the jour-nal of the Reconciling Congregations Program. At the time he wrote and preached the series, he "didn't know if what I was going to say was right or wrong." He knew of no precedent for reference and relied solely on contemporary literature and his relationship with persons through the CRH to craft his words. His goal was twofold: "The first was coming to know and respect women and men whose sexual orien-tation was different from my own. The second was my gut feeling where the spirit of Christ was lead-ing me" toward "acceptance and inclusiveness of people." Moore received varied responses from the sermon series. He records two. The first stated, "Sir, the Methodist Church hierarchy has reached a new low of gutter morals in allowing you to preach a sermon on accepting homosexuals." The second, more affirming, stated, "My desire to fit into some sort of artistic life in San Francisco, which I knew existed, brought me here. . . . I had known rejection, insults, and the smug-stone-throwing even . . . while in my teens. . . . I eventually found friends and the wonderful world of music, art and literature. But the great-est boon was to learn that there were other people like myself." Moore admits that his own personal views of homosexuality did not change quickly but that "coming to know lesbians and gay men was so important" for the evolution of his views ("Article for *Manna for the Journey*; folder: "Addresses and Pa-pers, 1966–1986," Moore Papers, 2144–4–3:1, Drew University).

summer of 1968, two women approached two clergy—most likely himself and Anderson, but the names of the clergy are left out of the article—and asked the clergy to help them make a "covenant for life" and declare their "intention to be 'one flesh'" in a church setting "publicly before God."[51]

With the wedding on the agenda of a United Methodist church, it received a substantial amount of local press. Due to local and, most likely, ecclesial pressure, the wedding never occurred in a Methodist sanctuary. Jones uses this story as a basis to deconstruct the Christian belief that homosexuals could change and to build a new Christian sexual ethic that viewed homosexuality as equal to heterosexuality and thus deserving of marriage. He argued, "It is crucial that the Christian silence his natural hostility to the homosexual" and recognize that "the traditional Christian insistence on 'cure' is unrealistic."[52] To support this statement, he cited the Wolfenden Report. Originally a 1956 report by the Church of England, the Wolfenden Report was published in America in 1963. It called for the end of sodomy laws because they discriminated against homosexual persons. This report claimed that "evidence leads us to conclude that a total reorientation from complete homosexuality to complete heterosexuality is very unlikely indeed."[53] Therefore, "The most valuable form of therapy" clergy "can in fact provide is not to cure a homosexual of his homosexuality but to help him come to terms with it and live with it."[54]

Clergy were then left with "over seven million homosexuals that must be served now, as they are, without cure or even possibility of cure being a factor in defining our responsibility to their needs."[55] Therefore, when two persons of the same sex asked to make a life-long commitment to each other in front of God, what reason did the clergy have to deny them that right? The new Christian sexual ethic, the "new morality," required a separation between "morality and immorality" and "the presence or absence of homosexual feelings, attitudes, and acts." Instead of an "ethics and homosexuality" approach, Jones called ministers to live into an "ethics of homosexuality," which required

---

51 W. Paul Jones, "Homosexuality and Marriage: Exploring on the Theological Edge," *Pastoral Psychology* (December 1970): 29.
52 Jones, 30.
53 Jones, 30.
54 Jones, 31.
55 Jones, 31, emphasis his.

approaching and treating homosexuality as if it were heterosexuality.[56] If one did this, then the end goal of a committed, loving relationship was marriage.

Jones concluded, "Profound relations between two members of the same sex *is not only morally permissible but is to be sought, encouraged, supported, and enabled with all the power at our command.*" He continued, "An act" whether sexual intercourse or marriage, "which expresses true affection between two individuals and gives pleasure to them both, does *not seem to us to be sinful by reason alone* of the fact that it is *homosexual.*"[57]

By 1970, many liberal Protestant clergy accepted the notion that homosexuality was a natural, God-given, sexual minority and should be treated and evaluated in the same manner as heterosexuality.

THE EVANGELICAL RESPONSE

However, not all Protestants held the same views of homosexuality. Conservative evangelicals, as previous chapters have shown, found a renewed voice in the 1960s, especially in regard to sex education and in opposition to the "new morality." One of the reasons they opposed the new morality was not only that it allowed for premarital sex; it also argued for the acceptance of homosexuality as God-given sexual identity. They preferred a morality that was based on scripturally mandated rules, a black-and-white view of what was right and wrong, moral and immoral. For them, "the pleasures of sex had unambiguous boundaries," and "rules—clear ones—guided godly men and women toward marriage and blocked off the various detours from [that] ultimate goal."[58]

Prior to the 1960s, most conservative evangelicals did not speak of homosexuality. After the 1960s, as the topic became more popular in the Christian press, they began to assert their view of homosexuality as a condemnable sin, according to the authority of Scripture, and as a sin that could be cured through a proper relationship with God. Evangelicals continued the mainline liberal Protestant view of sexuality and homosexuality that was preached in the 1950s and 1960s, but carried this sexual ethic into the 1970s and beyond.

Many, but not all, liberal Protestants were slowly becoming more accepting of homosexuality as a minority identity and of the "new morality" in the

---

56 Jones, 32.
57 Jones, 37, emphasis his.
58 White, *Reforming Sodom*, 127.

1960s. Thus, the main contention in the 1960s between liberal Protestants and conservative evangelicals remained sex education, not homosexuality. However, homosexuality would become a point of contention by the late 1970s when conservative evangelicals produced a "biblically authorized, revelation-bound, born-again sexual gospel."[59]

An article from *Christianity Today* best summarizes the conservative evangelical position. It began by calling out "straight Christians" who, due to their "neglect, fear, [and] hatred" of homosexual persons, "brush these people under the rug." Instead of ignoring homosexuals, Tom Minnery, the article's author, argued that Christians should accept homosexual persons "sin and all" and guide them in their "deliverance from homosexuality."[60] The author followed this statement with a few stories of persons who had "conquered" their homosexuality due to the "acceptance and love" of Christians and of God. Minnery believed that the most effective way to change a homosexual person was not through aversion therapy or electric shock treatment. Instead of seeing homosexuality as a sign of immature psychological development, he stated, evangelical Christians view it as "a sign of Christian immaturity." Homosexual persons "would learn how to be heterosexual as they developed Christian maturity."[61] This frame of mind led to the creation of the idiom "love the sinner, hate the sin" and the formation of "ex-gay ministries," both of which are still promulgated throughout many evangelical denominations and within some evangelical wings of mainline Protestantism.

Evangelical Christian condemnation of homosexuality turned more political in the late 1970s through the campaign efforts of Anita Bryant. Bryant reiterated conservative beliefs when she said, "God loves them. I love them. I love them enough to tell them the truth—that homosexuality is wrong, not by my standards but by God's."[62] Residents of Miami, Florida, in 1977, passed an antidiscrimination ordinance that prohibited discrimination against gay persons in housing, employment, and other forms of public accommodation. Bryant, appalled, began a campaign to overturn the ordinance, which quickly gained national attention as she was already a television personality. Believing that gay

59   White, 129.
60   Tom Minnery, "Homosexuals Can Change," *Christianity Today*, February 1981, 37.
61   Minnery, 38.
62   Nickell, *We Shall Not Be Moved*, 93.

men sought to "molest" or "recruit" children to a homosexual lifestyle, she began Save Our Children, a campaign that made Miami the epicenter of the gay rights campaign for six months.[63] To the surprise of many local residents and gay rights activists, Bryant won. Afterward, she took her organization to the national level with the help of Jerry Falwell. Together, the two created an antihomosexuality platform that, along with abortion, "mobilized conservative evangelicals throughout the nation," reinvigorated the New Christian Right's campaign against secularism in American society, and "launched the political careers of several future leaders of the Christian Right."[64]

As discussed in previous chapters, the New Christian Right in the 1970s was convinced that the "traditional family" was under assault. The rising divorce rate, premarital sex, *Roe v. Wade*, and the Equal Rights Amendment threatened the family from within and without. And now, gay liberation was an additional threat. Throughout the 1970s, gay liberation organizations worked at the federal level to lobby for legislative protection from discrimination. In response, and after Bryant's fall from fame due to a divorce and negative publicity, the Christian Voice united several existing anti-gay organizations and established an agenda to elect congresspersons who held or endorsed anti-gay platforms.[65]

In 1979, Jerry Falwell and Pat Robertson realized the potential political power of the New Christian Right and set out to create a comprehensive political agenda that would be enacted through the lobbying efforts of the Moral Majority. The Moral Majority was the first true attempt of the New Christian Right at partisan political influence.[66] Their efforts were supported by demographic changes. Evangelical denominations, such as the Southern Baptist Convention—that, due to fundamentalist dominance in the denomination, became more conservative in their social stances—and megachurches with at least two thousand members sprang up across the nation. Evangelicals were more educated in the 1970s, and evangelical authors wrote best sellers such as Hal Lindsey's *The Late, Great Planet Earth*.[67] The Moral Majority, and other organizations like it, advocated American exceptionalism, the idea that the United States played a major role in God's plan. Proponents of American exceptionalism

---

63 Self, *All in the Family*, 242–43.
64 Williams, *God's Own Party*, 147.
65 Williams, 146–53.
66 Williams, 160.
67 Williams, 162.

CHAPTER FIVE

believed that overt threats to the American family in the 1970s—along with the energy crisis, economic crisis, and international disputes—proved that God was angry with Americans because of their sexual laxity.[68]

Over time, the conversation shifted from preventing antidiscrimination legislation to preventing same-sex marriage through the Federal Marriage Amendment (FMA). In much the same way that the New Christian Right sought to add a Human Life Amendment to the U.S. Constitution to protect the rights of the unborn, they sought to define marriage in the U.S. Constitution as between one man and one woman. Civil unions gained popularity during the 1990s, and President Bill Clinton signed into law the Defense of Marriage Act (DOMA), which gave states the right to deny recognition of civil unions performed in other states. DOMA, however, could easily be overturned by future leaders, and the New Christian Right sought a more permanent resolution to the question of same-sex marriage. By 2004, the New Christian Right was powerful enough (and the evangelical voting bloc large enough) to force President George W. Bush to endorse the FMA in his reelection campaign.[69]

Toward the end of the 1970s, James Dobson, best described as a Christian psychologist, began his career as a host on *Focus on the Family,* a radio show that gave parental and marriage advice to concerned parents raising children and trying to maintain a moral lifestyle. The show was broadcast for over two decades, and by 1995, it was the third most popular radio show in America.

Throughout the 1980s, Dobson used this radio program as a political platform. In 1983, he created the Family Research Council to engage in more direct political lobbying.[70] One of these efforts was the FMA. He believed that "the homosexual activist movement" had achieved too much in its fifty years of political engagement and was "poised to deliver a devastating and potentially fatal blow to the traditional family" if homosexual persons continued to seek the right to marry.[71] He found homosexual marriage to be a direct threat to the institution of marriage. According to Dobson, homosexuals were too sexually promiscuous to maintain the biblical standards for marriage and would eventually seek to eliminate marriage altogether. After *Lawrence and Garner v. Texas*

---

68 Williams, 172–77.
69 Williams, 256–58.
70 Williams, 236–37.
71 Williams, 257.

struck down Texas's anti-sodomy laws based on the "right to privacy," and af-ter the Episcopal Church appointed its first openly gay bishop, the New Chris-tian Right was even more determined to put an end to the gay rights movement by permanently blocking same-sex marriage. After the repeated failure of the FMA, the debate moved to the states.[72] According to historian Mark Smith, "Be-tween 1998 and 2010, states voted a total of thirty-one times to pass a statute or amend the state constitution to define marriage as an institution between one man and one woman." Thirty of these elections ended with a legal prohi-bition against same-sex marriage. On the other side of the debate, Massachu-setts was the first state to legalize same-sex marriage in 2004, and by 2014, thirty-five states legalized same-sex marriage.[73] Thus, in a similar manner to abortion, the country was, once again, divided over sexuality.

UNITED METHODISTS AND GAY RIGHTS

By 1970, a divide was present between how liberal Protestants and conservative evangelicals viewed homosexual persons. This divide was present within United Methodism from its inception. The new denomination sought to produce a new set of social pronouncements in a context of rapid social change. It was evident to the 1968 General Conference that "the united church faced a new world sit-uation, both in the complexity of old social problems and the urgency of aris-ing new ones."[74] The original statement on human sexuality was written after four years of work by the Social Principles Study Commission, a commission tasked by the 1968 General Conference to present to the 1972 General Confer-ence a revision of the entire Social Principles. This section of the book will fo-cus on the subsection "The Nurturing Community," specifically, its paragraph "Human Sexuality," which has created more divisiveness in The UMC than any other paragraph. In the 1970s, Methodists began to form caucus groups at an unprecedented rate. After this paragraph was amended in 1972, they be-came highly political, advocating for amending the paragraph or defending its wording. During the next four decades, other, more restrictive paragraphs were added and limited the rights and the status of those who identify as gay or

---

72 Williams, 258–260.
73 Smith, *Secular Faith*, 110.
74 "Report of the Social Principles Study Commission," Charles D. White, ed., *Journal of the 1970 Special Session of the General Conference of The United Methodist Church*, 869.

lesbian in the denomination. With each General Conference, Methodist caucus groups advocated on behalf of extreme ideological and theological ends, pulling and tugging at those who positioned themselves in the middle.

THE 1972 GENERAL CONFERENCE

At the 1972 General Conference, the Study Commission presented the following text on "Human Sexuality." It will be analyzed a few sentences at a time. It began:

> We recognize that sexuality is a good gift of God, and we believe persons may be fully human only when that gift is acknowledged and affirmed by themselves, the church, and society. We call all persons to disciplines that lead to the fulfillment of themselves, other, and society in the stewardship of this gift.[75]

This should sound familiar, as it reflects what Rev. John V. Moore stated in 1965 (discussed above). Lacking any mention of heterosexual or homosexual identities, these two sentences call the church to help all persons acknowledge and affirm their unqualified sexuality as a divinely created part of their full personhood, and to use whatever "disciplines" were available to them to help them fully actualize their true selves, including their sexuality. It continued, "Medical, theological and humanistic disciplines should combine in a determined effort to understand human sexuality more completely." In 1972, the APA had not yet removed homosexuality as a sexual perversion, and many doctors still considered it a disease or thwarted maturation. Here, the Study Commission believed more work needed to be done in order to better understand the psychology and biology of various sexual orientations. "Although men and women are sexual beings whether or not they are married," it continued, "sex between a man and a woman is only to be clearly affirmed in the marriage bond." Here, a normative definition of sex limits its affirmation to only those acts that are between a man and a woman and only within marriage; thus, the denomination was willing to impose certain rules or restrictions to sexuality. However, the opening phrase, that men and women are sexual no matter their marital status, seems to undermine the conclusion by acknowledging that sex can and does occur outside

---

75 *Daily Christian Advocate* (Nashville: United Methodist Publishing House, 1972), 484. Hereafter cited as *DCA* with the year following.

of marriage. In accordance with previous phrases, these acts were still a part of God's good gift. It continued:

> Sex may become exploitive within as well as outside of marriage. We reject all sexual expressions which damage or destroy the humanity God has given us as birthright, and we affirm only that sexual expression which enhances that same humanity, in the midst of diverse opinion as to what constitutes that enhancement.

Again, these two sentences reflect the words of Rev. John Moore. In his first sermon, "Man, Sex, and the Gospel," he argued that objectification of persons occurred both within and outside of marriage, alienated people from their sexual encounters, and hindered their sexual expression. The two sentences above agree with Moore. Only sexual encounters that allowed persons to live into and express their full humanity (including all aspects of their sexuality) honored God. The last phrase openly stated that there was a "diverse opinion" on what types of sexual expression enhanced humanity. This was confirmed in the next sentence, which established the heterosexual/homosexual binary: "Homosexuals no less than heterosexuals are persons of sacred worth, who need the ministry and guidance of the church in their struggles for human fulfillment, as well as the spiritual and emotional support of a fellowship which enables reconciling relationships with God, with others and with themselves." Even though a binary was established in this last quotation, the Study Commission nevertheless believed that no matter a person's sexual orientation, he or she was of "sacred worth." The rest of the sentence can be interpreted in two ways. One, it fully welcomes homosexuals into the church and states the church should help these persons in their struggles to affirm and acknowledge their sexuality identity as homosexuals, in order to have the best possible relationship with God, with community, and with self. Or, two, it fully welcomes homosexual persons into the church and states it is the church's job to guide them through their sexual struggles to affirm and acknowledge their true (hetero)sexual selves through a right relationship with God, with others, and with self. In other words, this sentence could be read as either affirming nonheterosexual identity or seeking to change nonheterosexual identity. Thus, this sentence should be understood as reaching out to all Methodists, despite their political leanings, allowing them to interpret the denomination's stance as they best see fit. The final sentence, "Further we insist that homosexuals are entitled to have their human and civil rights insured," spoke against the legal and civil discrimination against homosexual persons and implied that homosexuality should be protected as a minority status, but did not state how the denomination would be involved in protecting civil rights.[76]

The proposed statement was discussed Wednesday, April 26, 1972, and the proceedings of the floor of General Conference were recorded in the *Daily Christian Advocate* (*DCA*). What ensued on the floor of General Conference can only be described as chaos. The original report was amended multiple times, with each amendment also amended or substituted. Due to the complicated nature of parliamentary procedure, delegates exhibited confusion as to what motions were before them and whether or not their affirmative or negative vote would accept or reject the motion. Add to this interruptions in the form of applause or derision from observers, and the beginning of a pattern of divisiveness over human sexuality was evident, one that would plague each General Conference from 1972 to the most recent in 2016.

After a brief discussion on abortion, the General Conference moved to discuss subsection C, "Human Sexuality." The discussion began with a question about the last phrase that ensured that the civil rights of homosexual persons were protected. The question, asked by Russell Kibler of South Indiana, was simply, "What does this mean?" Mr. Robert W. Moon of California-Nevada presented and spoke on behalf of the Study Commission. Moon stated that the last phrase was a statement against the firing of persons from their place of employment simply because they were homosexual; he called this a "violation of a natural right that is theirs."[77] After hearing Moon's and the Study Commission's reasoning, Kibler moved to delete the sentence because "homosexuals are preying upon the young men" in his hometown, and thus he believed their firing, especially from places of educational instruction, was valid. Before anyone could speak for or against Kibler's amendment, his amendment was amended by Carlton Dodge of Eastern Pennsylvania, who moved to delete the last two sentences of the original paragraph.[78] Dodge believed that if the paragraph was

---

76 The entire paragraph can be found in the *DCA* (1972), 484. The entire report of the Study Commission is found on pages 483–87.

77 *DCA* (1972), 705.

78 "Homosexuals no less than heterosexuals are persons of sacred worth, who need the ministry and guidance of the church in their struggles for human fulfillment, as well as the spiritual and emotional support of a fellowship which enables reconciling relationships with God, with others and with themselves. Further we insist that homosexuals are entitled to have their human and civil rights insured" (*DCA* [1972], 484).

going to name an "abnormal sexual behavior," it must include more than just homosexuality, and he believed the church should take a "forthright stand on the moral issues of the day" instead of condoning them.

After these two opinions, McKinnon White of Southern New England argued that the delegates were not understanding the full intent of the paragraph, which was to ensure that civil rights for all humans were guaranteed and to recognize homosexuals as persons in the eyes of God. The dialogue proceeded back and forth with some continuing the argument that homosexuals prey upon little boys (Kenneth Cooper, Alabama-West Florida) and others continuing to argue that homosexuals were persons in need of acceptance by the church (Katherine W. Wilcox, West Michigan). All relied on their personal and professional experience with homosexual persons. According to the General Conference rules, before a vote could be taken there must be two speeches for and two against the motion. However, after hearing two speeches for and two against, an amendment to delete the last two sentences and a substitution to the motion were brought forth. The substitution would keep the last two sentences but would change the last sentence to read: "Further we insist that all persons are entitled to have their human and civil rights insured." With this new motion before the delegates, an argument for and against were heard. After parliamentary confusion and inquiry, a vote was taken that supported the substitution. Thus, the conclusion of this part of the debate amended the final two sentences to read:

> Homosexuals no less than heterosexuals are persons of sacred worth, who need the ministry and guidance of the church in their struggles for human fulfillment, as well as the spiritual and emotional support of a fellowship which enables reconciling relationships with God, with others and with themselves. Further we insist that *all persons* are entitled to have their human and civil rights insured.[79]

After the vote was taken and another motion made, the previous vote was called into question over the concern that delegates were unsure of what they voted for. According to parliamentary procedure, a motion was made to "call for the previous question on what is before us." This awkward phrasing essentially means that the next vote would, first of all, affirm or deny the substitute

---

79   *DCA* (1972), 709, amended language in italics.

as the main motion, and second, conclude any changes made to the paragraph. After the motion was sustained, the conversation moved on to paragraph B, "Marriage." Immediately, parliamentary inquiries were brought to the floor, and the previous motion was reconsidered.

The proceedings continued and turned to discuss the paragraph on marriage. As presented, the paragraph affirmed marriage between "a man and a woman." The question here was whether or not this sentence also condemned same-sex marriage. Moon stated that the Study Commission "made no affirmation" as to the morality of same-sex marriage. An amendment was brought forth, which would add "We do not recommend marriage between two persons of the same sex."[80] The ensuing debate concerned the theological basis of marriage. Would marriage between two persons of the same sex "fulfill God's purposes in establishing [the] institution"? Some believed that not condemning same-sex marriage would drive current members away from the church. Others believed that the church had not "thought [sexuality] out well enough."[81] Walter Muelder (Southern New England) pleaded for "compassion and justice" and asked the General Conference "not to make prejudged or final issues or judgements on any one aspect of [sexuality] which would pre-judge all future thinking and reflection in our church on its social principles."[82] Upon vote, the amendment to add a statement not recommending same-sex marriage was added. After the vote, the DCA recorded an "INTERRUPTION ON FLOOR OF CONFERENCE."[83] There was no indication of what type of interruption occurred or if it was in support of the vote or against the vote.

In the middle of a discussion to amend the word "support" to "care" in the paragraph entitled Human Sexuality, another amendment was made. Don Hand, lay delegate from Southwest Texas, proposed adding "though we do not condone the practice of homosexuality and consider this teaching incompatible with Christian doctrine" to the last sentence of the paragraph.[84] This amendment has come to be called the "incompatibility clause" and is the most

---

80 DCA (1972), 710.

81 DCA (1972), 711.

82 DCA (1972), 710.

83 DCA (1972), 711, emphasis original.

84 It then read, "Further we insist that homosexuals are entitled to have their human and civil rights insured, though we do not condone the practice of homosexuality and consider this teaching incompatible with Christian doctrine." DCA (1972), 712. Later on, the word doctrine would be changed to teaching. DCA (1972), 718.

debated clause in the Social Principles, if not in United Methodist history. Hand believed, if amended, this final sentence would not "do violence to either side."

The debate on this one paragraph was nearing the end of its second hour, and in order to continue the debate, a vote was taken to extend the time of plenary.[85] Thus, the most hotly contested phrase in the history of The United Methodist Church was conducted at the end of the morning session, under extended time, with delegates desiring to break for lunch. After a failed substitution, which would have endorsed what have come to be called ex-gay ministries, and a few more parliamentary inquiries as to what motion was before the delegates, the floor returned to Hand's incompatibility clause. The amendment and a vote on the entirety of Section C, "Human Sexuality," were both supported.[86]

Twenty-two years later, Don Hand was interviewed by United Methodist News Service about the origins of his amendment. Hand's statement was reprinted by UM Voices of the Institute on Religion and Democracy, a far-right group. As a lay representative to the 1970 Southwest Texas Annual Conference, Hand experienced his first "glimpse of disruptive and disrespectful behavior by a clergy member." The clergy in question was charged and convicted with heterosexual misconduct, and his clergy credentials were suspended. The following year, another clergy, Gene Leggett, was charged with homosexual misconduct and his clergy credentials were also revoked.[87] Hand was appalled that Leggett brought with him "a large group of males attired in white robes," who continuously "disrupted the meeting creating stress and disorder." They "berated Bishop Slater" during worship, and Hand, a trial attorney, informed the gentlemen that "they were violating state law by disrupting a church service and could be prosecuted." Hand believed this disruption was an "expression[n] of entitlement by pastors and supporters who were unwilling to abide by centuries-old standards of Christian morality." Due to his efforts, he was elected a lay delegate to General Conference.

Here it is worth taking a moment to explain how votes were taken and how persons were called on to speak on the floor of General Conference. In the early

---

85   Don Hand, in a later interview, refers to the time spent on the debate just prior to his amendment. "Don Hand: Homosexuality and the 1972 Social Principles—Did the Conflict Begin with 'the language'?" *Juicy Ecumenism* (blog), July 4, 2014, https://juicyecumenism.com/2014/07/04/don-hand-homosexuality-and -the-1972-social-principles-did-the-conflict-begin-with-the-language/.

86   *DCA* (1972), 713.

87   Leggett's credentials were suspended by the 1971 Southwest Texas Annual Conference by a vote of 144 to 117. Holmen, *Queer Clergy*, 464.

1970s, delegates were given color-coded placards that corresponded to their vote and included opportunities to ask questions, make motions, or make a parliamentary inquiry. At the 1972 General Conference, there were around one thousand delegates present. The bishop sat on a raised platform at the front of an arena with the delegates spread out before him.[88] From here, the bishop was, in theory, able to see all of the delegates. However, as is evident from reading any *DCA* from 1972 onwards, persons toward the back of the room were ignored because they were hard to see. Bishops also tended to favor certain persons over others; the same names are called to the microphone again and again. During the proceeding that discussed the paragraph "Human Sexuality," Bishop Slater of the Southwest Texas Annual Conference presided. Don Hand was a lay representative of Southwest Texas, and the previous year had shown his immense respect for the bishop by quelling the disruption during annual conference session. Thus, it is not a surprise that Don Hand, out of the one thousand persons present, was acknowledged on the floor of General Conference.

At the 1972 General Conference, Hand noticed "a growing sense of uneasiness and despair among the delegates regarding the statement on human sexuality due to its ambiguity and inconsistency with traditional Christian doctrine." He continued:

> For example, the proposal states that "sex between a man and a woman is to be clearly affirmed only in the marriage bond," and yet provides no statement governing any other form of non-exploitative sexual activity between other persons other than to assert that "we affirm only that expression which enhances that same humanity, in the midst of diverse opinion as to what constitutes that enhancement." This language reflected the ideology of the sexual revolution of the late 1960s and early 1970s in its embrace of recreational sexual intercourse as a means of personal gratification and a civil right. As such, it was a serious departure from the teachings of the Christian tradition that risked conforming the moral standards of the Church to the licentious behavior of the world. Many delegates were fearful that the adoption of the proposed statement would result in the immediate division of the four-year-old denomination.[89]

---

88 All United Methodist bishops were men until 1980, when Marjorie Matthews was elected in the North Central Jurisdiction.

89 "Don Hand."

The idea that homosexuality and heterosexuality were biblically mandated or condoned has already been dealt with in this chapter. Hand disagreed that the Social Principle was a middle-of-the-road statement. He viewed it as a full endorsement of a lax morality. As such, he felt compelled to reinsert morality into the statement.

Not everyone viewed Hand's amendments as positive for the denomination. Victor Paul Furnish, a United Methodist New Testament scholar, believed that the incompatibility clause drastically changed the tone of the Social Principles:

> What had started out to be solely an expression of pastoral concern for homosexual persons ended up including a clause which appeared to give theological warrant to a widespread opinion that all homosexuality is "sinful" and that homosexual persons are dangerous to both themselves and society.[90]

Scholar Jane Ellen Nickell concludes that the 1972 debate on human sexuality carried a "fearful" tone, "reflecting not only a fear of gay men as sexually dangerous, but also fear of change."[91] Some feared that welcoming anyone into the church would diminish the church's moral authority; others feared that being too exclusive would diminish the church's social witness and mission. In its passing, Hand, unknowingly ensured that progressive and evangelical factions of The UMC would become highly politicized and would debate or defend the seventeen words of the incompatibility clause for the next forty-four years and counting.

REACTIONS TO THE 1972 GENERAL CONFERENCE

The aftermath of the 1972 General Conference and its incompatibility clause was immediately felt by politically minded persons within The UMC. However, most United Methodists just felt confused as to where their denomination actually stood on homosexuality, specifically, and sexuality, in general. Nickell points out some of the reasons for their confusion. During 1972:

> Delegates expressed fear of gay men as sexual predators; resistance to same-sex marriage as an erosion of traditional values and morality; support for the rights of gay and lesbian persons from those who

---

90 Nickell, *We Shall Not be Moved*, 95.
91 Nickell, 98.

disapproved of their sexual behavior; affirmation of both gay identity and same-sex sexual acts; and general confusion over the causes and effects of homosexuality and the nature of sexuality in general. Some saw homosexuality as an immoral choice, while others understood it as a sinful proclivity to be resisted, and a smaller group claimed it as a normal sexual variant.[92]

Delegates had a right to be confused; due to the nature of the amendments, certain paragraphs were both affirming of all sexualities and condemnatory of certain sexualities. These contradictions had ramifications as United Methodist caucus groups sought to interpret the Social Principles in ways that benefited themselves and their cause. The incompatibility clause also fueled both extremes and energized their political actions to either remove or defend the clause.

In the spring of 1973, Rick Huskey and Gene Leggett took the initial steps in forming a network of gay United Methodists. Leggett, an out gay clergyman, was suspended in 1971, in Southwest Texas. Rick Huskey, a gay man who was out in certain social circles but not within The UMC, graduated from Garrett Theological Seminary and attended General Conference 1972, where he met Leggett. When they heard of Steve Webster's attempt to attend seminary and seek ordination as an openly gay man, they sent him a letter of encouragement. Webster was not confirmed by his congregation, which was the first step needed to be accepted into a United Methodist seminary on an ordination track. Denied ministry in one form, Webster took it upon himself to join the efforts of Leggett and Huskey and fight for the rights of homosexual persons in the denomination. The three were joined by Richard Cash, a college student and board member of several UM agency boards who was interested in gay activism. These four organized over the next few years and held the initial meeting of the United Methodist Gay Caucus—soon to be called Affirmation—in the summer of 1975, when about twenty Methodists gathered in Evanston, Illinois, at Wheaton UMC.[93] Their primary purpose for 1975 was to prepare for 1976 General Conference, where they hoped to overturn the incompatibility clause.[94]

The conservative reaction to 1972 was mostly negative. They believed that

---

92 Nickell, 101.
93 Also in attendance were Rev. Earnest Reaugh (New York), Peggy Harmon (Dallas), Keith Spare (Kansas City) and Michael Collins.
94 Holmen, *Queer Clergy*, 464–66.

progressives won in 1972, in all areas except in regard to homosexuality. The six-teen thousand petitions sent in on behalf of Good News were "mishandled."[95] They protested Rev. Cecil Williams's sermon as part of a General Conference worship service, believing him to be "the denomination's most radical and con-troversial preacher of the left," largely for his involvement and endorsement of the CRH.[96] Evangelical-leaning Methodists felt further shunned when Billy Gra-ham was ridiculed from the floor of General Conference for "being indifferent to social needs," a move that they tried to have stricken from the record, but that was voted down.[97] Good News also protested the creation of new agen-cies; the Commission on the Status and Role of Women, the Commission on Religion and Race, the General Council on Ministries, the Board of Social Con-cerns, and the United Methodist Youth Council.[98]

The 1972 General Conference welcomed more ecumenical relationships with other Protestant groups and with Jewish persons, avowing not to seek to convert Jews in their combined ministerial efforts.[99] Finally, the General Con-ference declared "doctrinal pluralism" as the basis for the new denomination's approach to theology. Good News believed doctrinal pluralism was an "indi-vidualistic, anti-Biblical approach to theology" or a "Smorgasbord theology."[100] The only positive Good News saw out of 1972 General Conference was the in-sertion of the incompatibility clause to the Social Principles. Thus, they vowed to step up their efforts between 1972 and the 1976 General Conference to "cure the church" of its liberal tendencies. Keysor, the head of the Good News Move-ment and editor of its periodical, argued, "There is nothing unchristian about politics practiced for a Gospel purpose." Instead of calling his followers to form a new denomination, he called his new followers to be political:

> Therefore, let us organize at every level; let us take full advantage of the freedom that is ours. Let us elect lay delegates to Annual Con-ference. Let us elect delegates to General and Jurisdictional Confer-ences. Let us elect bishops too. Let evangelicals work systematically to gain control of key positions in the local church: the Committee on

---

95   "Editorials: In the Aftermath of Atlanta," *Good News*, Summer 1972, 34–35.
96   "Editorials: In the Aftermath of Atlanta," 36.
97   "Editorials: In the Aftermath of Atlanta," 36.
98   "Editorials: In the Aftermath of Atlanta," 39–40.
99   "Editorials: In the Aftermath of Atlanta," 39.
100 "Editorials: In the Aftermath of Atlanta," 43. Doctrinal pluralism was adopted by a vote of 925 to 17.

> Nominations, first, then Pastor-Parish relations, Education, Missions, Finance and Administrative Board. Remember that a small, dedicated, unified group banded together and supporting candidates by block voting can win against a large, disorganized, apathetic majority.[101]

And political they became. In April 1974, Good News held a board meeting where "the board recommitted itself to the cause of renewal, to spiritual encouragement, and set a course that would include greater political involvement." A large part of this political involvement would include efforts to keep the current wording of the human sexuality paragraph, if not make it more restrictive. By the spring of 1974, "the board . . . realized, perhaps for the first time, that the issue of homosexuality would be a point of controversy in the months (and years) to come."[102] This stance was corroborated in an article in the Spring 1974 issue of Good News, which read, "The signs are incredibly clear that a major homosexual storm is gathering. It seems to be part of a nationwide effort to eliminate the stigma against homosexuality . . . not only in the church, but in public education, government, and everywhere."[103] Good News viewed the American Psychiatric Association's removal of homosexuality from its list of sexual perversions and the increased efforts of the gay liberation movement as threats to their families and to their religion. Furthermore, they believed that their own denomination was "a top . . . target in the effort to legitimize homosexual practice."[104] They named six ways that The UMC was bending toward accepting homosexuality, which contributed to their efforts in 1976 to ban the funding of gay caucuses and their first attempt to ban the ordination of homosexual persons.

(1) In 1974, the Judicial Council, which decides the constitutionality of General Conference pronouncements, affirmed that Gene Leggett, who was suspended for being homosexual in 1971, was eligible for appointment. (2) The newly formed United Methodist Council on Youth Ministries set aside $400 to fund the "The National Task Force on Gay People in the Church," an ecumenical gay rights group, a move that inspired the conservative efforts to ban funding of gay rights organizations by official Methodist agencies at the 1976

101 Charles Keysor, "Where Do We Go from Here?" Good News, Summer 1972, 52–53.
102 Case, Evangelical and Methodist, 207.
103 Charles Keysor, "Editorial: The Gathering Storm," Good News, Spring 1974, 19.
104 Keysor, 19.

General Conference.[105] (3) The Council on Youth Ministries requested that homosexuality "'not be a bar to the ministry' and that 'homosexuality in itself not be in any way synonymous with immorality.'" According to Good News, it was evident that the Council on Youth Ministries was working directly with the newly formed Gay United Methodist Caucus to write legislation for 1976 General Conference.[106] (4) *New World Outlook*, the periodical of the United Methodist Board of Global Ministries, printed an article in support of homosexuality in its May 1973 issue. According to Good News, "The historic, biblical teaching of the Christian church as against homosexuality is not presented—on the contrary, it is scorned by the whole tone of this article."[107] Good News believed that the printing of this article "amounts to a *de facto* endorsement of homosexual practice by the Board," and argued that since apportionment dollars funded the magazine, United Methodist "dollars are being used to promote homosexual practice."[108] (5) Global Ministries recognized the existence of the National Task Force for Gay People in the Church through a $500 contribution to the organization.[109] (6) The California-Nevada Annual Conference sent ministers to attend an ecumenical "Consultation on Homosexuality" at Berkeley, which, according to a Good News report, declared the church "wrong and guilty" of homophobia and recognized homosexuality as "good, beautiful, spiritual, poetic, lovely, one of God's gifts."[110] These six things worried Good News about The UMC's focus on social activism more than evangelism, and they were the catalytic moments for their politicization against homosexuality.

THE 1976 GENERAL CONFERENCE

The General Conference of 1976 would set the tone for the next forty years. Would the denomination maintain its 1972 stance on homosexuality? Good News and Affirmation came to General Conference ready to lobby for their respective causes. Affirmation hosted worship services with their allies, the

---

105 The ban became paragraph 906.13 of the *Book of Discipline*. It read, "The council shall be responsible for ensuring that no board, agency, committee, commission, or council shall give United Methodist funds to any 'gay' caucus or groups, or otherwise use such funds to promote the acceptance of homosexuality. The council shall have the right to stop such expenditures." *BOD* (1976), 337.
106 Keysor, "Editorial: The Gathering Storm," 20.
107 Keysor, 20. The *New World Outlook* article is "The Church Comes Out" by Charles Lerrigo.
108 Keysor, 20.
109 Keysor, 20–21.
110 Keysor, 21.

Women's Caucus, the Council on Youth Ministries, and the Methodist Federation for Social Action. Keith Spare, an openly gay man and representative of Affirmation, was allowed to speak before the delegates, pleading his case for inclusion from the floor of General Conference.[111] Good News was the only official group at General Conference to declare in writing that it supported the incompatibility clause.[112] According to Good News, General Conference that year received eleven thousand petitions dealing with some aspect of human sexuality.[113] Both Affirmation and Good News spoke directly with delegates about sexuality in an effort to try and sway votes. To the dismay of Affirmation and the satisfaction of Good News, the incompatibility clause was sustained.

Good News's political efforts against official agency funding of gay caucuses were successful. This was seen as a direct attack on Affirmation and on the Council on Youth Ministries. Finally, the General Council on Ministries, Women's Division, Commission on the Status and Role of Women, and Board of Discipleship all brought forth a proposal for a "quadrennial study of the Christian faith and human sexuality." They believed that this should be not just a "general study" but a study of human sexuality at all levels of the church, including the local church, where it might have the most impact.[114] Such a study would allow for a deeper exploration and possible understanding of all aspects of human sexuality in the context of rapid social change and would help the church respond to these changes in an effective and appropriate manner.

A minority report agreed that a study was needed but disagreed with the type of study. It wanted the General Council on Ministries to provide resources for local congregations to conduct their own studies of human sexuality, if they chose to do so. The minority report was accepted by a vote of 477 to 446, and

---

111 Holmen, *Queer Clergy*, 466–67. His words can be found in the *DCA* (1976), 783. They read, "Sisters and brothers of the United Methodist Church, we of the United Methodist Gay Caucus are painfully sensitive to the complex nature of the issues which are before us in the matter of Gay people in the life and struggle of our Church. We come before this body breaking a history of silence and invisibility which has surrounded this issue. This silence has been a perpetuation of untold suffering not only of our Gay brothers and sisters and their families, but the entire Christian community. As we move toward a new horizon of what we hope to be a grace-filled dialogue we cannot ignore the inevitability of residual fears and misunderstandings. Yet our Christian duty demands we acknowledged that all persons have fallen short in the glory of God and need the saving grace of our Lord and Savior Jesus Christ. Throughout this week our caucus has attempted to hold before you this model of openness and dialogue. We pray now in the issues that are before you that the action of this Conference will reflect a willingness of our Church to continue in this dialogue. Thank you."

112 Case, *Evangelical and Methodist*, 208.

113 Nickell, *We Shall Not Be Moved,* 102.

114 *DCA* (1976), 887.

any study on human sexuality was up to the local churches.[115] Despite not securing a ban that would prevent homosexual persons from becoming ordained
ministers, the results had Good News, *Christianity Today,* and *Christian Century*
declaring 1976, "the year of the evangelical," not only within American politics with the election of born-again Jimmy Carter, but also within The UMC.[116]
Christianity Today declared, "Conservatives in the 9.9 million-member United
Methodist Church are still pinching themselves to make sure that The UMC's
sudden shift to the right is not just a dream."[117] Similarly, *Christian Century*
stated, "After the smoke cleared, it was evident that the conservative . . . Good
News' movement, which had worked for two years to affect decisions made
here, could take satisfaction in its success in moving the church to respond to its
concerns."[118] Good News celebrated their legislative victories during 1976, but
also recognized that there was much still to do. For both Good News and Affirmation, it was clear after 1976 that General Conference was to be *the* place for
political activism in the years to come and *the* social-religious battlefield where
the two extremes would fight for their causes.

Events between 1976 and 1980 affirmed that homosexuality was to remain a topic of conversation at the next General Conference. In 1975, Rick Huskey informed his bishop that he was gay, and his bishop removed him from his
current appointment. In 1977, the Minnesota Annual Conference revoked his
clergy credentials.[119] Also in 1977, a *New York Times* article brought Paul Abels
to the United Methodist headlines. Reverend Abels was pastor of Washington
Square United Methodist Church in New York City where he "had a vibrant
ministry to the gay community of Greenwich village." The *New York Times* article discussed "covenant services" that Abels had performed on behalf of his
congregants. Abels informed his bishop that he was gay, and the bishop immediately attempted to remove him. However, this time, the Annual Conference upheld Abels's appointment and so did the Judicial Council, which found
that as a minister, Abels was "in good standing."[120] That year, United Methodist
seminaries (Garrett-Evangelical Theological Seminary, Iliff School of Theology,

---

115 *DCA* (1976), 898.
116 Case, *Evangelical and Methodist*, 210.
117 Ed Plowman, "United Methodists: The View from Portland," *Christianity Today,* June 18, 1976.
118 "Methodism's Spirit of '76: Don't Rock the Church," *The Christian Century,* May 26, 1976, 508.
119 Holmen, *Queer Clergy*, 468.
120 Holmen, 468.

and St. Paul's School of Theology) began to expel or refuse admission to homo-sexual persons.

Apostles of Reaction

In 1978, the Methodist Federation for Social Action began a two-part series in its periodical, *Social Questions Bulletin*, entitled "Apostles of Reaction." The se-ries was meant to be an exposé on the Good News Movement. MFSA believed that Good News espoused orthodox renewal as a theological disguise to gain followers. The real intentions of Good News, they argued, were to "negate the church's commitment to social justice and to align the denomination with reac-tionary tendencies, both theologically and politically."[121] It explored the theol-ogy, political intent, and tactics of the movement to show that it was not simply concerned with a renewal of orthodoxy.

Given the movement's theology, MFSA believed Good News to be more concerned with "a rigid, traditional fundamentalism" and less with Wesley-anism.[122] They argued that a more apt United Methodist theology appreciated the theological diversity of church history and of current society. Politically, MFSA argued that Good News "reflect[ed] an extremely negative attitude to-wards the denomination's social witness" in areas such as "peace in Vietnam, women's rights, and economic and racial justice."[123] This negativity was espe-cially great in their stance against sexuality, including abortion and homosexu-ality, a subject that "evoke[d] the longest and strongest editorial blasts in *Good News* magazine."[124] Tactically, MFSA believed that Good News relied on ex-aggeration or "misrepresentation" of their opponents' stances in order to ad-vance their social-political agenda," and in regards to homosexuality, they relied on "witch hunts" that "identify transgressors, drive them out into the open, and punish them in public."[125] Their targets included homosexual persons, lib-eral bishops, and general agencies (specifically United Methodist Women and the Board of Church and Society). After discussing Good News's plans for the

121 "Apostles of Reaction: A Critical Evaluation of the 'Good News Movement: Part I,'" *Social Questions Bul-letin* (November–December 1978): 19, further substantiated on p. 21.

122 "Apostles of Reaction . . . Part I," 19.

123 "Apostles of Reaction . . . Part I," 20.

124 "Apostles of Reaction . . . Part I," 21.

125 "Apostles of Reaction . . . Part I," 21; "Apostles of Reaction: A Critical Evaluation of the 'Good News Movement: Part II'" *Social Questions Bulletin* (January–February 1979): 1.

General Conference of 1980, MFSA concluded that "the leadership of the 'Good News' movement constitutes the presence and influence of the New Far Right in United Methodism today," a scathing indictment of the movement.[126]

The purpose of this two-part article was to warn United Methodists that Good News was concealing "their reactionary politics under a camouflage of 'evangelical' concerns" and to prepare United Methodists who wanted a "just and loving vision" of the church that was "grounded in Scripture and based on economic justice, racial and sexual inclusiveness, and respect for human dignity" to join hands with MFSA and its partners in the years to come.[127]

At this point, it is easy to conclude that politically oriented members of United Methodism were split into two extremes who fought over the future of the denomination as it pertained to social issues, specifically homosexuality. During the next few General Conferences, evangelical Methodists would continue to thrive. Scholar Jane Ellen Nickell claims that by 1980, the fear of homosexuality present in previous General Conferences was gone, and it was replaced by overt moralism based in opposing views of Scripture.[128]

THE 1980 GENERAL CONFERENCE

In 1980, it was also evident that the Social Principles statements against homosexuality were not clear enough and impeded ministry. The Social Principles were meant to be guides and were not legally binding. Although homosexuality was condemned, homosexual persons continued to serve either "out" or closeted within the ordained ministry. Some were charged and defrocked; others were allowed to keep their ministerial appointments.

Across the board, delegates at the 1980 General Conference displayed

---

126 This section of the article defines the "New Right" as groups that tend to be "*pro*: death penalty, nuclear power, local police, FBI, CIA, greater defense spending, prayer in the schools, property rights, free market economics, 'right to work' laws, and a constitutional convention to prohibit abortion. Usually they are *anti*: busing to desegregate schools, gun control, ERA, abortion rights, government regulation of business, women's rights, union, religious ecumenism, homosexual rights, sex education, and the Panama Canal treaties." They tend to be "apocalyptic," believing worldliness is "the realm of evil against which they must defend themselves and which they must ultimately conquer." Finally, the New Far Right tends to "concentrate on single issues" in order to grow their support. MFSA believes that the Good News is a wing of the New Far Right because Good News's positions on "the death penalty, free market economics, governmental regulation of business, ERA, abortion, religious ecumenism, women's rights, homosexual rights, the Panama Canal treaties, and racial and ethnic quotas" reflect the position of the New Far Right ("Apostles of Reaction . . . Part II, 3.)

127 "Apostles of Reaction . . . Part II," 4.

128 Nickell, *We Shall Not Be Moved*, 102.

annoyance with "the church's preoccupation with [homosexuality]."[129] Affirmation and MFSA prevented the ban on the ordination of homosexual persons in 1980, although a rather long footnote in a paragraph on ordination was amended to include a reference to the incompatibility clause.[130] The Board of Discipleship presented *A Study Document on Human Sexuality* to the 1980 General Conference in hopes that the denomination was ready for a serious examination of sexuality. Trying to be middle-of-the-road, the report was based on the fact that the nuclear family was no longer the dominant family model, and thus the church needed to reevaluate its stance on all aspects of sexuality, including heterosexual relationships, single persons, adolescents, divorced persons, widowed persons, and homosexual relationships. The report was rejected for denominational study, and in a similar manner to 1976, was available to local churches if they chose to study sexuality.[131]

Between 1980 and 1984, Joanne Carlson Brown, who openly identified as lesbian, was ordained by Bishop Wheatley in the Rocky Mountain Annual Conference. Bishop Wheatley was known in the denomination as a liberal-leaning Methodist for his refusal to sign the Episcopal Address of 1980: it condoned the incompatibility clause, and he supported Julian Rush, an openly gay youth minister, whose coming out caused his dismissal from his congregation. Wheatley appointed Rush to St. Paul's, where he was allowed to maintain his clergy

129 As quoted in Nickell, 103.

130 The footnote was to paragraph 404, "Candidacy for Ordained Ministry," which discussed the "moral and social responsibility of ministers." Prior to the reference to the incompatibility clause, this footnote primarily discussed the use of tobacco and alcohol. *BOD* (1980), 182. The section on the incompatibility clause is found on p. 183.

131 The report focused on all aspects of sexuality, including male/female relationships, same-sex relationships, single persons, divorced persons, and widowed persons. It stated that too often "open and helpful dialogue is blocked, and personal needs are ignored." Its goal was to correct this. The study would "examine the biblical and theological roots of our understanding of human sexuality" with "careful consideration . . . given to the context in which Scripture was written." Specifically, the study would address: "a) health care and health education related to sexuality; b) psychological dimensions of sexuality; c) the institutional practices in society that have kept women in an inferior role or status; d) legal justice, including efforts to assure civil rights for homosexuals; e) legal rights relating to contraceptives, abortion, rape and incest; f) economic exploitation of sexuality and dehumanization of persons, such as is evident in advertising, pornography and prostitution . . .; g)the tremendous increase in teenage pregnancy, its causes and implications." It "recognize[d] at least five mistaken ways of viewing sexuality": "1) to worship it as an ultimate concern; 2) to sacramentalize sexuality as so holy, so extraordinarily divine that it becomes threatening and dominating over our lives; 3) to debase sex and sexuality, viewing these aspects of life as essentially evil; 4) to trivialize sex and sexuality, denying the deep meanings of human relationships; 5) to abuse sex and sexuality by using it as a means of manipulating and controlling others." After providing statistics that showed how the family was changing from a nuclear family to include non-traditional roles, the report turned to the biblical view of sexuality and the current problem of homophobia (*Journal of the 1980 General Conference*, 796–802). The report was published in 1983, along with a guide to help annual conferences and local churches through the study.

credentials.[132] Brown's ordination, like Paul Abels's in 1977, was upheld by the Judicial Council, which ruled that the fitness of ordinands was not reliant on their sexual orientation, and she was the first openly gay person to be ordained in The UMC.[133]

THE 1984 GENERAL CONFERENCE

In response to these ordinations and appointments, Good News doubled their efforts to enact a ban on the ordination of homosexual persons with over one thousand petitions requesting such a ban be implemented.[134] Nickell argues that "at every step it was clear that many delegates sought a specific ban on ordaining gays and lesbians."[135] The Committee on Ministry dealt specifically with ordination qualifications, and their recommendation was to add the phrase "fidelity in marriage and celibacy in singleness" to the requirements for ordination. Two minority reports were offered to this recommendation. The first, Minority Report A, sought to use more lenient language, "faithfulness and constancy in all relationships." The second, Minority Report B, sought to use more restrictive language, "Since the practice of homosexuality is incompatible with Christian teaching, self-avowed practicing homosexuals are not to be accepted as candidates, ordained as ministers, or appointed to serve in The United Methodist Church."[136]

Originally, delegates voted for the recommendation of the Committee on Ministry adding the phrase "fidelity in marriage and celibacy in singleness" to the requirements. These "seven last words," as they came to be known, in theory, banned sexually active homosexuals from ordination since homosexual persons could not legally marry.[137] However, after a point of inquiry and a Judicial Council ruling that stated that the seven words were not strong enough to prohibit homosexual persons from the ministry, the delegates went back to the floor for discussion and adopted Minority Report B. Thus, in 1984, in a vote of 568 to 404, self-avowed, practicing gays and lesbians were prohibited from all steps of ordination according to the *Discipline*.[138]

---

132 Holmen, *Queer Clergy*, 474–75.
133 Holmen, *Queer Clergy*, 474; Nickell, *We Shall Not Be Moved*, 108. See Judicial Council decision 513.
134 Nickell, 108.
135 Nickell, 110.
136 Nickell, 111.
137 This phrase was added to five paragraphs in the 1984 *BOD*: 404, 414, 429, and 431.
138 Nickell, *We Shall Not Be Moved*, 111–12.

The impetus behind the ban was fear. Evangelical Methodists were concerned that if a homosexual person was ordained in one Annual Conference and appointed to serve a congregation, then according to the connectional structure of The UMC, that person could at some point serve in their Annual Conference and be the minister of their local congregation. Evangelicals argued that the connectional system had to be uniform in its moral standards for all clergy, because any clergyperson had the potential to serve in any context. More progressive Methodists, however, argued that the General Conference overstepped its power with this ban. The power of who is or is not qualified for ordination, according to the *Discipline*, lies in the Annual Conference, specifically with the Board of Ordained Ministry (BOOM). By enacting a ban on a specific set of persons, General Conference impeded the powers and the will of the BOOM. Some United Methodist clergy began to test the limits of the ban, as it did not define "self-avowed, practicing." Thus the phrase was open to interpretation by the BOOM, by juries, and by bishops, a loophole that was taken advantage of in the years to come.

In 1983, a new United Methodist program was established, the Reconciling Congregations Program (RCP, later known as Reconciling Ministries Network, or RMN). Originally a local ministries wing of Affirmation, RCP/RMN has grown substantially since its inception in 1983, and its split from Affirmation in 1988.[139] Currently there are 907 reconciling congregations.[140] Immediately after the 1984 General Conference, the first two congregations, Washington Square UMC in NYC and Wesley UMC in Fresno, California, joined. In 1985 and 1987, California-Nevada Annual Conference and Wisconsin Annual Conference, respectively, recommended that their congregations consider joining RCP. In 1986, Northern Illinois Annual Conference became the first Annual Conference to declare itself a member of RCP, and it was quickly joined by three others: California-Nevada, Troy, and New York.[141] After 1988, RCP/RMN became the LGBTQ advocacy group within The UMC, and Affirmation focused on local ministry "providing a sanctuary for those who didn't have a welcoming home church."[142]

---

139 Holmen, *Queer Clergy*, 481.

140 Home Page, Reconciling Ministries Network website, accessed 1/23/2017, https://www.rmnetwork.org/newrmn/.

141 Holmen, *Queer Clergy*, 480, 485 n. 22.

142 Holmen, 481.

THE 1988 GENERAL CONFERENCE

In 1988, the main arbiter of homosexual inclusion was not Affirmation, MFSA, or RCP; it was the General Commission on the Status and Role of Women, which believed that homophobia and sexism were two fruits of the same seed.[143] They proposed the deletion of "fidelity in marriage and celibacy in singleness" from all five paragraphs of the *Discipline*, the removal of the incompatibility clause from the Social Principles, the deletion of the ban of gay and lesbian persons, and the deletion of the funding restrictions against homosexual groups and interests.[144] Similarly, The General Board of Church and Society called for the removal of the incompatibility clause and an amendment to the restrictions on funding that would allow for "research, education, and consultation on homosexuality" and for "ministries or efforts to protect rights of gay men and lesbians."[145] The General Board of Higher Education joined in and asked that the prohibition on homosexual ordination be removed, stating that "'our understandings are not sufficient' to make 'absolute judgments' on the issue."[146] According to a United Methodist News Services article, seventy-three regional conferences asked for some sort of change to the ban on ordination, either asking for more restrictive, clear language or more lenient, affirming language.[147] This was not the first time that annual conferences and general agencies had endorsed a change, in one way or another, of the language regarding homosexuality. Persons at all levels of the church had tried to alter the language within the Social Principles since its inception. However, these groups believed that there were unforeseeable ramifications to the ordination ban. The denomination was increasingly seen as unwelcoming by outsiders, and some of its boards believed that the ban prohibited the denomination from being able to fully live into its mission of ministry to all.

Delegates to the 1988 General Conference "ranked homosexuality as the

---

143 COSROW, in 1986, began a study on homophobia that led to their conclusions for and petitions to the 1988 General Conference. "Commission Set Plans to Study Homophobia in 1986," *Newscope* (September 27, 1985): 1–2.

144 "Homosexuality, God Language Placed on 1988 Agenda," *Newscope* (January 30, 1987): 3. COSROW also called for the use of gender-neutral language at all levels of The UMC and in all UM publications.

145 "Social Action Agency Completes Petitions to General Conference," *Newscope* (October 16, 1987): 1.

146 "General Conference Asked to Delete Prohibition on Ordaining Gays," *Newscope* (October 23, 1987): 1.

147 "Untitled Press Release," United Methodist News Service, October 19, 1987, 3.

No. 1 item at this year's meeting," according to a *New York Times* article.[148] In 1988, two small concessions were made. The language of the incompatibility clause was "made slightly more loving and less self-righteous" and read, "Although we do not condone the practice of homosexuality and consider this practice incompatible with Christian teaching, *we affirm that God's grace is available to all. We commit ourselves to be in ministry for and with all persons.*"[149] In 1988, the ban on ordination of "self-avowed, practicing homosexuals" was upheld by a vote of 676 to 293, the incompatibility clause was upheld by a vote of 765 to 181, and the prohibition against the use of church funds "to promote the acceptance of homosexuality" was upheld by a vote of 634 to 286.[150] Members of Affirmation and RCP were "disappointed but not surprised" by the retention of the incompatibility clause.[151] After the discussion of homosexuality, 150 members of the Affirmation and RCP gathered in the hallways for the first time to sing in protest. They stated, "We are gentle, angry people, and we are singing, singing for our lives."[152] However, delegates, by a two-thirds affirmative vote, mandated "an unprecedented study process," a denomination-wide, four-year study of homosexuality whose findings would be presented to the 1992 General Conference.[153] General Conference authorized the General Council on Ministries to direct the study "using consultants as it deems appropriate, including persons representative of the major existing points of view on homosexuality within the church and persons well-versed in scientific and theological method."[154] The committee was tasked with three objectives:

a) Study homosexuality as a subject for theological and ethical analysis, noting where there is consensus among biblical scholars, theologians, and ethicists and where there is not.

b) Seek the best biological, psychological, and sociological information and opinion on the nature of homosexuality, noting points at

---

148 "Methodists Vote to Retain Policy Condemning Homosexual Behavior," *New York Times*, May 3, 1988, A22.
149 Bradley Rymph, "Liberation and Justice Inevitably Advancing," *Christian Social Action* (July–August 1988): 29; Holmen, *Queer Clergy*, 481, emphasis mine.
150 *DCA* (1988), 273.
151 "Methodists Vote to Retain Policy," A22.
152 "Methodists Vote to Retain Policy," A22. Each General Conference since 1988, all of which have upheld the incompatibility clause, have witnessed this type of demonstration by members of the various LGBTQ caucuses.
153 Rymph, "Liberation and Justice Inevitably Advancing," 29.
154 "Study Process on Homosexuality," *BOR* (1988), 120.

which there is a consensus among informed scientists and where there is not.

c) Explore the implications of its study for the Social Principles.[155]

Affirmation and RCP, despite their joy in the creation of a study, were disappointed that the commission included only one representative from each caucus on its twenty-six-member study committee. The groups argued that at least two representatives from both caucuses were necessary to fulfill the mandate of General Conference, and that if this were any other "matter," such as one "concerning senior citizens or women or ethnic/racial minorities," there would be, without question, more representatives of the minority presented.[156] Good News, in the same manner as Affirmation and RCP, was disappointed at the lack of orthodox United Methodists represented on the panel. James Heidinger, the new president of Good News, stated that he hoped the study committee would clarify "points of confusion" found throughout the *Discipline*. He asked the committee to reaffirm Scripture as "the final authority" and "put to rest the widely held myth that homosexuals cannot change from their lifestyles."[157]

THE 1992 GENERAL CONFERENCE: THE STUDY COMMITTEE ON HOMOSEXUALITY REPORTS

After eight meetings over the four years, the Study Committee brought its report to the floor of General Conference in 1992. Nancy Yamasaki described the work of the study committee, which had heard from representatives from all of the political caucus groups (MFSA, Affirmation, RCP, Good News, and Transforming Congregations); they held "listening posts" in each jurisdiction where local clergy, ministers, and churches "could dialogue with committee members." The final report was voted on only once and it was "a unanimous vote," despite the vast differences represented on the committee.[158] The final report was printed on pages 265–81 of the 1992 *DCA*. It covered a vast array of

---

155 "Study Process on Homosexuality," 121.
156 "Two UM Caucuses Disappointed in Gay Membership on Panel," *Newscope* (December 9, 1988): 3. The full list of committee members can be found in the November 11, 1988, *Newscope* article, "GCOM Names Study Committee on Homosexuality."
157 Untitled Press Release, United Methodist News Service, December 5, 1989, 3.
158 *DCA* (1992), 399–400.

topics, the full analysis of which would require its own chapter or its own book. Here is a brief summary:

After providing a history of the "Church's Struggle" to ground the reasoning behind the existence of the committee, the committee examined "the human reality of homosexuality," where they heard personal testimonies from homosexual couples, parents of homosexuals, ex-gay persons, and so on;[159] the "theological affirmations and moral quandaries" where the committee examined biblical references, sexual ethics, and the oppression of homosexual persons in society.[160] They asked "what can be known about homosexuality?" in hope that biology, psychology, and sociology might enlighten views.[161] Then they asked "what can the church teach responsibly?" looking to church tradition to find its "central affirmations," and they acknowledged the differences within the committee and within the denomination.[162] Finally, they laid out "implications for the life and ministry of the church."[163]

They had six recommendations for the 1992 General Conference. (1) They wanted the General Conference to accept its report and "make it available for study and use across the whole church." (2–3) They wanted the UM Publishing House to assist in the "development of educational study materials on the issue of homosexuality" at all levels of the church, from the general church level to the individual level. (4) They recommended the formation of an Advisory Council, eight persons representing all points of view, to assist in the development of these materials.

(5) They recommended a change to the final two sentences of paragraph 71F (Social Principles' paragraph on Human Sexuality) and provided a majority and minority report with suggested language.[164] Both the majority and

---

159 *DCA* (1992), 268–69.
160 *DCA* (1992), 269–73.
161 *DCA* (1992), 273–75.
162 *DCA* (1992), 275–78.
163 *DCA* (1992), 278–79.
164 The majority report's final two sentences would read, "We acknowledge with humility that the church has been unable to arrive at a common mind on the compatibility of homosexual practice with Christian faith. Many consider this practice incompatible with Christian teaching. Others believe it acceptable when practiced in the context of human caring and covenantal faithfulness. The present state of knowledge and insight in the biblical, theological, ethical, biological, psychological, and sociological fields does not provide a satisfactory basis upon which the church can responsibly maintain the condemnation of homosexual practice. The church seeks further understanding through continued prayer, study, and pastoral experience. In doing so, the church continues to affirm that God's grace is bestowed on all, and that the members of Christ's body are called to be in ministry for and with one another, and to the world" (*DCA* [1992], 280).

minority reports recognized that the denomination was divided on whether or not homosexuality was acceptable, what would come to be called "agree to disagree." The majority report, signed by seventeen members, stated that with modern scientific, medical, sociological, and theological understandings, the denomination could not maintain its current condemnation of homosexuality; the minority report, signed by four members, stated that with modern scientific, medical, sociological, and theological understanding the denomination could not alter its current stance on homosexuality. (6) They recommended the addition of a new paragraph to the Social Principles, which would succeed the Human Sexuality paragraph and would concern the "Rights of Homosexual Persons."[165]

Before the report made its way to the plenary floor of General Conference, its legislative committee, most likely Church and Society, removed recommendation number five, which would have amended paragraph 71F, from the report. Thus, when the plenary dealt with the report, they dealt with recommendations one through four and six. After a long, parliamentary-intensive battle, the first recommendation of the report was adopted with only one amendment, to add an annotated bibliography to the resources available. The second through fourth recommendations were accepted with minor amendments.[166] The sixth recommendation, to add an additional paragraph ensuring the rights of homosexual persons was accepted (739 to 210), and the entire amended report was received by General Conference in a vote 767 to 190.[167]

The minority report would replace the final two sentences with, "We acknowledge with humility that the church has been unable to arrive at a common mind on the compatibility of homosexual practice with Christian faith. Many consider this practice incompatible with Christian teaching. Others believe it acceptable when practiced in a context of human caring and covenantal faithfulness. The present state of knowledge and insight in the biblical, theological, ethical, biological, psychological, and sociological fields does not provide a satisfactory basis upon which the church can responsibly alter its previously held position that we do not condone the practice of homosexuality and consider this practice incompatible with Christian teaching. The church seeks further understanding through continued prayer, study, and pastoral experiences. In doing so, the church continues to affirm that God's grace is bestowed on all, and that the members of Christi's body are called to be in ministry for and with one another, and to the world" (*DCA* [1992], 280).

165 The new paragraph would read, "Certain basic human rights and civil liberties are due all persons. We are committed to support those rights and liberties for homosexual persons. We see a clear issue of simple justice in protecting their rightful claims in same-sex relationships where they have: shared materials resources, pensions, guardian relationships, mutual powers of attorney and other such lawful claims typically attendant to contractual relationships which involve shared contributions, responsibilities and liabilities, and equal protection before the law. Moreover, we support efforts to stop violence and other forms of coercion against gays and lesbians." *DCA* (1992), 280.

166 *DCA* (1992), 411–15.

167 *DCA* (1992), 477.

In the legislative committee, the majority wanted to delete all of recommendation five and keep paragraph 71f as is, including the incompatibility clause. A minority report was issued from the legislative committee, which took "two additional truths seriously: first, that there is no generally accepted theory about the nature and origin of homosexuality . . . second, that large numbers of homosexual persons function quite normally."[168] It was defeated by a full plenary vote of 594 to 372; and the majority report, which kept the Social Principles' statement on human sexuality in its 1988 status, was accepted by a vote of 710 to 238.[169] Thus, while the report of the Study Committee would go on to be published and would produce supplemental resources for local congregational education on homosexuality, and ensured that homosexual persons had their civil rights protected, the major piece of the report, recommendation number five, which sought to affirm that, "the present state of knowledge and insight in the biblical, theological, ethical, biological, psychological, and sociological fields does not provide a satisfactory basis upon which the church can reasonably maintain the condemnation of homosexual practice," was rejected by a substantial vote.[170]

In the early hours of the debate, twenty persons demonstrated on the floor, most likely members of RCP, Affirmation, and MFSA, "carrying a banner reading 'The Stones Will Cry Out.'" The twenty persons remained standing at the front of the plenary floor for the remainder of the debate, giving a human presence to the debate over homosexuality. Accompanying them, around two thousand persons in the galleries stamped their feet in objection to various points of the proceedings.[171]

Good News, prior to the 1992 General Conference, believed that the fifth recommendation of the Study Committee, which sought to undo the incompatibility clause, was "divisive" and "unbiblical" and reflected "a flawed process because of the biased make-up of the committee." In a report sent to the Study Committee, they asserted their dissatisfaction with no orthodox representation on the committee, and requested that the committee consider three points in their deliberations:

---

168 *DCA* (1992), 478.
169 *DCA* (1992), 482.
170 "Daily Report," *DCA* 4, no. 7 (Tuesday May 12, 1992): 321.
171 "Daily Report," 321.

1. First, confirm for the church that the scriptures are clear that homo-sexual practice, regardless of how widespread it may be in society today, is not the will of God for humankind. . . .

2. Second, we would hope you would clarify for the church that the major corpus of Christian tradition supports the Biblical view as stated above. . . .

3. Finally, we hope you would help put to rest the widely-held myth that homosexuals cannot change from their lifestyles but must learn to accept it and live with it. [172]

Good News felt ignored by the Study Committee's final report; and these feelings were reiterated in a scathing indictment of the Study Committee in the January/February 1992 edition of *Good News*.[173]

Finally, in January 1992, eighty United Methodist evangelicals gathered in Memphis, Tennessee, and "issue[d] a declaration of faith—complete with standards and recommendations—to support at the upcoming General Con-ference." Referred to as the Memphis Declaration, the statement "articulates many long-held concerns of Good News" and "challenge[s] United Methodists to live faithfully as the body of Jesus Christ."[174] It reaffirmed the authority and primacy of Scripture, the divinity of Jesus Christ, marriage as between one man and one woman, homosexuality as a sin, the local church as the primary mis-sion field, the reduction of general church agencies, and the need to remodel seminary education. It called the General Conference to reaffirm the primacy of Scripture and its traditional language, abolish the General Council on Ministries, reduce the size of general agency staffs and boards, establish a General Board of Evangelism, move the General Board of Global Ministries, reaffirm the exist-ing stance on homosexuality and reject the report of the Study Committee, and affirm that a "personal decision" to accept Christ is necessary after an infant baptism.[175] This statement was signed by many evangelical United Methodists, members of Good News, the Confessing Movement, and Transforming Congre-gations. Their efforts created the Memphis Declaration in 1992, and sought to undermine the efforts of the Study Committee on Homosexuality.

The year 1992 proved to be a pivotal year for Methodist political caucus

---

172 "Report to the Homosexuality Study Task Force" *Good News*, December 1, 1989, 4–5.
173 *Good News*, January/February 1992.
174 "Issues Before Us: The Memphis Declaration," *Good News*, March/April 1992, 32.
175 "Issues Before Us," 32–33.

groups. All caucus groups left General Conference with renewed energy to block the efforts of others and implement their agendas at the local church and annual conference levels, in hopes of swaying future General Conference votes. Furthermore, Methodists had multiple political caucus groups to choose from by the 1996 General Conference. In 1993, RCP created a new Reconciling Pastor's Action Network whose purpose was "to provide a vehicle for UMC church professionals to witness to full inclusion of lesbian, gay, and bisexual persons." By 1994, RPAN had recruited over one hundred clergy. They also created a Youth/Young Adult Task Force to specifically address the concerns of lesbian, gay, and bisexual youth.[176] Progressive United Methodists continued to turn toward RCP, Affirmation, and MFSA for support and advocacy.

THE HOUSTON DECLARATION

Evangelical Methodists continued to turn toward Good News but had two new organizations to choose from. In 1987, the Houston Declaration affirmed "three crucial truths . . . the primacy of Scripture, the nature and name of the one God, Father, Son, and the Holy Spirit, and the high and holy character of ordained ministry."[177] Sixty-six clergy and laypersons, gathered in Houston in 1987, signed this statement and laid the foundation for what would officially become, in 1995, a new evangelical caucus group, the Confessing Movement.[178]

In a similar manner, in 1988, another caucus group was born, Transforming Congregations, an ex-gay ministry, which upheld "that homophobic (fearful,

---

176 "1993" Reconciling Ministries Network website, accessed 1/12/2017, https://www.rmnetwork.org/newrmn/who-we-are/history/.

177 "The Houston Declaration," Confessing Movement website, accessed 1/12/2017, http://www.confessingumc.org/our-story/the-houston-declaration/.

178 The group's stated purpose was: "The purpose of this Confessional Statement is to call The United Methodist Church, all laity and all clergy, to confess the person, work, and reign of Jesus Christ. This Statement confronts and repudiates teachings and practices in The United Methodist Church that currently challenge the truth of Jesus Christ–the Son of God, the Savior of the world, and the Lord of all. Aware of our own sinfulness, we who make this Confession submit our common witness and our lives to the judgment and mercy of God, as attested in Scripture, the written Word of God." All members had to agree and sign a confessional statement: "This, then, is our confession: We confess that Jesus Christ is the Son, the Savior, and the Lord, according to the Scriptures. The United Methodist Church has never had an institutional guarantee of doctrinal diversity without boundaries. We implore other United Methodists, laity and clergy, to join us in this confession. Relying upon the power of the Holy Spirit, we vow to make this confession in the congregations, boards, divisions, agencies, seminaries, and conferences of our denomination.

We will faithfully support United Methodist activities, groups, programs, and publications that further this confession, and we will vigorously challenge and hold accountable those that undermine this confession. All the while, readying for the coming of Jesus Christ in power and glory, we welcome ecumenical partnerships in the advancement of this confession." "Our Story," Confessing Movement, accessed 1/12/2017, http://www.confessingumc.org/our-story/.

hateful and rejecting) and accommodationist (uncritically accepting and affirming) responses were both contrary to scripture." Transforming Congregations "sought instead a compassionate approach that would offer the hope of transformational healing to those struggling with unwanted same-sex attraction and behavior."[179] The Confessing Movement and Transforming Congregations would go on to work hand in hand with Good News in the years to come, especially in preparation for General Conference. Thus between 1992 and 1996, United Methodists across the political spectrum had a broad coalition of caucus groups to advocate on behalf of their agendas.

After General Conference, a conglomeration of evangelical United Methodists took it upon themselves to defend the denomination and increased their efforts to dominate the United Methodist discussions of homosexuality. In fall 1992, Good News began a newsletter, "Focus," which sought to inform United Methodists on "critical issues facing the church." It included the "names and address of UM leaders whom readers are encouraged to write" with their "thoughtful opinion . . . on the substantive and controversial issues we face." The first issue dealt with only homosexuality, as many subsequent issues would deal with only homosexuality. "Focus" became the forum through which Good News carried out its agenda against LGBTQ inclusion. The first issue focused on a service of holy covenant where five United Methodist clergy performed a same-sex blessing; on the sexuality of the Reverend Jeanne Knepper, a lesbian woman who was recently appointed to a church in Oregon; and on Emory University, which recently opened a position for a "full-time director of its Office of Lesbian, Gay, and Bisexual Life."[180] Thus, after the 1992 General Conference, Good News amped up its efforts to maintain a strict biblical notion of anti-homosexuality at the General Conference level and at the grassroots level. Historian R. W. Holmen argues that between 1992 and 1996, the evangelical United Methodists "voices . . . grew louder and more shrill," especially in response to and in the hopes of blocking the successful efforts achieved by RCP, Affirmation, and MFSA at the annual conference and local church levels.[181]

Prior to the 1992 General Conference, the Reverend George McClain, of

---

179 "Who We Are: Our History," Transforming Congregations, accessed 1/12/2017, http://www.transcong
.org/1history.htm.
180 James Heidinger II, "Focus on The United Methodist Church: Information to Act On" *Focus* (Fall 1992).
181 Holmen, *Queer Clergy*, 499.

MFSA, remarked that the Study Committee's majority report moved in the right direction but did not go far enough in the acceptance of homosexual persons in the full ministry of the church.[182] After General Conference, RCP and Affirmation increased their work at the local church and annual conference levels, working mainly with the three conferences that were reconciling (New York, Troy, and California-Nevada). In the Minnesota Annual Conference, three reconciling congregations issued a resolution that "affirmed 'services of blessing and celebrations of committed relationships for couples of the same gender.'" While the resolution was ruled out of order by the bishop, it was a minor step forward for local churches. The California-Nevada conference "adopted a resolution recommending that congregations study ministry with lesbian, gay, and bisexual persons. In addition, each district superintendent was instructed to question each congregation as to its openness to such ministries at each annual charge or church conference." Oregon-Idaho and Rocky Mountain Annual Conferences voted to block "civil initiatives that seek to limit the rights of gay, lesbian, and bisexual persons." Northern New Jersey affirmed the right of all persons to be full members in their congregations. Northern Illinois denounced local hate groups that singled out persons based on their sexual orientation and declared that the denomination's current stance condemning homosexuality only gave power to these types of hate crimes.[183] Thus, while the General Conference refused to make large strides for the full inclusion and acceptance of LGBTQ persons in the life and ministry of the church, Affirmation and RCP worked at the local level to push the denomination toward these endeavors.

Post-1992, some Methodists were dissatisfied that the incompatibility clause and other prohibitions against homosexual persons were maintained; other Methodists were disappointed that the General Conference received the Study Committee report, believing that "receiving" the report constituted condoning it. Despite general dissatisfaction, the resources created and published for local church use were of good quality. By March 1994, *The Church Studies Homosexuality* was available as a six–ten-week study for "small, adult groups in local churches." It helped these groups "to tackle biblical and theological discussions

---

182 "Caucuses' Views Differ on Homosexuality Proposal," *Methodists Make News* (March 1, 1991): 3. The report of the study committee did not discuss the ban on ordination of homosexual persons or the restriction on funding.

183 "RCP Report," *Open Hands* (Date unknown): 22.

and discourse on the church's relationship to and ministries with gay men and lesbians."[184] The study also included "a summary of the committee's work . . . definition of terms, a resource list, passages of church law concerning homosexuality, and traditional and alternative interpretations of Scripture sometimes used to bolster the church's anti-homosexuality stances."[185] It is unknown how many local congregations took advantage of such resources, but it is admirable that the resources were available for those who wished to do so.

THE 1996 GENERAL CONFERENCE: SAME-SEX UNIONS

Some Methodists had condoned and conducted blessings of same-sex unions since the early 1970s. According to an article in *Open Hands*, the journal of RCP, "As gay men and lesbians increasingly seek public and legal recognition of their relationships, their demands must be considered legitimate on the basis *both* of Scripture *and* of Church tradition." This conclusion was substantiated by the findings of Dr. John Boswell, professor of history at Yale University, who argued that there was "clear evidence that same-sex weddings are a part of Christian tradition" and "were well established by the sixth century and continued in a relatively common use for several centuries thereafter."[186] Due to articles in *Good News* and efforts of the Metropolitan Community Church, there was an increased publicity of the blessings of same-sex unions by Methodist clergy by 1996. According to the *Discipline*, the decision of who was allowed to or prepared to marry was left to the pastor's discretion. Same-sex unions would be the subject of much concern at the 1996 General Conference.

The 1996 General Conference began with controversy. First, the progressive United Methodist caucuses tried and failed to have the location of General Conference moved from Denver, Colorado, due to a discriminatory ordinance against LGBT persons. Second, fifteen bishops (eleven active and four retired), who came to be called the "Denver Fifteen," released a statement that publicly expressed their "pain . . . over our personal convictions that are contradicted by the proscriptions in *The Book of Discipline* against gay and lesbians within our church and within our ordained and diaconal ministers," the first act

---

184 M. Garlinda Burton, "United Methodist Study on Homosexuality Based on 1992 General Conference Actions," United Methodist News Service, March 23, 1994, 1.

185 Burton, "United Methodist Study on Homosexuality," 2.

186 Dick Burdon, "Same-Sex Marriage: It's Nothing New," *Open Hands*, Fall 1989, 16–17, emphasis original.

of ecclesiastical disobedience since Bishop Wheatley's 1980 refusal to sign the Episcopal Address.[187]

Conferences and caucuses responded differently to this statement. Northwest Texas, Alabama-West Florida, West Ohio, Mississippi, North Arkansas, and Little Rock either passed resolutions disagreeing with the bishops' statement or upholding the incompatibility clause in the *Discipline*. Others—New York, California-Pacific, California-Nevada, Oregon-Idaho, Kansas-East, Kansas-West, and Peninsula-Delaware—expressed appreciation of the bishops' statement. Wisconsin, as a result, voted to become a Reconciling conference, and Desert Southwest almost became a Reconciling conference (180 no to 172 yes).[188] Good News and evangelical United Methodists, however, denounced RCP by officially affiliating with Transforming Congregations, and they passed a resolution calling for the resignation of the fifteen bishops.[189]

During General Conference, controversy continued as a proposal to acknowledge that United Methodists were not of one mind on homosexuality, reflecting the tenor of the Study Committee's report, was rejected in favor of sustaining the incompatibly clause.[190] Furthermore, a proposal to ban same-sex blessings was supported in the last hours of plenary by a vote of 598 to 304.[191] This new prohibition removed any hope of progress. However, with the bishops' willingness to stand up for their advocacy efforts, progressives found increased courage to engage in acts of ecclesiastical disobedience, which, as of 2000, they called *biblical obedience*. Thus after 1996, the number of same-sex blessings performed by United Methodist clergy and within United Methodist churches increased. In 1997, progressive United Methodists released their own

---

187 Nickell, *We Shall Not Be Moved*, 122; Holmen, *Queer Clergy*, 500. The full statement reads, "We the undersigned bishops wish to affirm the commitment made at our consecration to the vows to uphold the Discipline of the church. However, we must confess the pain we feel over our personal convictions that are contradicted by the proscriptions in the Discipline against gay and lesbian persons within our church and within our ordained and diaconal ministers. . . . We believe it is time to break the silence and state where we are on this issue that is hurting and silencing countless faithful Christians. We will continue our responsibility to the order and discipline of the church but urge our United Methodist churches to open the doors in gracious hospitality to all our brothers and sisters in the faith." Those sections are paragraphs: 71F (last paragraph), 402.2, and 906.12; and the footnote on page 205." Language pertains to the incompatibility clause, the ban on ordination, and to the funding restriction.

188 "Conferences Respond Differently to 15 Bishops' Statement" *Newscope* (July 12, 1996).

189 "'Good News' Challenges Bishop, 'Reconciling' Programs," *United Methodist Reporter* (October 11, 1996).

190 Holmen, *Queer Clergy*, 500–501.

191 "Church Holds Line on Homosexuality," *Good News*, May/June 1996, 17. It was added to the paragraph on "Marriage" in the Social Principles and read, "Ceremonies that celebrate homosexual unions shall not be conducted by our ministers and shall not be conducted in our churches" (*BOD* (1996), 87.

statement, *In All Things Charity*, which challenged the church's current anti-gay stances and laid forth six affirmations to continue to work for full inclusion.[192]

In 1997, Jimmy Creech, pastor in Nebraska, performed the ceremony for a lesbian couple in his congregation. This was not new for Creech or for other United Methodist ministers, but same-sex unions were now condemned in the *Discipline*. As a result, the Nebraska Annual Conference charged him with violating the *Discipline* and brought him to trial. The charges were dropped because the prohibition against same-sex blessings was in the Social Principles, which are "instructive" and "not to be considered church law." However, in 1998, the Judicial Council, in an unprecedented move, ruled that despite the prohibition's placement in the Social Principles it "has the effect of church law . . . and therefore, governs the conduct of the ministerial office." In April 1999, Rev. Creech again blessed a same-sex union. He was tried and defrocked later that year.[193] Others joined Reverend Creech. The Reverend Gregory Dell of Chicago, Illinois, blessed a same-sex union for two of his congregants. He was convicted and suspended in 1999. The "Sacramento 68," sixty-eight clergypersons from the West Coast, presided over a same-sex union, and after deliberation, charges were not drawn.[194]

The increase in trials, suspensions, and convictions for both same-sex unions and of LGBTQ clergy, along with the arrest of two hundred protestors at the 2000 General Conference, ensured that General Conference 2004 would be heated. As Good News's President Heidinger stated, "The last several General Conferences have evolved into two-week battles over homosexuality."[195] He could not have been more correct. In 2004, evangelical United Methodists were angry that an out lesbian clergywoman, the Reverend Karen Dammann, was not charged for being so. In an effort to garner support for their stance, the presidents of Good News (James Heidinger II) and the Confessing Movement (Bill Hinson) threatened to bring forth a proposal that called for an amicable split of the denomination. Realizing that this was not desired by the majority of delegates, progressive and evangelical alike, they backtracked their statements.[196]

---

192 Part of the text can be found in Holmen, *Queer Clergy*, 507–8.

193 Holmen, *Queer Clergy*, 508–9.

194 Holmen, 509–11.

195 James Heidinger II, "A Bittersweet 2004 General Conference." *Good News*, May/June 2004, 3.

196 Maxie Dunnam, "Truth Getting Distorted about 'Amicable Separation,'" *Good News*, July/August 2004, 26–27.

Instead, they focused their efforts on a statement that would create chargeable offenses for being a "self-avowed, practicing homosexual" and for presiding over same-sex unions.[197] The evangelical voice had been gaining ground since 1996, due to the increase of Central Conference delegates (delegates from outside of the United States). In 1984, Central Conference delegates represented 6.8 percent of the total; by 2004, they accounted for 13 percent; and by 2012, they represented 39 percent of the total delegation. Jane Ellen Nickell argues:

> The influx of African delegates had a significant impact on the discussion and vote on homosexuality. While delegates from these countries represent a variety of perspectives, many of them are theologically conservative, so they were courted by conservative caucuses and informed about key pieces of legislation; indeed, as the number of overseas delegates increased, so did the margin on votes related to homosexuality.[198]

Homosexuality has been portrayed by evangelicals as a U.S. "issue"; liberals view the rights of LGBTQ persons as a global concern that the church should address no matter the location. However, within the United States, progressive United Methodists would continue in acts of biblical obedience, conducting same-sex unions, and coming out as LGBTQ persons of faith.

By 2012, most clergy trials resulted in twenty-four-hour suspensions, acquittals, or "just resolutions." The problem was that General Conference had never defined what exactly "self-avowed, practicing homosexual" meant. The Judicial Council in 2001 "mandated that a question must be asked during an investigation—whether the accused is engaged in genital sexual acts with a person of the same gender." No one had dared ask this private question until Thomas Lambrecht, vice president and general manager of Good News, repeatedly asked it of Amy DeLong during her trial for both conducting a same-sex union and for being a lesbian clergy. She declined to answer.[199]

CONCLUSION

At the General Conference of 2012, delegates again declined to "agree to disagree." Nickell argues that within The UMC there are four positions on homosex-

---

197 These were added to paragraph 2702 (*BOD* [2004], 719).
198 Nickell, *We Shall Not Be Moved*, 125.
199 Holmen, *Queer Clergy*, 544–45.

uality: "total rejection, partial rejection, qualified acceptance, and full accep-tance." The UMC is officially somewhere in the middle, with evangelicals (and many in the middle) believing the denomination upholds qualified acceptance, and progressives believing the denomination upholds partial rejection.[200]

While each side was frustrated with the amount of time and energy spent on homosexuality during General Conference, both sides experienced harm and hurt during these proceedings. Evangelical United Methodists were often ridi-culed, called outdated, and deemed divisive. They truly believe that homosex-uality is a sin and that it is their Christian duty to help homosexual persons find holiness, that is, heterosexuality, in order to be right with God. They feel that The UMC rejects them and their orthodox beliefs, and they are frequently told that their beliefs are not truly Wesleyan. Progressive United Methodists experience personal harm, as others try to convince them that their natural, God-given sexuality is wrong, sinful, and immoral. They are told that their lives are not worth full inclusion in the denomination. And they continually witness their denomination refusing to recognize their loving, committed relationships. There is no easy answer to this divide without doing further harm to one side or the other. The problem became only more pressing since the United States legalized same-sex marriage in 2015. As representatives of the state, United Methodist clergy are now increasingly asked to perform same-sex marriages and are facing the impossible situation of having to deny marriage in a home congregation to their members or face a loss of credentials.

In January 1979, the Commission on Faith and Order of the National Coun-cil of Churches issued a study document entitled, "A Call to Responsible De-bate on Controversial Issues: Abortion and Homosexuality." It recognized that many Protestant denominations were internally divided over how to approach abortion and homosexuality. The reasons these two aspects of human sexual-ity are so divisive is that there is a lack of "a moral consensus in . . . society." Eighteen years ago, this same committee realized that "positions on these is-sues have become so hardened, emotions so inflamed, reason so confused that careful public debate is very rare." The UMC has become only more hardened, more harmed, and more inflamed in recent years. It continues to be divided on

---

200 Nickell, *We Shall Not Be Moved*, 129.

abortion and homosexuality because it is divided "on the larger questions of the nature and meaning of human sexuality and responsible relationships."[201]

The Methodist Church's understanding of homosexuality has changed drastically. In 1964, some Methodists sought to reconcile and create relationships with the homophile community through the Commission on Religion and the Homosexual. Eight years later, the General Conference declared homosexuality incompatible with Christian teaching. Such drastic change can be understood only in the context of the late 1960s and early 1970s when evangelical Americans sought to undo the revolutionary fervor of the 1960s and return to what they understood to be the ideal 1950s. The homosexual/heterosexual binary came to the forefront of American society, American politics, and American Methodism in the 1970s. Since then, the status and rights of persons has been subject of vitriolic debate. In addition, many United Methodists do not know or understand the historic context through which the incompatibility clause emerged. They also do not know how often the General Conference of The United Methodist Church has authorized study commissions to find a way to balance the wide variety of views within the denomination. This chapter has provided the social and political context through which the incompatibility clause and its accompanying restrictions emerged. As the New Christian Right became more conservative on matters of sexuality, specifically the rights of LGBTQ persons, so, too, did United Methodism. Evangelical caucus groups moved the church in a more conservative direction in 1972. As the New Christian Right gained power in American politics, evangelical caucus groups gained power in The United Methodist Church. The parallel origin, nature, and rhetoric of these coalitions cannot be overstated. Much like America today, American United Methodists are increasingly divided.

---

201 "A Call to Responsible Debate on Controversial Issues: Abortion and Homosexuality," January 1979; folder: "Homosexuality and the Church," records of the General Commission on Christian Unity and Interreligious Concerns, 2434-6-8:5, GCAH.

CONCLUSION

The United Methodism presented in the two previous chapters leads us to the question, "What is The United Methodist Church?" Is it the church of the "old-fashioned, devil-fighting, sin-killing, hanky-waving, amen-shouting, foot-stomping" revivals, or is it the church that breaks down racial barriers, that empowers women, that uplifts the poor, and defends the marginalized? Is it both? If so, how? Evangelical-leaning United Methodists claim to be "orthodox" and truly Wesleyan. To them, it is the progressive United Methodists who took over the administrative ranks of the denomination and forced it to change. But on the ground, in the small, rural pulpits where United Methodism lives and breathes, it is the evangelicals who hold on to a legitimate, authentic past, or so they believe.

For many progressive United Methodists, this rhetoric ignores progress. It assumes that religion either cannot or should not evolve alongside society; and that religion is a permanent doctrine that is completely separate from outside influence. To others, this is not even Wesleyan. Wesley was a preacher of the people. As people and society changed, the message needed to change to speak to the largest number of people. Methodism grew quickly in the early nineteenth century, because it used "plain speak," the language of the uneducated, of the frontiersman, of the slave to spread the message that God loved all. As society settled, as social classes developed, as education boomed, and as social justice increased, religion had to evolve to be able to fully speak to all people. This is the rhetoric that has contributed to a stark divide among United Methodists, a divide that has been exponentially widened with changes in sexuality.

The most recent General Conference of The United Methodist Church in 2016 did not discuss any legislation regarding sexuality. Instead, it voted, yet again, to form a study commission that might bring forth some new ways of existing as United Methodists despite differences. In a historic and unprecedented move, a special session of General Conference will be held in early 2019 solely to discuss persons who identify as gay and lesbian, their lives, and their ministry in The United Methodist Church.

After the 2016 General Conference, United Methodists took drastic steps in hopes of guiding the denomination one way or the other. At the same time, a wave of non-conformity measures swept across the United States Annual Conferences. The New England, Desert Southwest, California-Pacific, California-Nevada, and Pacific Northwest Annual Conferences have all stated, in a variety of ways, that they will no longer comply with the statements in the *Discipline* against LGBTQ persons, statements that prohibit them from living into the full mission and ministry of the church. Some of the conferences sought to uphold a commitment to women's health and independently joined the Religious Coalition for Reproductive Choice, the reproductive rights organization from which The UMC officially withdrew its membership during General Conference 2016. Just prior to General Conference, on May 9, 111 clergy and clergy candidates officially came out as gay in a joint statement, and their action was supported by 500 openly LGBTQ clergy from other denominations.[1] The New York Annual Conference ordained and commissioned four openly gay clergy in June 2016.[2] Others nominated openly LGBTQ persons as candidates for bishops and ordination.[3] In July 2016, the Western Jurisdiction unanimously elected the first openly lesbian woman to the episcopacy, Karen Oliveto, who was also the first female senior pastor of Glide Memorial Methodist Church and who increased the local church's membership to over twelve thousand persons.[4] A fellow bishop, Bishop Grant Hagiya remarked, "We understand there may be some political implications, but in our mind [she] was the best person. It was not a question of [sexual] orientation, it was a question of who was the best spiritual leader."[5] In response, the

---

1   Heather Hahn, "500 clergy support gay United Methodist clergy who came out," United Methodist News Service, May 9, 2016, http://www.umc.org/news-and-media/111-clergy-clergy-candidates-come-out-as-gay.

2   Joanne Utley, "27 Ordained, Commissioned in 'Historic' Service," New York Annual Conference, accessed 1/19/2017, http://www.nyac.com/newsdetail/33-ordained-commissioned-by-new-york-conference-5012427.

3   Jeremy Smith, "Non-Conformity and the Hope from Creative Minorities in the UMC," Hacking Christianity (June 28, 2016), accessed 1/19/2017, http://um-insight.net/perspectives/jeremy-smith/non-conformity-and-the-hope-from-creative-minorities-in-the-/.

4   Karen Oliveto, "Strangely Warmed Hearts, a United Methodist In (Queer)y," public lecture (Garrett-Evangelical Theological Seminary, Chicago, IL, January 13, 2017).

5   Kathy Gilbert, "Married Lesbian Consecrated United Methodist Bishop," United Methodist News Service, July 16, 2016, http://www.umc.org/news-and-media/married-lesbian-consecrated-united-methodist-bishop.

South Central Jurisdiction requested that the Judicial Council make a "declaratory decision regarding gay and lesbian church leaders."[6] Predictably, responses varied. Progressive United Methodists proclaimed Oliveto's election as "a seismic shift towards LGBTQ inclusion in The United Methodist Church!" They understood her election as a move that was "bound to propel the dialogue within the church to a higher and more urgent level."[7] Evangelical-leaning United Methodists believed these moves pushed the denomination toward schism:

> It is deplorable that the Western Jurisdiction, along with many annual conferences, has ignored the Council of Bishop's proposal. . . .
> If the Western Jurisdiction wanted to push the church to the brink of schism, they could not have found a more certain way of doing so.[8]

Soon after, a new movement within The UMC, the Wesleyan Covenant Association (WCA), held its organizational meeting in Chicago, Illinois, on October 7, 2016. The WCA is "orthodox Wesleyan," and its members are "unashamed by the gospel of Christ."[9] The WCA seeks a "new day for Methodism," and a return to nineteenth-century Methodist revivals and emphasis on social accountability.[10] Those gathered had one goal: "reclaiming, renewing, and rebuilding the old Methodist identity," for they believe, "what it means to be Wesleyan

---

6   Gilbert, "Married Lesbian Consecrated." See Judicial Council decision 1341, released April 28, 2017: http://www.umc.org/decisions/71953.

7   Gilbert, "Married Lesbian Consecrated."

8   "West Elects Oliveto," Good News, accessed 1/17/2017, http://goodnewsmag.org/2016/08/west-elects -oliveto/

9   "Purpose and Beliefs," Wesleyan Covenant Association, accessed 1/19/2017, https://wesleyancovenant .org/purposebeliefs/, opening video, WCA Oct. 7, 2016, unpublished. An orthodox Wesleyan is defined as one who upholds Scripture as "the church's primary and final authority on all matters of faith and practice;" who affirms "the historic faith" as professed in the Nicene Creed, the Articles of Religion of the Methodist Church (from 1808), the Confession of Faith of the Evangelical United Brethren Church (from 1963), the Standard Sermons of John Wesley, the Explanatory Notes upon the New Testament by John Wesley, and the General Rules of The Methodist Church (from 1868); who believes that men and women are created equally; who believes that "all persons are of sacred worth;" who affirms that "marriage is the uniting of one man and one woman in a single, exclusive union;" who upholds that "God intends faithfulness in marriage and celibacy in singleness;" and who believes "that every persons must be afforded compassion, love, kindness, respect, and dignity," accessed 1/19/2017, https://wesleyancovenant .org/purposebeliefs/.

    Many persons believe that the formation of the WCA was a reaction to actions during and after General Conference 2016. However, the public documentation of their incorporation as a nonprofit organization clarifies that this group filed organization papers a few months prior to General Conference. For more on the formation of the WCA see Jeremy Smith's "Three Takeaways from the Wesleyan Covenant Association's Founding Documents," http://hackingchristianity.net/2018/01/three-takeaways-from-the -wesleyan-covenant-association-founding-document.html.

10   Rob Renfroe, keynote address, WCA, October 7, 2016, unpublished.

and what it means to be Methodist are no longer the same thing."[11] Their opening video placed their members picking up where the circuit riders left off, spreading a renewed, historic United Methodism to all.[12] Speakers warned that the denomination was growing increasingly concerned with culture and less concerned with Scripture. The WCA believes that the acculturation of The UMC has allowed "social construct [to] become [its] God," and has increasingly affirmed those who are not "right on the inside."[13] The WCA does not view itself as a political caucus; instead, it is a "bottom-up" movement within United Methodism.[14] They believe that renewal groups within The UMC have been trying to keep the denomination in one place, but the denomination's administration keeps pulling the denomination in way that equates "social justice as personal holiness."

Since the formation of the WCA, other caucus groups have formed. The United Methodist Queer Clergy Caucus is an organization of lesbian, gay, bisexual, transgender, queer, and intersex persons who are either called, commissioned, or ordained clergy within The United Methodist Church.[15] Uniting Methodists is another group that seeks to "be a unifying and clarifying voice in a divided conversation and a polarized culture."[16] The formation of the WCA, the Queer Clergy Caucus, and Uniting Methodists underscores how divided the denomination remains.

This book has mapped the changes in sexuality since World War I in America and has shown how Methodist denominations responded to those changes. It has argued that Methodists sought to create a new notion of healthy sexuality throughout the 1930s and 1940s, one that allowed for sexual intimacy within marriage without the risk of conception and one that openly endorsed the use of artificial contraception as a responsible part of heterosexual Christian

---

11   Andrew Thompson, address, WCA, October 7, 2016, unpublished.

12   The video that opened the WCA event in Chicago (among other videos) is available on the WCA website: https://wesleyancovenant.org/wca-intro-video/

13   Kenneth Livingston, sermon, WCA, October 7, 2016, unpublished.

14   Rob Renfroe, in his keynote address, emphasized that the WCA was a separate entity from Good News, the Confessing Movement, and Transforming Congregations, a statement complicated by the fact that the main leaders of these organizations are also the main organizers of the WCA: Rob Renfroe, the president of Good News, gave the keynote address. Tom Lambrecht, the vice president of Good News, moderated the event. Maxie Dunnam, honorary chairman of the Confessing Movement, also gave an address.

15   For more, visit their website: https://www.umqcc.org/.

16   http://unitingmethodists.com/.

marriage. It has shown how this healthy sexuality had to change to accommo-date the rise in divorce and the beginnings of the sexual revolution in the 1950s. It problematized the Methodist notion of sexuality as upholding one type of family, exemplified through the Methodist Family of the Year and through the pages of *Together* magazine, thus liberating heterosexual married couples and alienating those who were sexual outside of marriage or who identified as non-heterosexual. In response to the sexual revolution, Methodists upheld the new morality, the idea that sexuality is directly tied to a God-given identity and thus to honor God one must honor one's sexuality, no matter its orientation. The new morality peaked in the 1960s with radical new approaches to sex edu-cation through courses like *Sex and the Whole Person*, a full endorsement of abortion rights, the ministry of the Reverend John V. Moore, and the Council on Religion and the Homosexual. However, the new morality coincided with a po-litical turn, evident through the increased presence of and a new voice for evan-gelicals, *Good News* and Charles Keysor. These evangelical Methodists critiqued the new morality as "value-neutral," "psycho-babble," and anti-scriptural.[17] The evangelical desire for a morality solely reliant on scriptural mandates collided with the new morality and led to intense debates over sex education, abor-tion, and the inclusion of LGBTQ persons from the 1970s onward. Since 1972, United Methodists have continually debated the lives and ministry of persons who identify as LGBTQ at each General Conference; and every four years, the denomination questions whether or not it will be able to remain united amid its diversity.

This book has shown the benefit of following one denomination and ana-lyzing its responses to cultural change. It has shown how intertwined religious change is with social change. Protestantism, throughout the twentieth century, strived to maintain relevancy in the changing social, specifically sexual, climate. Following Methodists throughout the century allows for an understanding of how one Protestant denomination altered its theology and its sexual morality according to cultural change, despite denial and protest. Furthermore, it showed how vulnerable to political influence a denomination can be. This book traced the rise of the New Christian Right and argued that, as it gained power, evan-gelical Methodists gained power. Studies of the New Christian Right have traced

---

17   Booth, *Forgetting How to Blush*, 245.

its political influence, but none have traced the evolution of the New Christian Right alongside one denomination to see how the movement influenced intra-denominational rhetoric, relationship, polity, and doctrine. This book begins to uncover this relationship.

The term *evangelical* seems now more synonymous with the GOP than with a classification of Protestantism. When many hear someone described as evangelical, they automatically assume that the person is white, socially conservative, and has voted Republican in recent elections. The New Christian Right's political influence peaked with the election of George W. Bush to the presidency in 2000 and 2004.[18] Since then, evangelicals associated with the New Christian Right have struggled to maintain power in a society that seeks to give credence to the voices of minorities. In addition, they are no longer cohesive as a political entity. Many evangelicals today disagree on environmentalism, immigration, and LGBTQ rights. This has led many scholars to question whether or not the word or category of *evangelical* is useful anymore. With the most recent presidential election of 2016, evangelicals still voted predominantly for the GOP candidate Donald J. Trump, despite his overt lack of morality and his tenuous religious affiliation.[19] However, if the term no longer means "one that is concerned with evangelism" is it a useful theological term or should we concede it to the political realm?

United Methodism today is anything but united, for it cannot agree on what it means to be a sexual human being. This book does not presume to offer a way forward for United Methodism, but it offers a critical and contextual reexamination of our past. Prior to the rise and influence of the New Christian Right, American Methodists were willing to adapt policies and views of sexuality with the changing times. Recalling Heather White's *Reforming Sodom*, in order for the gay rights movement to be successful, it had to have the support of the clergy. This book has elaborated on this point and shown how vital the support and rhetoric of the clergy can be. Margaret Sanger understood that in order for the birth-control movement to progress, she had to have the support of the clergy. Likewise, in order for divorce and sex education in public schools to be accepted, clergy had to advocate for it. SIECUS and the Clergymen's

---

18   Williams, *God's Own Party*, 105–6.
19   For the most recent account of evangelicals—their power and the term—see Frances FitzGerald, *The Evangelicals: The Struggle to Shape America* (New York: Simon & Schuster, 2017).

Consultation Service on Abortion provided platforms for clergy to make their support of sex education and abortion known. Affirmation, Reconciling Ministries Network, the Methodist Federation for Social Action, among others, have provided platforms for clergy to advocate for the full rights of LGBTQ persons within the life of The UMC and the world. However, these groups have faced and continue to face intense pushback.

Once sexuality began to include nonwhite, nonmarital, and non-heterosexual persons, white males and females felt threatened, and the New Christian Right emerged as the new political and religious power-house. White, male and female, American Methodists felt this threat too. They understood the sexual revolutions of the 1960s as a threat to their religious authority as clergy and to the authority of Scripture, for neither dictated what sexual acts were right or wrong anymore. In order to combat this threat, they formed their own internal political caucus groups and used the successful rhetoric of the New Christian Right within the newly formed United Methodist Church. In response to their actions, other United Methodists formed political caucus groups to combat their narrow definition of sexuality and their limited notion of sexual morality.

It is not likely that members of The United Methodist Church will stop forming political caucus groups. It is not likely that the current political caucus groups will dissolve or will cease campaigning. It is not likely that the denomination will recover from its political turn of the late 1960s and early 1970s. And it is not likely that political rhetoric will stop being used to advocate for certain positions within The UMC. But perhaps this book can shed light on how the political, and religious context are intertwined such that neither can be spoken of without reference to the other, and thus enlighten United Methodists and American Protestants as to how politics and political rhetoric influence the social and moral stances of a denomination.

SELECTED BIBLIOGRAPHY

PRIMARY SOURCES

Archival Material

The following are taken from the General Commission on Archives and History of The United Methodist Church, or GCAH.

Abortion: A Human Choice. Division of General Welfare, Department of Population Problems, Board of Christian Social Concerns of The United Methodist Church. May 1971. 5. Folder Title: "Abortion Packet 1972." Folder Number: 1443-4-2:6. Box Title: Administrative Records of the Division of General Welfare of the General Board of Church and Society. GCAH.

"Abortion Packet." Folder Title: "Abortion Packet." Folder Number: 1443-4-2:6. Box Title: Administrative Records of General Welfare of the General Board of Church and Society. GCAH.

Butterfield, Oliver M. "Now You Are Engaged." Nashville: Methodist Publishing House, 1955. Folder Title: Now You Are Engaged/leaflet. Folder Number: 2355-5-4:2. Box Title Administrative Records of the General Board of Discipleship. GCAH.

"The Christian Family and Rapid Social Change." Nashville: Methodist Publishing House, 1962. Folder Title: Christian Family and Rapid Social Change/leaflet. Folder Number: 2356-2-4:29. Box Title: Administrative Records of the General Board of Discipleship. GCAH.

Fagley, Richard M. "Responsible Parenthood from a Christian Perspective." Nashville: Methodist Publishing House, 1964. Folder Title: Responsible Parenthood from a Christian Perspective. Folder Number: 1445-1-4:2. Box Title: Administrative Records of General Welfare of the General Board of Church and Society. GCAH.

Genne, Elizabeth and William. "Sex Facts for Adolescents." Folder Title: Sex Facts for Adolescents/pamphlet. Folder Number: 2355-6-1:37. Box Title: Administrative Records for the General Board of Discipleship. GCAH.

"Guidelines for Using *Sex and the Whole Person: A Christian View*." *Sex Education Resource Packet*. Nashville, TN: The General Committee on Family Life, 1969. Folder Title: "Sex Education Resource Packet 1964-66." Folder Number: 2355-6-1:38. Box Title: Records of Health and Welfare Ministries. GCAH.

Hagler, Albert Dale, "Every Marriage Has Problems." Folder Title: Every Marriage Has Problems/leaflet. Folder Number: 2356-3-3:35. Box Title: Administrative Records of the General Board of Discipleship. GCAH.

Moore, John V. "Chastity and the Pill (Consideration of Ethics and Sex)." January 24, 1965. Folder Title: Sermons 1965. Folder Number: 2144-4-3:3. Box Title: Moore Papers. GCAH.

———. "Church, Community, and Homosexuality." Folder Title: Sermons 1965. Folder Number: 2144-4-3:3. Box Title: Moore Papers. GCAH.

———. "Man, Sex and the Gospel." January 10, 1965. Folder Title: Sermons 1965. Folder Number: 2144-4-3:3. Box Title: Moore Papers. GCAH.

"Preparation for Marriage Filmstrips: A Leader's Guide," 1955. Box Title: The Television, Radio, and Film Commission of the Methodist Church. GCAH.

"RCAR's Program 1976–1977," Folder Title: "Religious Coalition for Abortion Rights 1979." Folder Number: 2589-6-4:1. Box Title: Records of the Women's Division of the General Board of Global Ministries. GCAH.

"Report to the Annual Conference from the Task Force on Homosexuality." Folder Title: Resource Materials-Church Studies on Human Sexuality 1974–1980. Folder Number: 2133-4-1:21. Box Title: Affirmation. GCAH.

"Sex Education Folder." Nashville, TN: The General Committee on Family Life, 1969. Folder Title: "General Committee on Family Life—Sex Education Task Force." Folder Number: 2080-7-8:4. Box Title: Records of Health and Welfare Ministries. GCAH.

Vance, Lee. "Sex Education for United Methodist Youth." *Sex Education Resource Packet*. Nashville, TN: The General Committee on Family Life, 1969. Folder Title: "Sex Education Resource Packet: 1964-66." Folder Number: 2355-6-1:38. Box Title: Records of Health and Welfare Ministries. GCAH.

Weir, Frank E. *Sex and the Whole Person*. Nashville, TN: Abingdon Press, 1964. As quoted in "SIECUS Assists in Understanding Sexuality," *Sex Education Folder*.

Websites and Online Primary Sources

"The Connectional Table," The United Methodist Church. Accessed 1/30/2017. http://www.umc.org /topics/the-connectional-table-home.

"Council on Religion and the Homosexual." The Lesbian, Gay, Bisexual, and Transgender Religious Archives Network. Accessed 1/8/2017. https://www.lgbtran.org/Exhibits/CRH/Exhibit.aspx.

"The Durham Declaration." Lifewatch. Accessed 12/20/2016. https://www.lifewatch.org/durham.html.

"Home Page." Reconciling Ministries Network. Accessed 1/23/2017. https://www.rmnetwork.org /newrmn/.

"The Houston Declaration." Confessing Movement. Accessed 1/12/2017. http://www.confessingumc .org/our-story/the-houston-declaration/.

"An Offering for a Way Forward." Accessed 1/19/2017. http://s3.amazonaws.com/Website_Properties /general-conference/2016/documents/council-bishops-statement-offering-way-forward-may-18 -gc2016.pdf.

"Our History." Reconciling Ministries Network. Accessed 1/12/2017, https://www.rmnetwork.org /newrmn/who-we-are/history/.

"Our Story." Confessing Movement. Accessed 1/12/2017. http://www.confessingumc.org/our-story/.

"Playboyism, A New Religious Alternative." *Night Call*. September 29, 1969. GCAH Digital Archives. Accessed 1/23/2017. http://catalog.gcah.org/DigitalArchives/NightCall/Dr_Moore_DA_1067.mp3, 2:01–2:17.

Wesleyan Covenant Association (Feb. 28, 2017) 1:01–1:09. Accessed 3/2/2017, https://wesleyancovenant .org/welcome/.

"What We Believe." The United Methodist Church. Accessed 1/15/2017. http://www.umc.org/what-we -believe/responsible-parenthood

"Who We Are: Our History." Transforming Congregations. Accessed 1/12/2017. http://www.transcong .org/1history.htm.

"Who We Are." The United Methodist Church. Accessed 1/17/2017. http://www.umc.org/who-we-are /constitutional-s

Published and Printed Primary Sources

"Apostles of Reaction: A Critical Evaluation of the 'Good News Movement: Part I.'" *Social Questions Bulletin* (November–December 1978).

"Apostles of Reaction: A Critical Evaluation of the 'Good News Movement: Part II.'" *Social Questions Bulletin* (January–February 1979).

Blanchard, Anne C. *Youth Views Sexuality.* Nashville, TN: Graded Press, Methodist Publishing House, 1971.

The Book of Discipline of The United Methodist Church (BOD). Nashville, TN: The United Methodist Publishing House, 1968–2016.

The Book of Resolutions of The United Methodist Church (BOR). Nashville, TN: The United Methodist Publishing House, 1968–2016.

Call to the Colors. Philadelphia, PA: Methodist League for Faith and Life, 1925–1926.

Charles, Marjorie. "Love, The New Security: A College Senior Writes on Truth as Motivation for Relationships." *motive* magazine, December 1941, 25, 28.

"The Church and Homosexuality: A Changing Picture." *New World Outlook* (September 1970): 25–29.

"The Churches and Birth Control." *Federal Council Bulletin*, 14, no. 4 (April 1931): 19.

The Church Studies Homosexuality. Nashville, TN: Cokesbury, 1994.

"The Controversy over Sex Education: What Our Children Stand to Lose." *Redbook*, September 1969.

Daily Christian Advocate. Nashville, TN: United Methodist Publishing House, 1972–2016.

Doctrines and Disciplines of The Methodist Church. Nashville, TN: The Methodist Publishing House, 1940–1964.

Doctrines and Disciplines of The Methodist Episcopal Church. New York: Methodist Book Concern, 1928–1936.

The Essentialist. Haddenfield, NJ: Bible League of North America, 1927–1930.

"The Federal Council on Birth Control." *Christian Advocate* (April 2, 1931): 3–4.

Heidinger, James, II, "Perspectives in the Church." *What about Abortion?* Wilmore, KY: Good News, 1977: 24–32.

High, Stanley. "Methodism's Pink Fringe." *Reader's Digest* 56, no. 2 (February 1950): 134–38.

"In the Aftermath of Atlanta." *Good News*, Summer 1972, 34–53.

"The Junaluska Affirmation." Wilmore, KY: Forum for Scriptural Christianity within The United Methodist Church, 1975.

Keysor, Charles. "Coming out of Exile." *Good News*, July/September 1970, 22.

———. "The Crisis in Methodist Curriculum." *Good News*, July/September 1970, 18–35.

———. "Cyanide in the Church School." *Good News*, January/March 1970, 32.

———. "The Double Roots of Abortion." *What about Abortion?* Wilmore, KY: Good News, 1977: 33–39.

———. "Editorial: The Gathering Storm." *Good News*, Spring 1974, 19–23.

———. "Methodism's Silent Minority." *Christian Advocate*, July 14, 1966, 9–10.

———. "The Story of Good News." *Good News*, April/June 1972, 12–19.

Kuhn, Donald. "Goals for Sex Life." *Concern*, July 15, 1964, 12.

"Meet: Methodist Family of the Year," *Together: The Midmonth Magazine for Methodist Families*, November 1958, 14–17.

"The Memphis Declaration." *Good News* (March/April 1992): 32–33.

"The New Durham Declaration." *Good News* (May/June 1992).

"1962 Methodist Family of the Year." *Together: The Midmonth Magazine for Methodist Families*, May 1962, 17–20.

"Now That We Are Married." *motive* magazine, November 1944, 15–18.

Phillips, James H. *Sex Education in Major Protestant Denominations.* New York: National Council of Churches in the U.S.A., 1976.

"A Protestant Affirmation on the Control of Human Reproduction.' *Christianity Today*, October 11, 1968, 18–20.

"Report of the Social Principles Study Commission." Edited by Charles D. White. *Journal of the 1970 Special Session of the General Conference of The United Methodist Church.* Nashville, TN: United Methodist Publishing House, 1970.

Robb, Edmund W. "The Predicament of Methodism." *Christianity Today*, October 1963, 8–10.

"A Sanctuary from Abortion." *Good News*, May/June 1992, 31.

Sanger, Margaret. *Motherhood in Bondage.* New York: Brentano's, 1928.

———. *The Woman Rebel* 1, no. 1 (March 1914).

Schuler, Bob. "Methodists Go Socialist." *The Methodist Challenge* (December 1944).

Smith, Leon. "Religion's Response to the New Sexuality." SIECUS Report 4, no. 2 (November 1975): 1, 14–15.

Tippy, Worth M. "The Protestant View of Sex, Love, and Marriage." *Current History* 29, no. 5 (February 1929).

"What about Abortion?" *What about Abortion?* Wilmore, KY: Good News, 1977: 1–39.

Wiese, Otis. "Live the Life of McCall's." *McCall's*, May 1954, 27.

Unpublished Primary Materials

Livingston, Kenneth. "Untitled Address." Sermon, Wesleyan Covenant Association, Chicago, IL, October 7, 2016.

Oliveto, Karen. "Strangely Warmed Hearts, A United Methodist In(Queer)y." Public lecture, Garrett-Evangelical Theological Seminary, Chicago, IL, January 13, 2017.

Renfroe, Rob. "Stepping into That New Day" Keynote address, Wesleyan Covenant Association, Chicago, IL, October 7, 2016.

"The Third Way Talking Points." Working paper, General Conference 2016, Portland, OR, May 2016.

Thompson, Andrew. "Untitled Address." Sermon, Wesleyan Covenant Association, Chicago, IL, October 7, 2016.

SECONDARY SOURCES

Bebbington, David. *Evangelicalism in Modern Britain: A History from the 1730s to 1980s.* London: Unwin Hyman, 1989.

Behney, J. Bruce, Paul H. Eller, and Kenneth W. Krueger, eds., *History of the Evangelical United Brethren Church.* Nashville, TN: Abingdon, 1979.

Beisel, Nicola. *Imperiled Innocents: Anthony Comstock and Family Reproduction in Victorian America.* Princeton, NJ: Princeton University Press, 1998.

Booth, Karen. *Forgetting How to Blush: United Methodism's Compromise with the Sexual Revolution.* Fort Valley, GA: Bristol House, 2012.

Carlson, Allan. *Godly Seed: American Evangelicals Confront Birth Control, 1873–1973*. Piscataway, NJ: Transactions, 2011.

Case, Riley B. *Evangelical and Methodist: A Popular History*. Nashville, TN: Abingdon Press, 2004.

Cole, Stewart Grant. *The History of Fundamentalism*. New York: R. R. Smith, 1931.

Colello, Kristin. *Making Marriage Work: A History of Marriage and Divorce in the Twentieth-Century United States*. Chapel Hill: University of North Carolina Press, 2009.

Coontz, Stephanie. *The Way We Never Were: American Families and the Nostalgia Trap*. New York: Basic Books, 1993.

Critchlow, Donald T. *Intended Consequences: Birth Control, Abortion, and the Federal Government in Modern America*. New York: Oxford University Press, 1999.

Davis, Morris L. "The Methodist Merger of 1939: 'Successful' Unification?" *Unity of the Church and Human Sexuality: Toward a Faithful United Methodist Witness*. Nashville, TN: General Board of Higher Education and Ministry Publishing of The United Methodist Church, 2018.

Davis, Rebecca L. *More Perfect Unions: The American Search for Marital Bliss*. Cambridge, MA: Harvard University Press, 2010.

Davis, Tom. *Sacred Work: Planned Parenthood and Its Clergy Alliances*. New Brunswick, NJ: Rutgers University Press, 2005.

Emilio, John D. and Estelle B. Freedman, *Intimate Matters: A History of Sexuality in America*. 3rd ed. Chicago: University of Chicago Press, 2012.

Fletcher, Joseph. "The New Look in Christian Ethics." *Harvard Divinity Bulletin* 24 no. 1 (1932?): 7–18

———. *Situation Ethics: The New Morality*. Philadelphia, PA: Westminster Press, 1966.

Fraterrigo, Elizabeth. Playboy *and the Making of the Good Life in Modern America*. New York: Oxford University Press, 2009.

Griffith, Marie. "The Religious Encounters of Alfred Kinsey." *Journal of American History* (September 2008): 349–377.

Hall, Amy Laura. *Conceiving Parenthood: American Protestantism and the Spirit of Reproduction*. Grand Rapids: Eerdmans, 2008.

Hartman, Andrew. *A War for the Soul of America: A History of the Culture Wars*. Chicago, IL: University of Chicago Press, 2016.

Hatch, Nathan O., and John H. Wigger, eds. *Methodism and the Shaping of American Culture*. Nashville, TN: Abingdon Press, 2001.

Heitzenrater, Richard P. *Wesley and the People Called Methodists*. Nashville, TN: Abingdon Press, 1995.

Hempton, David. *Methodism: Empire of the Spirit*. New Haven, CT: Yale University Press, 2005.

Holmen, R. W. *Queer Clergy: A History of Gay and Lesbian Ministry in American Protestantism*. Cleveland, OH: Pilgrim Press, 2013.

Hynson, Leon O. "Christian Love: The Key to Wesley's Ethics." *Methodist History* 14 no. 1 (October 1975): 44–55.

Knotts, Alice G. *Fellowship of Love: Methodist Women Changing American Racial Attitudes, 1920–1968*. Nashville: Kingswood Books, 1996.

Littauer, Amanda H. *Bad Girls: Young Women, Sex, and Rebellion before the Sixties*. Chapel Hill, NC: University of North Carolina Press, 2015.

Long, Edward LeRoy, Jr. "The History and Literature of 'The New Morality.'" *Pittsburgh Perspective* 3 (September 1966): 4–17.

Marsden, George M. *Fundamentalism and American Culture*. 2nd ed. New York: Oxford University Press, 2005.

Marquardt, Manfred. *John Wesley's Social Ethics: Praxis and Principles*. Nashville, TN: Abingdon Press, 1992.

May, Elaine Tyler. *America and the Pill: A History of Promise, Peril, and Liberation*. New York: Basic Books, 2011.

———. *Great Expectations: Marriage and Divorce in Post-Victorian America*. Chicago, IL: University of Chicago Press, 1983.

———. *Homeward Bound: American Families in the Cold War Era*. New York: Basic Books, 2008.

McConnell, Francis J. *Borden Parker Bowne: His Life and His Philosophy*. New York, NY: Abingdon Press, 1929.

Milhaven, John G., and David J. Casey. "Introduction to the Theological Background of the New Morality." *Theological Studies* 28, no. 2 (June 1967): 213–44.

Newburg, Kevin D. "The Split That Didn't Happen." *Unity of the Church and Human Sexuality: Toward a Faithful United Methodist Witness*. Nashville, TN: GBHEM Publishing of The United Methodist Church, 2018.

Nickell, Jane Ellen. *We Shall Not Be Moved: Methodists Debate Race, Gender, and Homosexuality*. Eugene, OR: Pickwick Publications, 2013.

Parker, Alison M. *Purifying America: Women, Cultural Reform, and Pro-Censorship Activism, 1873–1933*. Urbana, IL: University of Illinois Press, 1997.

Richey, Russell E., "Today's *Untied* Methodism: Living with/into/beyond Its Two Centuries of Regular Division." *Unity of the Church and Human Sexuality: Toward a Faithful United Methodist Witness*. Nashville, TN: GBHEM Publishing of The United Methodist Church, 2018.

Richey, Russell E., Kenneth E. Rowe, and Jean Miller Schmidt. *Methodist Experience in America [MEA]*. Vol. 1. Nashville, TN: Abingdon Press, 2010.

———. *The Methodist Experience in American [MEA]*. Vol. 2: *Sourcebook*. Nashville, TN: Abingdon Press, 2000.

Rowe, Kenneth. "How Do Caucuses Contribute to Connection?" in *Questions for the Twenty-First Century Church*. Edited by Dennis M. Campbell et al. Nashville, TN: Abingdon Press, 1999.

Schafer, Axel R. *Countercultural Conservatives: American Evangelicalism from the Postwar Revival to the New Christian Right*. Madison, WI: University of Wisconsin Press, 2011.

Schmidt, Jean Miller. *Grace Sufficient: A History of Women in American Methodism*. Nashville: Abingdon Press, 1999.

Schneider, A. Gregory. "Objective Selves versus Empowered Selves: The Conflict over Holiness in the Post–Civil War Methodist Episcopal Church." *Methodist History* 32, no. 4 (July 1994): 237–49.

———. *The Way of the Cross Leads Home: The Domestication of American Methodism*. Bloomington, IN: Indiana University Press, 1993.

Self, Robert O. *All in the Family: The Realignment of American Democracy since 1964*. New York: Hill & Wang, 2011.

Simmons, Christina. *Making Marriage Modern: Women's Sexuality from the Progressive Era to World War II*. New York: Oxford University Press, 2011.

Smith, Mark A. *Secular Faith: How Culture Has Trumped Religion in American Politics*. Chicago, IL: University of Chicago Press, 2015.

Smith-Rosenberg, Carroll. *Disorderly Conduct: Visions of Gender in Victorian America*. New York, NY: Oxford University Press, 1986.

Spann, Howard Glen. "Evangelicalism in Modern American Methodism: Theological Conservatives in the 'Great Deep' of the Church, 1900–1980." PhD diss., John Hopkins University, 1994.

Stephens, Darryl W. *Methodist Morals: Social Principles in the Public Church's Witness*. Knoxville, TN: University of Tennessee Press, 2016.

Tipton, Stephen M. *Public Pulpits: Methodists and Mainline Churches in the Moral Argument of Public Life*. Chicago: University of Chicago Press, 2008.

Tobin, Kathleen A. *The American Religious Debate over Birth Control, 1907–1937*. Jefferson, NC: McFarland Publishers, 2001.

Tone, Andrea. "Contraceptive Consumers: Gender and the Political Economy of Birth Control in the 1930s," *Journal of Social History* 29, no 3 (Spring 1996): 485–506.

———. *Devices and Desires: a History of Contraceptives in America*. New York: Hill & Wang, 2002.

Vickers, Jason E. "American Methodism: A Theological Tradition," in *The Cambridge Companion to American Methodism*. Edited by Jason E. Vickers. Cambridge: Cambridge University Press, 2013.

Vickers, Jason E., ed. *The Cambridge Companion to American Methodism*. New York: Cambridge University Press, 2013.

Weiss, Jessica. *To Have and to Hold: Marriage, the Baby Boom, and Social Change*. Chicago, IL: University of Chicago Press, 2000.

Wellings, Martin. "Methodism and the Evangelical Tradition," in *The Ashgate Research Companion to World Methodism*. Edited by Martin Wellings, Peter S. Forsaith, and William Gibson. Burlington, VT: Routledge, 2013. Accessed 11/15/2016; *eBook Academic Collection (EBSCOhost)*.

White, Heather R. *Reforming Sodom: Protestants and the Rise of Gay Rights*. Chapel Hill, NC: University of North Carolina Press, 2015.

Wigger, John. *Taking Heaven by Storm: Methodism and the Rise of Popular Christianity in America*. Repr. ed. Chicago, IL: University of Illinois Press, 2011.

Williams, Daniel K. *Defenders of the Unborn: The Pro-Life Movement before* Roe v. Wade. New York: Oxford University Press, 2016.

———. *God's Own Party: The Making of the Christian Right*. New York: Oxford University Press, 2010.

Winham, Melissa. "A Voice of Reason: The Story of the Religious Coalition for Reproductive Choice." Master's thesis, University of Southern California, 2004.

Ziegler, Mary. *The Lost History of the Abortion Debate*. Cambridge, MA: Harvard University Press, 2015.

INDEX

Abels, Paul, 241, 244

abortion: 18, 149; American history of, 151–76; overpopulation and, 155–57, 177; pro-choice and, 164–65; pro-life movement and, 150, 158, 159–64; Protestants and, 165–203; *Roe. v. Wade* and, 159–60, 162; state legalization of, 157–65; therapeutic abortion, 153, 154, 158. *See also* Clergymen's Consultation Service on Abortion; Religious Coalition for Abortion Rights

affirmation, 17, 236, 239, 246, 247, 248, 249, 252, 254, 255–56, 269

American Law Institute, 155, 158

American Medical Association, 38, 47, 50, 152, 158

American Way of Life, 70, 84, 87, 111, 122, 158

artificial contraception: 23; underground market, 24; increased sales, 35–36. *See also* birth control

birth control: 17, 20, 27, 155; birth control movement, 20, 21, Catholic Church and, 33; Clinical Research Bureau raid, 34–35; conservative evangelicals and, 47; endorsed by Methodist Church, 50; FCC's guarded approval of, 37; gains respectability, 47–48; Lambeth Conference, 32–33; MEC and, 40–41; as "proper medical practice," 36; *US v. One Package of Japanese Pessaries*, 36; *Youngs v. C. I. Lee*, 35. *See also* Sanger, Margaret; Planned Parenthood Federation of America; planned parenthood

Birth Control Federation of America, 47. *See also* Planned Parenthood Federation of America

Brown, Joanne Carlson, 205, 244–45

Christianity Today, 112–13, 118, 241; and abortion, 173–74; and homosexuality, 241

Circuit Riders, 87, 117

Clergymen's Consultation Service on Abortion (CCSA), 149, 151, 166–67, 177, 183, 184, 186, 268–69

Committee for the Preservation of Methodism, 117–18

Committee on Population Growth and the American Future, 156–57, 164, 170

Comstock Laws, 22, 29, 34, 153; dismantling of, 34–36; MEC and, 43–45

Comstock, Anthony, 22–23, 24, 153; moral establishment and, 23–24; *See also* Comstock Laws

Confessing Movement, 17, 109, 120, 253, 254, 255, 259. *See also* Houston Declaration. *See also* Memphis Declaration

Council on Religion and the Homosexual, 214–17, 219

Creech, Jimmy, 259

cult of togetherness, 67, 70–71, 79–84. See also *Together Magazine*

Dammann, Karen, 259

Daughters of Bilitis, 205

Dell, Greg, 259

divorce: 17, 89–96

Durham Declaration, 197–99

evangelical Methodists, 3, 4–5, 10–11, 15, 29, 72, 114–26, 140–46; abortion and, 176–79, 189–203; homosexuality and, 223–24, 227–62; sex education and, 143–46. *See also* Confessing Movement; Good News Movement; Methodist League for Faith and Life; Wesleyan Covenant Association

Evangelical United Brethren: 20; and abortion, 176; and birth control, 58; and divorce, 90; and race, 86

evangelicals: abortion and, 171–76; definition of, 3–4, 10, 268; homosexuality and, 223–27; rise of, 109–26; sex education and, 109–14, 120–26. See also neo-evangelical

family planning: abortion and, 155–65, 176, 177, 179, 182, 188, 200; birth control and, 48, 51, 53, 55, 58; sex education and, 124

Federal Council of Churches of Christ in America: birth control and, 37; Committee on Marriage and the Home and, 33–34, 37; Social Creed and, 29

Federal Marriage Amendment, 226–27

General Board of Church and Society, 118, 168, 179, 185, 188

General Commission on the Status and Role of Women, 247

General Committee on Family Life, 126; Sex Education Task Force and, 126–39

Good News Movement, 15, 84, 118–19, 139–46, 194; abortion and, 189–203; church–school curriculum and, 144–46; homosexuality and, 236–62

Graham, Billy, 112–13, 114; Methodists and, 112

Hand, Don, 232–35

Henry Foundation, 213, 219

homosexuality: 18, 205; American history and, 206–10; gay rights movement

and, 209–10; homophile movement and, 208–9; Protestantism and, 210–62

Houston Declaration, 254

Human Life Amendment, 160–61, 163, 164, 168

Hyde Amendment, 163, 168

Institute for Religion and Democracy, 118, 188, 198, 233

Keysor, Charles, 1, 15, 72, 139–46, 193–96, 237–39, 267. *See also* Good News Movement

Kinsey, Alfred, 57

Kuhn, Donald, 135–36

Lambeth Conference: birth control and, 32–33

Lifewatch. *See* Taskforce of United Methodists on Abortion and Sexuality

Magginis, Pat, 166

marriage counseling, 56, 88–96, 104, 127, 133, 213

marriage experts, 90–93

marriage revisionists, 31–32; companionate marriage and, 32

Mattachine Society, 208

Memphis Declaration, 253

Methodist Church (MC), 15; abortion and, 176; birth control/planned parenthood and, 49–50, 57–59; Central Jurisdiction and, 72; creation of, 48–49; divorce and, 88–96; family life and, 71, 74–75; homosexuality and, 205–6, 214–27; the new morality and, 108–9, 134–39; (pre)marital counseling and, 92–96; race and, 84–88; revised 1940 Social Creed of, 49–50; sex education and, 107–9, 127–47

Methodist Committee on Family Life, 20, 61. *See also* General Committee on Family Life; National Methodist Committee on Family Life

Methodist Episcopal Church (MEC): birth control and, 37–39, 40–41; divorce and, 89–90; family life and, 63; FCC's Committee on Marriage and the Home, 33–34; institutionalization of, 62–64; marriage reform and, 39, 40, 43–44, 89; social action/reform and, 30; Social Creed, 29; theological shift within, 11, 14, 30, 41–42, 64

Methodist Episcopal Church, South (MECS): 20, 62; divorce and, 89; marriage reform and, 40; Social Creed and, 29

Methodist Family of the Year, 61, 68, 72, 74–79, 111

Methodist Federation for Social Action, 87, 117–18, 240, 244, 247, 249, 252, 254, 255; against Good News Movement, 242–43, 269

Methodist Federation for Social Service (MFSS), 29; removal of Social Creed, 45–46; Social Creed creation of, 29, 30. See also Methodist Federation for Social Action (MFSA)

Methodist League for Faith and Life (MLFL), 14, 42; at General Conference, 42–46; organization of, 42; see also Sloan, Harold Paul

Methodist Protestant Church (MP): divorce and, 89; Social Creed and, 30

miscegenation, 95

Moody, Howard, 166

Moore, Allan, 99–103, 180, 181–82

Moore, John V., 1, 217–21, 229

motive Magazine, 19, 20; marital sex and, 52–57; premarital sex and, 52–57

National Association for Repeal of Abortion Laws, 159

National Association of Evangelicals, 47, 77, 110–13, 118, 129; birth control and, 47, 48

National Council of Churches: abortion and, 170

National Methodist Committee on Family Life, 68, 73–79

National Right to Life Committee, 160, 173, 187. See also abortion

neo–evangelical, 109–10; sex education and, 120–26. See also evangelical

New Christian Right, 2, 3, 2n4, 109, 113–14, 120–26, 128, 262, 267–68; abortion and, 174–76; homosexuality and, 224–27

new eugenics, 67

new morality, 1; abortion and, 150, 176, 181, 184; critique of, 136, 197, 223–24, 267; definition of, 3, 12–13; homosexuality and, 217–21, 222; Methodist ethics and, 13–14, 17, 100–101, 108–9, 134–39, 217, 220, 267

new woman (women), 24–27, 31; second generation of, 25–27

Night Call, 97; *Playboy* and, 99–103

Oliveto, Karen, 264–65

orthodox Methodists, see evangelical Methodists

personalism, 30, 64

planned parenthood: birth control and, 48; EUB endorses, 58; MC endorses, 58

Planned Parenthood Federation of America, 48, 132–33, 200; Methodist Church and, 50, 57–58; the National Clergymen's Advisory Council and, 50–52. See also Birth Control Federation of America

Playboy, 96–103

political caucus groups: abortion and, 150; definition of, 11, 16, 268–69; Good News Movement as, 194–202; homosexuality and, 236–62; purpose of, 17, 109; recent formations of, 265–66; Reconciling Ministries Network as, 246; rise of, 11, 15, 16, 228, 253–54

postmarital counseling, 46, 55–59, 88–96

premarital counseling/courses, 20, 50–52, 58, 88–96, 104, 188, 210

premarital sex, 52–57, 60, 67, 101, 105, 121, 135, 137, 139, 162, 213, 218, 223, 225

progressive Methodists, 4–5, 11, 118, 201, 246, 263, 265; definition of, 4, 109, 147

purity movement, 22–23; moral establishment and, 23–24; race and, 23

queer theory, 6–7

Reconciling Congregations Program, 246–48, 249, 252, 254, 255–56, 257–58. See also Reconciling Ministries Network

Reconciling Ministries Network, 5, 17, 246, 267, 269

Religious Coalition for Abortion Rights (RCAR), 168–70, 185, 198. See also Religious Coalition for Reproductive Choice

Religious Coalition for Reproductive Choice, 170, 185–89, 200–202, 264. See also Religious Coalition for Abortion Rights

responsible parenthood, 58–59, 177, 184–90, 198–99, 201–3

Robb, Edmund W., 118–20

Rockefeller, John D., III, 155–57, 168, 170

Roe v. Wade, 159, 162–65, 168, 174, 176, 185, 186, 192. See also abortion

same-sex union/marriage, 232, 257–60

Sanger, Margaret, 27–29, 30, 39; Catholic Church and, 33; Clinical Research Bureau raid and, 34–35

Schuler, Bob, 14, 114–20, 139

secular humanism, 121, 122–23

sex education: 17, 107–9, 120–39, 144–47, 160, 184–85; for married couples, 40, 55; right to, 49–50

Sex and the Whole Person, 107, 124, 134–39, 144, 146, 267

SIECUS, 124; Methodism and, 124–26, 129–34, 268–69

situational ethics. See new morality

Sloan, Harold Paul, 14, 42; Course of Study and, 42, 45–47. See also Methodist League for Faith and Life

Smith, Leon, 131–32

Taskforce of United Methodists on Abortion and Sexuality (Lifewatch), 197–99

Together Magazine, 61, 68, 71, 72, 98, 100, 111, 267; Methodist Family of the Year and, 72, 75–79; togetherness and, 79–84

Togetherness. See cult of togetherness

Transforming Congregations, 5, 17, 138, 249, 253, 254–55, 258

United Brethren in Christ: 20; divorce and, 89; marriage reform and, 39–40; Social Creed and, 30

United Methodist Church, The: abortion and, 149–50, 165, 166, 168, 176–203; homosexuality and, 205–6, 221–23, 227–62; "Responsible Parenthood" and, 188–89, 198–99, 201–3; sex education and, 126–47; theological pluralism and, 15–16

United Methodist Gay Caucus, 236. See also Affirmation

United Methodist Queer Clergy Caucus, 5, 266

Uniting Methodists, 266

Wesleyan Covenant Association, 5, 17, 109, 115, 265–66

Women's Division of Christian Service, 86–88, 117, 168, 179, 184, 185, 188

Printed in the USA
CPSIA information can be obtained
at www.ICGtesting.com
LVHW040958020823
754027LV00003B/183